SMALL CRAFT ADVISORY

SMALL CRAFT
ADVISORY

~~~~~

*A Book About the Building of
a Boat*

Louis D. Rubin, Jr.

THE ATLANTIC MONTHLY PRESS
NEW YORK
•

Published simultaneously in Canada
Printed in the United States of America

FIRST EDITION

Library of Congress Cataloging-in-Publication Data

Rubin, Louis Decimus, 1923–
Small craft advisory: a book about the building of a boat /
Louis D. Rubin, Jr.—1st ed.

1. Boatbuilding—South Carolina.   2. Rubin, Louis Decimus, 1923–
3. Algonquin (Boat)   4. Motorboats—South Carolina—Design and
construction.   I. Title.

VM321.R77 1991   623.8'231—dc20   91-19545

ISBN 0-87113-533-7 (pb.)

Design by Laura Hough

For Eva,
for Diane,
and for Eva Diane

ACKNOWLEDGMENTS

So many friends have been involved in my boating escapades and thus have, whether wittingly or unwittingly, contributed to the contents of this book that I can do no more than list their names. They include: Ellington and Ellen White, John and Shelley Barth, the late Willard N. James, Carroll and Alice Hollis, Bob and Mary Simpson, Bill and Susan Simpson, John McCallum, Stanley and Barbara Porter, Scholey Pitcher, Clyde and Susan Edgerton, Robert Alden Rubin, William Louis Rubin, John Nelson, Ed and Mildred Voorhees, Mary Warren Leary and the late Lewis Leary, the staff at Minnesott Beach Yacht Basin, Nick Lyons, Clem Willis, George Alletsee, and Larry Myers.

In a somewhat different version, the chapter entitled "Prologue, 1937: The First Boat" appeared in *Boats,* edited by David Seybold and published by Grove-Weidenfeld in 1990.

Portions of the chapter entitled "Sailboat for Sale" were first published in the September 1990 issue of *Southern Living*.

Some of the material pertaining to the building of the *Algonquin* appeared in the June-July 1991 issue of *Coastal Cruising* magazine.

I suppose I also ought to acknowledge the efforts of the crooked son of a bitch who made it possible for me to end this narrative on a humorous note, even if it cost me a tidy sum thereby.

CONTENTS

CONTENTS

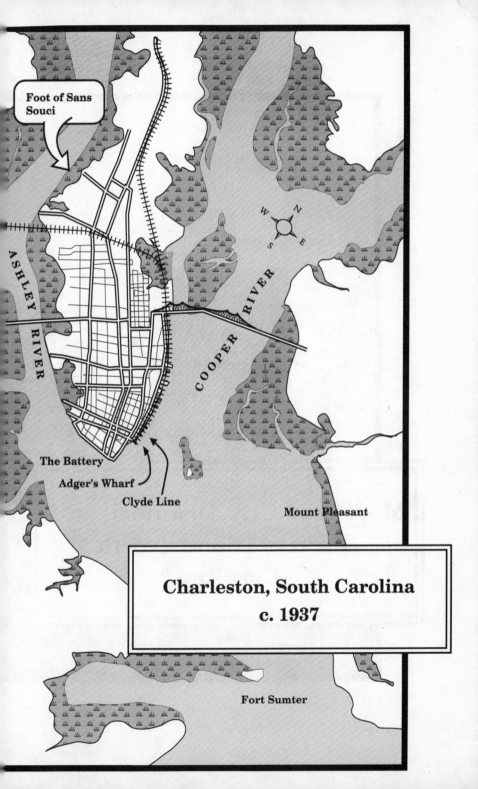

Foot of Sans Souci

ASHLEY RIVER

COOPER RIVER

The Battery

Adger's Wharf

Clyde Line

Mount Pleasant

Charleston, South Carolina
c. 1937

Fort Sumter

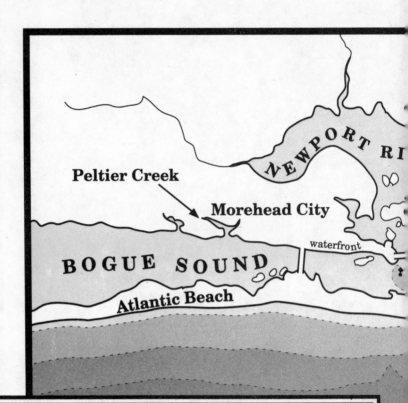

Peltier Creek

Morehead City

NEWPORT RI

waterfront

BOGUE SOUND

Atlantic Beach

Morehead City, Beaufort, and Harkers Island, North Carolina

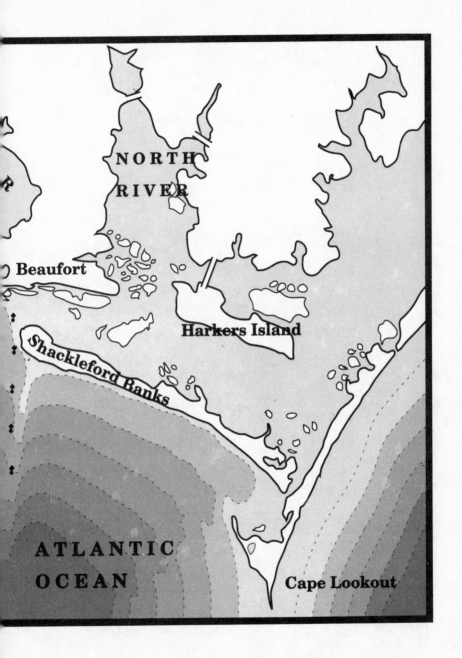

PROLOGUE, 1937
The First Boat

I grew up on salt water. Charleston, South Carolina, is a
peninsula with rivers on two sides. The local pleasantry,
endlessly repeated to tourists, was that the rivers, the
Ashley and the Cooper, met at the point of the harbor to
form the Atlantic Ocean. When I was eleven my parents
built a house up near the northwest boundary of the city,
at the foot of a street named Sans Souci for the old
plantation house that still stood there. (Like all French
names in Charleston it had long since been anglicized, and
was pronounced *Sands Susie.*) Our new house, built atop
nine-foot-high brick columns, was on a low hill, almost
the only hill along the entire Ashley River shoreline,
with a sloping drop-off to the edge of the salt marsh.
From our front porch, through a line of water oaks, we
had a clear view of the river.

An expanse of marshland lay between shoreline

and river, with a creek winding through to the river's edge beyond. Cattails fringed the border of the marsh along the shore. In the winter and early springtime, at low tide, the marsh was a carpet of gray-brown. As spring progressed the blades of reed grass turned green at their base, the new life creeping upward until by full summer the brown was all gone and the reed grass was a thick spread of green. When the tide was high the water often covered all except the edges, leaving only the tips of the reed grass visible, as if it were a lake, which on sunny days reflected back a prickled image of the sky overhead in a kind of *pointillisme*. The open river itself was perhaps a quarter mile wide at that juncture. Beyond it lay the dark green western shoreline of St. Andrews Parish, where in the late 1600s Charles Town had first been settled before being moved down to the tip of the peninsula for purposes of better defense against the Indians and the Spanish.

A mile upstream, out of sight behind a grove of trees, were docks belonging to some fertilizer and lumber companies. Several times a week ships passed by along the channel, preceded by a tugboat of the White Stack Towboat Company. The Seaboard Air Line railroad trestle spanned the Ashley a mile downriver to the south, and the hoot of the tug's siren signaling for the swinging drawspan to open, followed at once by a deep-throated

blast from the whistle of the ship, alerted us to the
imminence of traffic out on the river. My father had
bought several pairs of cheap binoculars when we moved
into the house, and whenever we heard the sound of a
ship's whistle we hurried to retrieve the glasses from his
bottom bureau drawer and went out onto the porch to
watch. If the oncoming ship was of any size at all I was
not satisfied to stop there, but ran down the steps into the
yard, through the gate, and across our neighbor's property
to the high point of the bluff to watch from closer up.

I came to be able to recognize which one of the
White Stack tugboats was escorting the ship—the *Cecilia*,
the *Robert H. Lockwood*, or the *James P. Congdon*. Smaller
and less powerful than the others, the *James P. Congdon*
was often assigned to the ships coming up the Ashley,
while the other two customarily performed duties in and
about the harbor and beyond, tending the vessels of
deeper draft that docked on the Cooper River waterfront,
including the Clyde–Mallory Line passenger ships. There
was another tugboat fleet based in the harbor, and I knew
those tugs—the *Hinton,* the *Waban,* and the *Barren-
fork*—by sight, too, but my loyalties were all for the
White Stack boats, whose operators, the Lockwoods, were
friends of our family.

From the shoreline below the bluff to the river,
out past the reed grass, was a distance of at most a few

hundred yards. Yet so far as getting to the river's edge was concerned, it might have been a thousand miles, for without a boat there was no way to get there. My father wasn't interested in boats, sailing, or fishing, and neither was our neighbor, Mr. Rivers, who lived at Sans Souci.

At the base of the bluff there was a little dock fronting on a creek; it was used mainly for catching crabs, which my mother and I sometimes did in the summertime. My Uncle Manning, who was a bachelor and lived downtown, owned a sailboat, and several times when tide and wind were right he sailed up the Ashley River to the mouth of the marsh creek, then rowed his way to the dock. He took me along with him once, and it was an exciting arrival that we made, moving to the shore from the river. But he did not otherwise think to invite me to sail with him, nor for that matter did it occur to me that he might have done so, and I would never have thought to ask. For unlike my older cousin, with whose family my uncle lived downtown, I showed no aptitude for boats and sailing. I did not even know how to swim.

I should have been thrilled beyond measure to go aboard a tugboat, to look on from the pilothouse as the tug churned its way out to the entrance to the inner harbor, made fast a towline to an incoming freighter, proudly led that freighter up the channel off James Island

and northward along the Cooper River waterfront past
the High Battery and Adger's Wharf to a dock, then
patiently pushed, nudged, and tugged the ship alongside
the pier where it could be made fast. To be allowed to
do that, however, would have been beyond all imagining;
no such prospect was even conceivable, and any thought
of it the wildest of fancies. I was no youthful Francis
Drake, growing up at Plymouth on the Devon coast,
listening to the tales of old mariners and plotting out the
voyages he would make when he grew to manhood. I
knew no mariners, ancient or otherwise. I only watched
them from afar, admiringly, down at Adger's Wharf at
the head of Tradd Street, where the shrimp boats and
small craft berthed. If I dreamed of voyages it was in the
most fanciful and remote terms, unconnected with any
actuality that I could foresee.

My friend John Connolly, who lived five blocks
away up Sans Souci Street, was my constant companion.
In our freshman year in high school, when I was twelve
years old, we tried out for the glee club. After a couple
of practices I dropped out, but not before we had learned
the words to a song:

> *I never see a sail afloat but in my heart's a song*
> *To guide it on its willing way and bring it back*
> *erelong.*

*I'd leave the harbor far behind if one would wait for
me,
But as I wait and vainly hope, I know 'twill never be*

Ships, boats, the river, the harbor, the water
everywhere about Charleston, the ocean that lay out
beyond Fort Sumter and the jetties at the entrance to the
harbor—for me these were inaccessible territory. They
constituted a realm of activity as closed to me as a
voyage to the stars. By fate, by family circumstance, they
constituted no part of my experience. It did not even
occur to me to resent the deprivation. On Saturdays
and on summer weekdays, when the *Cherokee* or the
Algonquin was in port for the day, I sometimes watched
the passengers coming down the iron-green overpass at
the Clyde Line wharves at Vendue Range, where the
taxicabs waited to take them sightseeing. I thought how
fine it would be, when I was grown up, to travel to
New York City or Jacksonville. But for now or in any
realistically conceivable future, the limits of my universe
were the city limits of Charleston, up to the water's edge
and no farther.

All the same, I should have liked to go out into
the marsh that fronted our house. The edge of the Ashley
River seemed so near. If only I were able to traverse
those acres of reed grass that lay between the shore and

the river, so that when a ship came along I could view it from up close. . . .

John Connolly owned a set of the *Book of Knowledge,* and once, looking through one of the volumes, I came upon a picture of a small boy seated in a boat that had a set of paddle wheels attached to the sides. The boat was wooden and blunt-ended, with uncurved sides. Recurrently thereafter I thought about that box-shaped boat with the paddle wheels. With such a boat I would be able to go out onto the creek and into the surrounding marshland.

Then one day the idea came to me. *We could build a boat.* Why not? The boat pictured in John Connolly's book was nothing more nor less than an elongated, open wooden box. Surely we could build a boat like that! We could take it down to the little dock behind Sans Souci, launch it overboard, and go paddling along the marsh creek in splendid fashion out to the river's edge. We could go exploring along some of the other creeks and pathways that led through the marsh, and at high tide move out onto the lakelike expanse of water that covered all but the tips of the reed grass.

I knew better than to mention any such ambitions to my mother, for she would at once bring up the inescapable fact that I could not swim, and therefore had no business in a boat, period. But if the boat were already built, when questioned about it I could assure her that all we had in mind was paddling about in the creek itself, close to shore, where the water was no more than a few feet deep and the thick marsh grass was close by.

Securing the materials for building the boat constituted no problem whatever. When we had first moved into our house there was half a mile or more of open fields between us and the nearest built-up area off to the east. But now other homes were being built, several of them just up the street from us. When the workmen were finished for the day, they left lumber lying about everywhere. As for nails, there would always be a half-filled keg or two left open somewhere.

To be sure, there were ethical considerations. We did not think of it as stealing, though; what could the taking of a few boards from among so many matter? True, it would be improper to remove planks from stacks of unused lumber. But once any portion of a board had been sawed off, what was left, whether two feet or ten feet in length, became scrap lumber, and therefore fair game. The same applied to nails. To pry the lid off an unopened keg would be wrong, but to requisition on one already opened was otherwise. Besides, the builder, Mr. Claude Blanchard, had been the contractor for our house as well, and surely a few pieces of scrap lumber and a pound or two of nails meant little to him, or he would not have left them exposed and unguarded. Nevertheless, it would not be discreet to be seen carting such things off in broad daylight. So, having cased the site at dusk after the workmen had left for the day, and having earmarked what we would need, we waited until after dark, then visited the scene with my younger brother's wagon and fetched home what we required.

We began the boat the next morning, setting up operations underneath the side porch. It was to be eight feet in length, and three feet in width. The sides would be made of two ten-inch-wide boards each. The lower part of the bow would not be completely box shaped, but would slant inward, in order to move through the water more easily.

By noontime we had sawed the lumber and nailed together the sides and the bow and the stern, and had begun sawing the planking for the bottom. The tide was scheduled to be high in the late afternoon, and we were bent upon finishing the boat and launching it that day.

My father soon noticed what was going on. The night before he had observed us bringing in the lumber, but had said nothing; he too had occasionally requisitioned materials from houses under construction. As for my mother, however, when she became aware of the project she had remarks to make, along the lines that I had anticipated. I could not swim; therefore I should not go out on the water. My argument about sticking close to shore and near the marsh grass did not appease her.

"What if I wear a life preserver?" I asked. The boy in the picture in the *Book of Knowledge* had been wearing a life preserver.

"You don't have a life preserver."

I thought for a minute. "I could wear an innertube."

"Where could you get an innertube?" she asked.

"From a service station."

"You haven't got any money to buy an innertube."

"They'll give me an old one, and I can patch it."

"Humpf."

But she did not say no, positively not, never under any circumstances, I forbid you to go out into the marsh in a boat. She did not force the issue. She let it drop.

The way was clear.

John Connolly and I rode our bicycles down Sans Souci Street ten blocks to King Street, and then over to the Chasonoil station at Mount Pleasant Street, and asked whether there were any old innertubes around that we could use for floats. The service station was one that John's father regularly patronized, and the proprietor was obliging. Not only did he locate a pair of innertubes for us, but he proceeded to inflate them, place them in a tub of water to find out where they were defective, and apply patches to the leaks. With the inflated innertubes slung around our necks, we bicycled happily back to my house.

We had sawed the bottom planks, which were to run crossways, to approximately the proper length, and were preparing to nail them into position, when another boy who lived nearby, Billy Muckenfuss, came over to observe for a few minutes.

"It's going to leak like a sieve," he predicted. "You have to cork the seams."

"What are you talking about?"

"If you don't use corking, water comes in between the boards. I know, because my old man told me that's what kept boats from leaking. He said the corking's pushed into the seams, and when it gets wet it swells up and holds the water out."

This was a new problem. There were some bottle corks in the pantry, but slicing them up thinly enough to line the planks would be difficult, and there wouldn't be nearly enough to do the job, either. I decided to consult my father, who was out in the garden working on his temple orange trees.

"It's not corking," he explained. "C-a-u-l-k-i-n-g.

It's a kind of string. It's made out of something called oakum." It was sold at marine stores such as J. W. Luden, on East Bay Street, he said.

"Is it expensive?" I asked.

"I don't know. I've never bought any."

My father returned to his tree-pruning, and John Connolly and I went into the house, looked up the telephone number for J. W. Luden, and called to ask the price of caulking. We were told that it sold for twenty-five cents a ball. Not only did I not have twenty-five cents—my weekly allowance was fifteen cents, and it was all spent by now—but even if we could assemble such a sum, to travel all the way downtown to the store on the Rutledge Avenue trolley car to buy the caulking and then back again would take up most of the afternoon, and we were eager to get the planks nailed on and the boat down to the dock and afloat.

We went back outside, and I reported the news to my father. "You'll have to save up your allowance," he said.

"Do we *have* to use caulking?" I asked.

"You could tar the seams."

"Have we got some tar?"

"No," he said, "but you could probably find some tarpaper scraps over at one of the new houses."

We wasted no time in proceeding to the nearest

---

construction site. I asked one of the workmen whether there were any tarpaper scraps around, and was told to look over next to the toolshed. We did, and soon returned home with several armfuls.

The question now was how to apply the tarpaper. By that time my father had gone inside for his afternoon nap, and waiting until he woke up to ask for advice on how to apply the tarpaper would mean a delay of several hours.

Clearly none of the tarpaper scraps was large enough to be spread over the entire bottom of the boat. If we tried to cover it by nailing smaller scraps together, the water would get in under the edges and up through the seams. We decided therefore that since the tarpaper was being used in lieu of caulking, and the way to apply caulking was to place it between the seams, we would simply cut the tarpaper into narrow strips and lay the strips between the planks. Then, while one of us pressed the planks together as tightly as possible, the other one would nail them in place.

The planks were not quite the same length, but we sawed off any protruding ends flush with the sides. Then we lifted the boat off the sawhorses, turned it right side up, and nailed two boards across the bottom for seats fore and aft. With my father's brace and bit I bored a small hole an inch below the edge of the topmost plank at the bow, found a length of clothesline rope, and tied it to the boat.

What had especially intrigued me about the boat pictured in the *Book of Knowledge* were the paddle wheels affixed to each side, with two little handles for turning them. I was not sure just how to build such devices for our boat, however, so we decided that for the present we would use paddles to power and guide the boat. My father had some lengths of one-by-two-inch boards stored underneath the front porch, so we nailed slabs of wood to the ends of two of them.

I had read somewhere that when a boat was launched it was considered proper to break a bottle of champagne across the bow. We had nothing like that, but my sister was making some Kool-Aid and, because John Connolly was involved, offered to pour some of it into a milk bottle for the occasion, so we decided to settle for that.

The boat was weighty, but we managed to load it onto my brother's wagon, and with the paddles and the innertubes placed inside it we hauled the boat out from under the side porch, around the house to the front gate, and then across the oak-lined property of Mr. Rivers down to the wharf at the foot of the bluff behind Sans Souci. My brother and a friend of his from up the street came along to watch, and my sister brought along the

milk bottle full of Kool-Aid. It was slow going, because
the grass under the oaks had grown high; then, when we
started down the slope leading to the dock, we had to
hold onto the boat and wagon to keep them from rolling
too rapidly. I glanced back at our house to see whether
our departure had been noticed. My mother was standing
on the porch watching. Finally we drew up to the dock.

While we considered just how to unload the boat
into the creek, I looked around, as if to fix the scene of
the occasion in my mind. It was late afternoon, but still
bright, and the water, though not at flood-tide stage, was
well up in the creek and the marsh. The yellow-green
reed grass, the tall brown-furred cattails along the shore,
the high sky overhead with a cluster of cumulus building
to the southwest, were all in place. The day was hot,
with no breeze to speak of. Off in the distance I could
hear the sound of hammers from the new houses.

In the seventh grade at James Simons School we
had memorized stanzas from Longfellow's poem "The
Building of the Ship." I remembered the words:

> *She starts,—she moves,—she seems to feel*
> *The thrill of life along her keel,*
> *And, spurning with her foot the ground,*
> *With one exulting, joyous bound,*
> *She leaps into the ocean's arms!*

While it was true that our boat had no keel, I decided that the general principle would still hold good.

We removed the innertubes and the paddles, slid the wagon out from underneath, and dragged and pushed the boat onto the dock. We decided that breaking the milk bottle of Kool-Aid across the bow might not be a good idea after all. All of us had bare feet, and there might be pieces of glass left about. Moreover, we did not have one of those bags of meshed cord used to swing the bottle of champagne against the ship's prow on such occasions, and if I held the milk bottle by its neck and tried to break it, I would certainly cut my hand. So we agreed to compromise by pouring the Kool-Aid over the bow. "I'll do it," John Connolly said, straddling the bow at the edge of the dock. "Give it here."

My sister reached over and handed him the bottle.

"I christen thee—Hey, what are we going to name it?" John Connolly asked.

"I don't know." The idea that the boat should have a name had not occurred to me. "Call it 'First Boat,' " I said.

"I christen thee First Boat!" John Connolly declared, and poured the Kool-Aid out of the milk bottle and onto the bow of the boat. It was grape-flavored, and it stained the unpainted wood purple.

He stepped back and out of the boat. With the end of the clothesline rope tied to my wrist, together we manhandled the boat off the edge of the dock into the creek. It plopped into the water and slid across the surface of the creek into the reed grass beyond. With the rope I hauled it back to the center of the creek, from where it drifted against the dock, as if it were saying, Let's get going!

It floats! I thought exultantly. It floats!

I looked down into the boat. There was a little water coming in along the sides.

"We need a bailing can," I said.

"Go get a couple of those empty tomato cans from under the basement steps," I told my brother, who had been watching the procedures silently and with great seriousness. He and his friend set out for our house, running up the slope at full speed.

"Well, let's try it out," I said. John Connolly collected the innertubes and paddles from where they lay on the shore, while I sat down on the end of the dock with my feet hanging over into the boat. "Give me the rope," John said. I removed the loop from my wrist and handed it to him. Then, with the innertube looped around my neck, I stepped down into the boat, first one foot, then the other. The boat at once slid away from the dock and I grabbed onto the sides to keep from falling. Then I took a seat on one of the cross planks. The boat was a little wobbly, but gave no signs of upsetting.

"Here, grab this." John reached out with one of

the paddles, I grasped it, and he hauled me back alongside the dock. Then he handed me the other paddle and stepped down into the boat, too. We swung away from the dock. Before I knew it the stern of the boat, where I was seated, had nosed into the reed grass. I thrust my paddle over the side to move us out. John did the same, and we turned into the creek.

At that point we both realized that our feet were in several inches of water. "Hey, it's leaking!" John said. Our combined weight was pushing the hull down into the creek, and the water was jetting up from between the planks in little fountains. Not only that, but the strips of tarpaper, far from swelling up and impeding its entry, were now floating around inside the boat.

"We better get back to the dock," I said.

About then my brother and his friend came back with the bailing cans. We maneuvered the boat alongside the dock and took the cans from them. After some minutes of urgent bailing we had scooped out a good deal of the water, getting thoroughly drenched in the process. The respite was only momentary, however, because more water was steadily coming in through the seams.

There was no doubt about it, our boat leaked like a sieve, just as Billy Muckenfuss had predicted. Still, with frequent pauses for bailing, we could venture down the

---

creek a little. So we paddled our way fifty feet along the marsh, until we reached a place where the creek forked. Several times as we moved along, marsh birds in the adjacent reed grass, frightened by the unexpected visitors, vaulted upward and soared off, startling us considerably. The tide was high, so we could see over the top of the reed grass and observe the expanse of marsh and water on either side. "Boy, this is great!" John Connolly said, and I agreed. However clumsily and wetly—and by then we were fully soaked—I was afloat, on the water at last.

It was hot, and the constant bailing quickly became a chore, so we headed back up the creek to the dock and climbed out, leaving behind the paddles, the bailing cans, and the innertubes, which by now were floating in the water inside the boat. John departed for home. My brother and his friend were eager to try out the boat. I was afraid to let them go off in the creek by themselves, but I let them climb inside and paddle around near the dock while I held onto the end of the rope. As for my sister, now that John had departed she was of no mind to try her hand at it.

That evening at supper I recounted the events of the day, and reported the failure of the tarpaper that my father had suggested to keep the boat from leaking. "You mean you just cut the tarpaper up and stuck it between the boards?" my father asked.

"We didn't have a piece big enough to cover the whole bottom with it," I explained.

He laughed. "What I meant was you could heat the tarpaper over a fire until it started melting, and then pour it along the cracks," he said. "The way you used it, you'd have been better off without the tarpaper at all."

But the chances were, he said, that the wooden planking would swell from being left in the water, and within a day or two the boat might not leak quite so badly.

John Connolly came over on his bicycle the next morning bearing a ball of heavy twine. "My father says to wedge it in the cracks with this"—he extracted a putty knife from his pocket and showed it to me—"and it will help keep the water out."

When we went down to the boat we found it a dozen feet away from the dock across and down the creek, high and dry on a mudbank, the clothesline rope extended to its limits. The tide was going out, and there was less than half a foot of water in the creek. If we could have pulled the boat off the bank and into the water we could have gotten to it, but it was now so heavy from being in the water that it was impossible to dislodge by tugging on the rope. So we waited until early afternoon, when the tide turned and enough water

___

was flowing back into the creek to float the boat off the mudbank. When we managed to pull the boat in, we found eight inches of water inside it.

"That's why we couldn't move it," John Connolly said. "That water must have gone in there from the last high tide, early this morning."

"I guess so."

"But if it didn't drain when the tide was out, then the seams must have swelled up some overnight," John said.

So they had. My father's prediction had been correct. When we climbed down into the boat and bailed it out, some more water did seep back in because of the additional weight of our bodies, but notably less abundantly than the previous day. It remained necessary for us to bail from time to time, but not nearly so often. Emboldened by the development, we headed down the creek and this time did not pause at the fork, but continued on. Neither of us said anything to indicate our intention. We only paddled onward, along the creek, which was beginning to widen. The tide was only halfway up, so that our eyes were at about a level with the top of the reed grass.

It took us a while to reach the vicinity of the creek mouth, because the creek doubled back on itself several times as it wound through the marsh, and also

because we were bucking the incoming tide. At length
we came to a point where the creek executed a sweeping
bend and, more than a dozen yards wide now, ran
parallel to the river, separated from the open water by no
more than a twenty-foot expanse of reed grass.

Not only was the water in the creek flowing
strongly but there was definite wave action, so that our
boat rose and fell as we paddled on toward where the
creek broadened into a little bay and fronted the Ashley
River itself. Then, prompted by an identical impulse, we
lifted the blades of our paddles from the water and rested
there to allow our boat's forward motion to cease, and
drifted in the current.

We did not stay in place for long. The powerful
incoming tide quickly swung the blunt bow toward the
edge of the marsh. Broadside to the current, the boat
rolled perceptibly as the low waves moved against the
sides and then slipped underneath us. There was a definite
feeling of instability. In an instant we were being
propelled swiftly back into the creek.

Seated in the bow, John Connolly dug the blade
of his paddle into the water to straighten us out, and I
did the same. We were now moving rapidly with the
current, and—I realized—*were no longer in full control of
our boat's motion.* I reached down to where the innertube
lay around my feet and lifted it across my knees.

"Head up into the marsh!" John said. Working strenuously, we were able to angle the boat across the creek and up to the reed grass. The current was flowing powerfully through the grass, the tips of which were no more than a foot above the surface of the water and bending with the flow.

John reached over and caught hold of a clump of reed grass, and I tried to shove the blade of my paddle into the mud at the base of the grass. For a second we hung there, but then the stern swung upstream with the current, the reed grass slipped from John's grasp, my paddle pulled loose from the mud, and the boat, now almost parallel with the edge of the creek, slid inexorably out into the creek again, this time stern first.

Paddling hard as we swung along, we succeeded in turning the boat, so that, bow first now, we went scooting up the creek until we reached the bend. The marsh grass was thicker and taller there. This time we let the boat be carried well up into the reed stalks, where after a moment we came to a halt.

"Boy!" John said. "That current's something! Good thing the tide's coming in, instead of out. We might have ended up out there in the deep water."

I was sweating from the effort of paddling, my breath was coming in gasps, and my heart was racing. I looked around. For now, at least, we were out of danger.

"Let's catch our breath," I said after a minute. "Once we get around this bend we'll be out of the river current."

So there we were, our boat caught in the reed grass, and the Ashley River no more than a few dozen yards away, flowing along powerfully, its mottled green surface flashing in the afternoon sunlight. We could see the docks upstream quite plainly, less than a mile distant, with a freighter alongside one of them. Downstream the black horizontal profile of the Seaboard railroad trestle was in full view, stretching from shore to shore. To the west, across the river, the far shore, which from our front porch had seemed so distant, was now visible in detail, the edge of the marsh distinct from the dark green trees on land.

Eastward, back where we had set out, was the grassy hill of Sans Souci, and atop it the house itself, white with a red roof. To its right the line of oak trees partially obscured our house, but I could make out the front porch. Was my mother watching from it? It was too far off to tell. I hoped not.

This was where I had wanted to be, at the river's edge. How many times had I yearned to be able to reach it, so that when ships passed up and down the channel I could watch them from close by. I glanced anxiously upstream and down, to satisfy myself that none were approaching; the last thing in the world I wanted now was for a ship to come along, with a tugboat preceding it. If that ever happened I wanted to be well back into the creek, safe from any wake that might be thrown up.

What I had not anticipated was the force of the current. I had assumed that the river would be placid and still, like the water that made a lake of the marsh at high tides. Instead, once we drew near the creek mouth and encountered the flowing water of the river, the boat we had built for ourselves, which had seemed so completely adequate and sturdy back in the confines of the marsh creek near the shore, had rocked and swayed from side to side unsteadily, and we had been unable to keep it steered properly.

We waited a few minutes longer, then, after bailing the water from inside the boat, we pushed against the roots of the reed grass with the paddles until we were out in the creek again. We set out for home, rounding the bend and then heading back up the creek, moving beyond the reach of the river's powerful flow. Another turn, and we were pointed toward the bluff. Stroking along almost without effort as the incoming tide bore us with it, I felt pride in our boat, and in what we had done.

I also had a sense of anticipation. However uncertain and even perilous the edge of the river itself might be, I was satisfied that the marshland itself, and the creeks that led through it, were thoroughly within my competence. No longer would I have to stand on the shore at flood tide and watch the water cover the reed grass. I could go out on it. And on our voyage down and back up the creek, I had seen that there were all kinds of smaller side creeks leading off into the marsh. Where did they go? From now on, when the tide permitted I could travel through the marshland as I wished.

We churned along rhythmically, matching our strokes. After a minute John Connolly began singing:

Ships that are sailing for Carthage
Boats that are heading for Rome

It was the chorus to "I never see a sail afloat," which he had sung in concert with the glee club, and I too had learned before I dropped out: I joined him and we sang together as we paddled.

Leaving the bay for fabled Cathay
When will they all come home?

We moved up the creek toward the dock. When we got there we pulled the boat up into the marsh grass next to the dock and tied it close, so that tomorrow morning when the tide was out we could try pressing the twine into the seams. But now that the boat was leaking only moderately, that was no longer so important. A little bailing here and there was no trouble to do, not for a boat that could take me to the edge of the river or wherever else I might want to go.

If my mother knew or suspected what we had done, she gave no indication of it. I told my father about the way his prediction about the planks swelling had worked out. He made no comment. Matters having to do with boats were without interest for him. In a box of old photographs up in our attic there was a yellowed picture of him, my Uncle Manning, and their friend Octavus Roy Cohen, who was a famous writer now, in a fishing boat of some kind, apparently taken when they were in their late teens. I had asked him about it, but he said only that they had rented boats occasionally and gone fishing out in the harbor. He must long since have ceased to take any pleasure in such activities, because I had never known him to go fishing or boating. What he cared about was his garden, in particular his temple orange trees and his rose bushes, and the poker game that he and Mr. Rivers and my Uncle Manning and several others played every Saturday night over at Sans Souci.

As boats go, of course, my first one was not a very good one. Indeed, it was so narrow and unseaworthy as to be positively dangerous. I tremble to think what might have

happened if, on that day when we first took our boat to
the edge of the river, the tide had been flowing out
rather than coming in. For, once swept out into the river,
I am by no means sure that we could have made our way
back into the mouth of the creek. With any kind of
wind and wave action the little flat-bottomed boat could
and probably would have capsized, or at the least been
swamped. And I could not swim a stroke! I could
only have clung to the side of the boat as it swept
downstream, or else held onto the patched-up rubber
innertube and tried to steer for the marsh's edge.

My mother *was* watching us that day from the
porch. I found this out years later, not from her but from
my sister. Yet what could she have done if she had seen
us being carried out into the river? Telephoned the
police, probably, or more likely, the Coast Guard. But so
far as I know there were no boats of any kind on that
section of the river that could have been dispatched to
our rescue, though someone might have had the presence
of mind to contact one of the industrial docks upstream,
and a boat sent after us from there.

But all that is conjecture. Very likely John
Connolly and I would have realized, if the tide had been
going out that afternoon, that we were having trouble
controlling the boat long before we reached the mouth of
the creek, and turned around and headed back.

* * *

John Connolly soon lost interest in exploring the marsh, but I did not. As the summer went on I came to be much more adept at handling the little boat. Not only did I go paddling all through the marsh, following the numerous side creeks and, on flood tides, cruising out upon the tidal lake that covered all but the tips of the reed grass, but on several occasions I went back to the mouth of the creek and even out onto the river itself. But it was always at times of slack tide, and only for brief periods.

On one such expedition I even attached a wooden pole vertically to the boat and fashioned a crude sail— out of very porous croker-sack material, fortunately, for without a keel the boat would certainly have been capsized by the first good gust of wind. I made my way along the edge of the river for several hundred feet before turning and paddling back up the creek.

That day, too, my mother was watching. I can only guess what anxiety she must have felt when she saw me out there by myself on the Ashley River, in a tiny coffin-shaped wooden box with a sail, in twenty-five feet of river water—for the ship channel led close to the marsh's edge at that point. Yet she never afterward said a word to me about it, never gave the slightest indication that she was aware of what I was doing with the boat!

My mother was otherwise in no way reticent about
expressing her opinion about my activities. Perhaps she
did not realize just how dangerous what I was doing was,
though that seems unlikely. Was it stoicism on her part?
Did she feel that she ought to allow me, as a boy, to take
risks on my own?

Whatever it was, I am reasonably sure that she
was more than a little gratified and relieved several years
later when a large peagreen-colored U.S. Army Corps of
Engineers dredge showed up in the Ashley River, along
with platforms, floats, lengths of pipe, and several
launches. In the months that followed there was much
tooting of whistles, blowing of sirens, ringing of bells,
and shifting of suction pipes as the dredge worked
methodically away at deepening and widening the ship
channel. In so doing, it pumped out thousands of tons of
white sand all along the edge of the marsh, creating a
chain of small islands and closing off the mouth of the
creek behind Sans Souci.

Many years later my mother and my aunt were
visiting us at our summer home on the York River in
Virginia, and I took her out fishing. As we were cruising
along in my outboard motorboat, en route to the edge of
a shoal half a mile away where the fishing was almost
always good, she remarked, "You're doing something
you've wanted to do all your life."

* * *

Building and using that little boat was one of the more
satisfying accomplishments of my life. I have thought
about it with pleasure many times, and have written
fiction about it. It was, I think, deeply emblematical. For
it was the first time I had ever done anything of my
own accord to *change* my life. I wanted to go out on
the water—leave the land, free myself from the
restrictions of the shore and the city where I lived—and
I built a boat and did so. In its own way it was a
Liberating Act.

By the time I built the boat I had begun to
write, and had even earned a certain amount of local
attention for my high school newspaper pieces. But this
had scarcely brought about anything like the buoyant
conviction of achievement that I felt when I was able to
go out upon the hitherto inaccessible waters of the
marsh and the creek. Literally overnight, I had achieved
a breakthrough, and effected not only an important
passageway out of my geographical and territorial confines but an expansion of my imaginative horizons as
well.

Years were to pass before I owned another boat,
but thereafter I have never been without at least one, and
usually several at a time. Yet the clumsy wooden boat
that John Connolly and I built more than half a century

ago meant most to me of all. In a very real sense, every
boat I have ever acquired as an adult, whether old or
new, sail or power, has represented an attempt to
reproduce that one early experience.

1

ADGER'S WHARF

Two summers ago, in 1989, when I was sixty-five years old, I made up my mind to have a boat built. It was to be made of wood, not fiberglass, and its workboat hull configuration was to be the same as that of many hundreds of small commercial fishing craft along the coast, although its cabin would be larger, designed not merely as shelter from the sun, wind, and rain, but with facilities to allow me to sleep aboard it for several days at a time.

For the same amount of money that the new boat would cost, I could have bought a new or late-model production cabin cruiser with a fiberglass hull, which would go much faster, with considerably more in the way of amenities, and be designed from the keel up for pleasure rather than commerce. When eventually I decided to sell it—and with boats that day inevitably comes—it would bring a far better price. But I did not want a production cabin cruiser. I wanted a wooden launch, as small craft like the one I had in mind used to be called before pleasure boats became big business and more glamorous designations such as cabin cruiser and sportsfisherman were bestowed upon them, one that resembled the kind used by coastal watermen to make a living.

A sailboating friend of mine once accused me of exhibiting a kind of reverse snobbery when it came to boats. I liked them old, preferably wooden, and I gave them names like *Bill James, Barbara P., Little Eva,* and *Mudtoad.* It got me to thinking; there was some truth to the accusation. The question, however, is Why? What is the particular attraction that workboats and other such utilitarian craft hold for me?

My admiration for workboats goes a long way back, all the way to my childhood and a place called Adger's Wharf. Located at the head of Tradd Street on the Charleston waterfront, Adger's Wharf was actually two wharves, a north and a south, and it was mostly given over to small commercial craft. When I was a teenager in Charleston in the 1930s and early 1940s, I spent many hours there and elsewhere along the city waterfront. In retrospect, I can see that the downtown waterfront in Charleston had a meaning for me that went

considerably beyond the customary attraction that such
things ordinarily have.

Let us assume, first of all, that no very
extraordinary psychological explanation is needed at this
point for why I, or any other adolescent male, might
have been fascinated with boats, trains, and the like. Let
us assume also that for a youth growing up in a small
southern city with ambitions for a career as a journalist
and writer, the ships and trains that left the city for other
places far and wide held a symbolic place in my
imagination for that reason in itself.

Beyond these, however, other factors are involved
which, if I am to tell the story properly, must be
explored and understood. It is necessary first of all to try
to explain my particular place, and my family's, in the
Charleston scene, and to show how Adger's Wharf, its
workboats, and the downtown waterfront in general fit
into the picture.

When I was young, there were not one but two
different and seemingly discrete Charlestons. For more
than one reason, they could be designated as Uptown and
Downtown.

Downtown Charleston was the old part of the
city, with buildings that dated back to colonial times. It
was the city that the tourists came to see, and where the
Old Charlestonians lived, the families whose forebears

were the antebellum rice planters and merchant princes. Downtown Charleston was a city of narrow, sometimes winding streets with quaint and historical names like Longitude Lane and St. Michael's and Price's and Bedon's and Stoll's and Do As You Choose Alleys and Tradd and Church and Water and Gibbes and Legaré and Lamboll and Orange and East Bay. In church affiliation it was Episcopalian and Huguenot and Presbyterian, with a few Unitarians and Congregationalists and Jews whose tenure often went back to colonial and early federal times. Downtown people were lawyers and doctors and professors and realtors and bankers and stockbrokers and businessmen and artists and writers and newspaper editors. Black people Downtown were Colorful and Primitive and wore bandannas and spoke Gullah and they went about the streets hawking fish and shrimp and produce and everyone knew their picturesque vending cries. The women wore uniforms and had names like Viola and Evalina.

Downtown was laden with history, and its residents talked about and some few even remembered the Firing on Fort Sumter, and Downtown was where there had been pirates and privateers and Revolutionary War heroes and blockade runners and Civil War generals. The big houses Downtown had outbuildings behind them which had once been slave quarters. Downtown there was

Culture and Art and Poetry, and painters and etchers made illustrations of the famous Sword Gates and St. Michael's Church and the Flower Ladies on its portico and other quaint scenes, and authors wrote poems and sketches extolling the uniqueness of the Carolina Low-country, and the Dock Street Theatre performed plays, and there were concerts and recitals. Downtown was the place of the College of Charleston, the nation's oldest municipal college, and the Historical Society and the Library Society and the New England Society, and also the St. Cecilia Society, where the females of the gentry made their debuts.

Downtown was White Point Gardens and the Battery, with Fort Sumter visible across at the harbor mouth, and where the Fort Sumter Hotel, and also the Villa Marguerita (which didn't accept Jews as guests), were located. Downtown families were named Alston and Ball and Barnwell and Drayton and FitzSimons and Huger and Lowndes and Manigault and Maybank and Mazyck and Smythe and Pinckney and Porcher and Rhett and Simons (with one *m* only) and Stoney and VanderHorst and Waring; sometimes they even bore two of the names at the same time. For recreation the Downtown residents kept sailing craft at the Carolina Yacht Club and the Yacht Basin, and they went sailing off the Battery and held regattas and raced Snipes and

scows and cruised in handsome yawls and ketches and
schooners. They played tennis and golf. They hunted
ducks in the abandoned rice fields of the Low-country.
They rode horseback and held fox hunts and steeplechase
races. Downtown, in sum, was patrician and cultured and
historical and scenic and romantic and literary. When you
read about Charleston in a poem or a book it was always
Downtown Charleston. If you saw a picture of Charleston in a magazine, or in a painting or watercolor,
Downtown Charleston was what was portrayed.

Uptown, by contrast, was plebeian and middle-
class and ordinary and not at all scenic and cultured
and literary. Uptown people were named Bowman and
Bierfischer and Blanchard and Bolchoz and Burmester and
Castanes and Cohen and Connolly and Condon and
Dennis and Finkelstein and Hesse and Jones and Karesh
and McLaughlin and Morse and Muckenfuss and Murphy
and Pearlstine and Rosen and Rubin and Shokes and
Simmons (with two *m*'s) and Smith (spelled with an *i*,
not a *y*) and Thomas and Wineberg. The Uptown streets
were straight and not narrow, and bore names like Maple
and Poplar and Cypress and Peachtree and Grove and
Line and Bogard and Allen and Cleveland and Alberta
and Dunnemann. Uptown there were no lanes and no
alleys.

Uptown people were Baptists and Methodists and
Lutherans and Catholics and Greeks and Jews. They were

storekeepers and carpenters and mechanics and salesmen and policemen and Navy Yard workers and clerks and certified public accountants and dentists and Power Company linemen and railroad men and streetcar conductors and bus drivers and branch managers and merchants and pharmacists. The black people who worked Uptown did not wear bandannas and uniforms and did not sell flowers and were not picturesque.

Uptown there was nothing Historical. There were railroad stations and freight yards and, north of the city limits, a few factories and the Navy Yard. There was a park with flowers and duck ponds and a zoo, and the campus of The Citadel, the Military College of South Carolina, but the park was not old and the campus was a new one, not the historic Old Citadel of pink stucco buildings that was there when the cadets fired on the steamship *Star of the West* at the outbreak of the War Between the States.

Uptown there were no old and quaint buildings and gateways. The houses had front porches, not piazzas, with lawns and gardens fronting the street and in clear view, not in the sideyard and back and visible only through closed gates. No tourists came from afar to see Uptown Charleston; the guide books did not describe its quaint charm. There were no historical societies Uptown, and girls who lived Uptown did not make their debuts.

For recreation the Uptown people went to the

movies, to baseball games at College Park, and to boxing matches, and played baseball and basketball and poker, and if they had boats they were powered by gasoline engines, not sails, and were used for fishing. They did not race in regattas. When they played golf it was at the Municipal Links, not the Country Club. They were interested in cars and they did not own horses and go fox hunting. Uptown people did not write or read poems, publish books, or do paintings and etchings. Uptown, in short, was middle-class and democratic and everyday and practical, and very, very Real.

Socially, the city of Charleston, South Carolina, in the 1920s, 1930s, and 1940s was a very class-conscious city. As usually happens in such a place, not only the descendants of the pre–Civil War plantation gentry, most of whom lived south of Broad Street, but all the other elements in the population, from the top to the bottom of the social scale, were divided into strata. Each successive stratum aspired to the next higher on the scale, and looked down on the stratum just below it. Another word for this is snobbery—and Charleston was a very snobbish place. This was true of the Protestants, the Roman Catholics, the Jews, the Greeks; it was true of the whites and the blacks. One reason for this was that there wasn't much money around Charleston in those days. Persons in search of prestige and status, therefore, could look for the manifestations of those only back in the past, before the War Between the States, and so inherited social position was all there was to be snobbish about.

The Jewish community was divided into two groups—Uptown and Downtown. K. K. Beth Elohim was the Downtown, Reform congregation—the oldest Reform temple in the United States. B'rith Sholom and another synagogue were the Uptown, Orthodox congregations. Their division was not really geographical, but reflected the degree of each group's assimilation into the local culture. The Reform congregation was made up of what remained of the old Sephardic Jewish families of colonial and early federal days, the German Jewish families of the middle and late nineteenth century, and some latecomers. The Orthodox congregations were mostly of more recent advent—Russians and Eastern Europeans who held on more closely to the customs, traditions, and language of the immigrant past, whereas the Reform congregation had largely dispensed with such things. Reform services were in English. Certain responses were written in Hebrew, but few members of the congregation could read them. There was a choir and organ music, and no cantor. The dietary laws were observed in very lax fashion, if at all. In short, the Jewish community was undergoing the same process of

assimilation that went on with every American immigrant
population from the 1800s onward, and because
Charleston was a small city, without enough people of
various ethnicities to group themselves into sizeable
enclaves, the assimilative process was more rapid.

When I look back and try to make sense of what
was involved, certain things strike me. The Downtown,
Reform congregation, to which my family belonged, was
very small; there were only three people in our Sabbath
School confirmation class. The congregation had dwindled
away over the years, as people moved away, intermarried,
were assimilated into the Protestant community, and so
on; in truth it was a dying community, and even in
certain respects no longer had an ethnic identity at all.
The result was that by the time of my generation—the
generation that grew up in the 1930s and 1940s—those
who remained held on self-consciously to their position,
looked down socially upon the Orthodox community,
and prided themselves on the supposed absence of ethnic
identity. Judaism, they told themselves, was not an ethnic
matter, but purely religious and theological (this, of
course, while across the Atlantic the Nazis were making
no such distinction at all).

Snobbery always involves pretense, of course. The
person who places a premium upon social status is trying
to prove something. My own family, for example, did

not extend back lengthy generations into Charleston life; my grandfather was European born—and in East Prussia or Lithuania, not in western Europe—and came to the city only in the 1880s. Yet for reasons not quite clear to me—perhaps because my New York City–born grandmother had a sister who was of considerably longer residence in Charleston and was married to a tailor who was a Confederate veteran—we were unquestionably part of the Downtown congregation.

As I look back, I realize the extent to which my generation imbibed this way of thinking and feeling from infancy on. In effect we were raised and tutored in such snobbery. Yet we were not wealthy, and moreover geographically we lived far uptown. My boyhood friends were almost all Uptown—but not Jewish; there were no Jewish families living within two miles of our house. But the Uptown/Downtown division I have sought to describe was by no means limited to or even especially characteristic of the Jewish population. It was part of a whole way of looking at the world. And in my own case the division was intensified by certain other factors.

The result was that in actuality I lived in two worlds when I was growing up. In the Uptown world I played baseball and hung around the Hampton Park Pharmacy and the playground during the summer, and worked and wrote sports stories for the newspaper and

went to the movies with girls. At the same time, I had
strong interests that were very much associated with
Downtown; I read history and was fascinated by it,
listened to classical music, read books of poetry and
fiction, began attending plays and concerts, and tried to
write poems and stories.

Living as I did in two worlds, I was not wholly
or fully of either, the more so because my literary
ambitions and my interest in music and history were
solitary activities, shared by none of my friends. Thus in
my imagination, as someone who would some day
become a writer, Uptown and Downtown were discrete
worlds, linked by the slender umbilical cord of the
Rutledge Avenue trolley and, later, bus that I rode from
our house far uptown to the downtown city on the point
of the peninsula.

And that is where Adger's Wharf and the
workboats come in. Their fascination for me, and the
fascination of the Cooper River waterfront in general, lay
in the unique fusion, geographical, psychological, and
cultural, of the two Charlestons that they offered to my
imagination.

The small craft berthed at Adger's Wharf were
shrimp trawlers, cargo launches that served the nearby sea
island communities, commercial fishing boats, the harbor
pilot boats, crab buy boats, and a variety of other small

boats. At the head of the south wharf were the three tugs
of the White Stack Towboat Company. At the base of
the north wharf was a large, mostly open-sided shed with
a wide galvanized tin roof, where the catches of the
shrimping fleet were bought, sorted by an array of black
women, iced down, and shipped out. Just upstream and
abutting Adger's Wharf was a boatyard with a marine
railway and a machine shop. The area was always busy.

Adger's Wharf was considered to be one of the
tourist attractions of the city; the trawlers and launches
were frequently extolled in magazine articles as
contributing to the "quaintness" and the "romantic
atmosphere" of an old seaport town. By the mid-1930s,
when I grew old enough to spend time down on the
waterfront, make-and-break gasoline engines had replaced
the sail power of the once-numerous "mosquito fleet" that
seined for shrimp outside the harbor. Before the advent of
good roads, and bridges linking the sea islands up and
down the coast to the mainland, water transport had
provided the principal means of moving passengers and
goods, and Adger's Wharf was where many of the small,
shallow-draft launches in the island trade had docked. By
my time these had mostly succumbed to competition
from automobiles and buses. The trawlers and other
workboats that did tie up at Adger's Wharf tended to be
motley affairs, many of them owned by black fishermen

and painted with garish colors and odd decorations, including more than one "eye" to ward off the evil spirits lurking in the deep.

With their nets hung out to dry, their trawl boards and donkey engines, and the pungent aroma of dead fish and shrimp spoiling in the hot sun, these workboats were picturesque enough, I suppose, as were the red-hulled Lockwood tugboats with their tall white stacks topped in black, from which wisps of smoke always trailed as their engines were kept ready for duty. And so were the numerous sea gulls that constantly dipped and soared overhead, in wait for whatever might materialize in the way of discarded fish, shrimp, or other organic refuse in the water about the wharf.

Yet *I* certainly did not think of Adger's Wharf and its inhabitants as scenic, picturesque, colorful, or anything of the sort. The boats I saw there were workboats—designed for commercial duties on the water—and if there was considerable glamour about them for me, it was in their sturdy, practical quality, just as the steam locomotives that came into the city across the Seaboard trestle downstream from our house, or the freighters and tugboats that passed by on the Ashley River, were fascinating to watch.

The sailing craft at the Carolina Yacht Club, downstream from Adger's Wharf, held no interest for me, nor did I feel any desire to go over to the foot of

Calhoun Street on the other side of town and look at the sailboats and power yachts that were berthed at the new Yacht Basin on the Ashley River. There was something artificial about these boats, and contrived. They were for show. They were Downtown. Adger's Wharf, and the docks and wharves along the Cooper River from there northward, were what held my attention.

A short distance farther upstream were the Clyde–Mallory Line docks, three large, green-painted closed wharves where the passenger ships that operated between New York City and various South Atlantic and Gulf Coast ports came in from the ocean to discharge and take on passengers and freight. Except for one ship, the *Henry R. Mallory,* which hauled more freight and fewer passengers than the others, the Clyde Line ships bore Indian names—the *Shawnee,* the *Iroquois,* the *Seminole,* the *Cherokee,* and the *Algonquin.*

They were all small ships as passenger liners went, designed for coastal service and displacing no more than about five thousand tons. In New York Harbor, where the great transatlantic liners were regular callers, they were doubtless considered insignificant affairs indeed; but to a youth who had never seen the likes of the *Berengaria, Aquitania, Mauretania, Bremen, Ile de France, Queen Mary, Normandie,* or any of the other famed transoceanic greyhounds, they seemed enormous.

The Clyde liner that I saw most often was the

Cherokee, a single-stacked ship that berthed along the outside wharf when it called at the docks, and so was visible from the shore. It was there every Saturday morning, and it departed in mid-afternoon. The *Algonquin,* which was only somewhat larger but which I never saw at that wharf, was my favorite liner, however. When I was six years old and we were spending the summer out on Sullivan's Island across the harbor, my father had gone to New York City on business and had returned aboard the *Algonquin.* The harbor channel led close to the island, and very early in the morning my mother had taken us down to the beach to see it come by. It was a gray dawn, and misty. My father tipped a deckhand to let him blink a ship's lantern at us from the deck. My father was coming home, to operate his electrical business on King Street and play golf and take me for walks. Thereafter the *Algonquin* was "my" boat.

I was never to achieve my ambition to travel aboard a Clyde-Mallory liner, however, because when World War II broke out, all coastwise passenger service was suspended, and never afterward resumed. I sometimes wondered what had become of those little ships. Years later I was returning aboard the *Constitution* from a summer of lecturing in southern France, and out on the stern one evening I struck up a conversation with a black crewman who it turned out had worked aboard the

Clyde-Mallory ships during the 1930s. The *Cherokee,* he told me, met a disastrous end. Its cabins and super-structure were constructed of plywood, he said, and during the war, pressed into duty with the Navy, it was torpedoed by a U-boat off Nova Scotia. The flimsy superstructure crumpled, and the ship went down within a matter of minutes. As for the *Algonquin,* it had eventually been sold to a Turkish shipping firm, and as far as he knew it was still in service somewhere in the Black Sea.

To the north of the Clyde-Mallory docks, at the foot of Market Street and behind the stately U.S. Custom House, were also numerous small craft, as well as the old Cooper River Ferry terminal. In the 1920s, before the immense twin-spanned Cooper River bridge was built across Charleston Harbor from the city to Mount Pleasant on the western shore, a pair of sizeable ferryboats, the *Palmetto* and the *Lawrence,* had provided transportation. The older of the two, the *Lawrence,* had a pair of tall smokestacks and a large walking-beam atop the cabin; the *Palmetto* was a diesel-powered craft without such conspicuous trappings. Years later I was struck by a description in William Styron's novel *Set This House On Fire* of the ferryboats that during his childhood had traveled between Newport News and Norfolk, Virginia: "those low-slung smoke-belching tubs which had always

possessed their own incomparable dumpy glamour." For
there *was* a glamour about such craft, boxlike and
double-ended, so perfectly adapted to their function.

To drive aboard them, en route to the beach, was
an exciting business, the family car clumping down the
serrated steel gangway between the huge clusters of
pilings ringed at the top, onto the deck and along a
narrow avenue to our assigned parking place. Then the
rattle of the chains in the sprocket-wheel hoist
mechanisms as the gangway was drawn up free of the
deck, and the throbbing rumble of the engines and the
rocking motion beneath the deck as the ferry moved out
from the slip and into the harbor. Usually we got out of
the automobile and went up a stairway to the upper
deck, to sit on wooden benches and watch as the ferry
made its way across the harbor. Midway across, the two
ferries, crowded with automobiles, passed each other,
engines churning away, firmly intent upon their missions.
Then, as the dock drew near and we returned to our
automobile, came the abrupt cessation of the engine's
pulsating vibration as it disengaged its gears. The ferry
glided silently dockward, only to have the engine roar
into action again as, this time in reverse, the forward
momentum was stemmed and the wide bow of the
slowed boat bumped into the pilings and slid by them as
they swayed back, then came to a stop in front of the

---

ramp. Then more rattling of chains as the ramp was lowered, the protective guard chains strung across the bow were removed, and one by one the waiting automobiles were flagged forward and bumped across the steel gangway and up the ramp to firm ground.

By the time I was able to visit the waterfront on my own, the *Palmetto* and the *Lawrence* had been out of service for several years, the new Cooper River bridge having usurped their clientele. The only ferry still in operation from the dock behind the Custom House was a much smaller, open-decked affair operated by a Captain Baitery, which, powered by a single diesel engine, plied the waters between Charleston and Sullivan's Island. Running an hour each way, it was a much longer journey than straight across to Mount Pleasant by bridge. I watched the boat seemingly creep across the harbor past Castle Pinckney, its engine emitting a thin, droning monotone as it moved along ever so slowly. Still, it was a working ferryboat, and worthy of its own dignity.

The docks farther up the river were where the freighters put in. There were certain regular visitors, such as the *Shickshinny,* and I could see their yellow masts and cargo above the roofs of the warehouses, but these ships were off limits, unapproachable behind chain link fences. The small, white-hulled steamships of the United Fruit Company's Great White Fleet called regularly, and their

operations were open to view from the land. Standing at
the foot of the wharf, I could watch the stalks of green
bananas coming ashore on roller ladders in a steady
stream, to be grasped by black laborers and borne toward
the yellow open-doored railroad refrigerator cars, where
checkers kept tally as the bananas were loaded for
shipment. Outside, beyond the entrance to the dock, long
strings of railroad cars were shunted into position.

Strung out all along the shore of the waterfront
were the rusty-railed tracks of the Port Utilities
Commission, linking the various wharves with the outside
world and with sidings leading to warehouses downtown.
Occasionally a locomotive would be working these tracks,
a small, grimy switcher with standing boards in front of
the pistons for brakemen to ride upon as the locomotive
distributed some boxcars and collected others. It was a
slow, painstaking operation, with the locomotive, one or
more boxcars attached, moving back and forth along the
tracks, occasionally proceeding up a side track as the
brakemen opened the switches. The iron wheels squealed
as curves were being negotiated, the locomotive spotting
a boxcar or two and emitting considerable smoke and
much noise as it came and went.

From Adger's Wharf to the ferryboat dock
behind the Custom House was my territory. I knew it
all, every step of it, every pier and piling. Most of all,

however, it was Adger's Wharf itself that drew me like a magnet. On Saturday mornings I would linger there for hours at a time watching the proceedings, waiting for the tugboats to cast off their lines and go over to the Clyde Line dock to help the *Cherokee,* now bedecked with pennants, extricate itself and back out into the channel, then swing its stern upstream and proceed southward under its own power, very slowly at first, past Adger's Wharf and the High Battery until it turned eastward in the Ashley River channel and headed off to sea. Eventually the ship was no more than a long low shape in the water out beyond Fort Sumter, and was bound for New York or Jacksonville. But by then it was getting toward late afternoon and time for me to walk up Broad Street to Meeting Street, to the post office. There I would board the Rutledge Avenue car that would take me all the way uptown to Sans Souci Street and home.

It would be many years before I would begin to realize why Adger's Wharf had such significance for me. But one reason I was so drawn to the Charleston water-front—its ships and cargo launches and tugboats and trawlers—was that it seemed to fuse two discrete realms of my experience; it was the stuff of literature and the imagination, and yet was *not* self-consciously picturesque or quaint but immediate and real and important to me.

The workboats *belonged* on the Downtown scene, as that
scene figured in my experience, yet they were Uptown in
what they did and in how they looked and in the people
who worked aboard them. Workboats didn't sail in
regattas, or go cruising along the High Battery with
fashionable people aboard; they carried freight and pulled
barges and trawled for seafood. But they did those things
on the waterfront and in the harbor and along the sea
islands, where the Civil War and the British attack on
Charleston had taken place and the pirate ships had sailed,
about which the poems and stories were written. To be
associated with a workboat was to unite those two realms
of existence. They were almost the only part of my
experience back then that I could identify as representing
what I hoped some day to attain: a place for grounding
my imagination in actuality.

Nowadays Adger's Wharf is gone from the Charleston
waterfront, as are the Clyde-Mallory wharves that were
next to it. The area has been made into a park. The ship
channel no longer runs along the downtown waterfront,
and ships enter the harbor and depart over beyond Castle
Pinckney. To see the shrimp trawlers and other such
workboats one must travel over to Mount Pleasant, across
the harbor. But that is part of Charleston, too, now. It is
only in my memory that the city of sixty-two thousand

inhabitants, bordered on the north by Mount Pleasant Street and on the south, east, and west by water, divided into an Uptown and Downtown of which I was part of both and of neither, still exists.

When I come back to Charleston now I am a visitor, a tourist, even. I have not lived there for almost half a century, and most of my friends and almost all of my family there are gone as well. Yet my imagination still inhabits the place as it was in the 1920s and 1930s and early 1940s; and what the intervening years have done is not to change the place that my imagination knows, but only the perspective from which I view it.

By having my boat, designed for purposes of pleasure and for going about on the water, built on a workboat hull, I would be contriving an emblem of that transaction.

2

SAILBOAT FOR SALE

When Robert E. Lee surrendered to U. S. Grant in April of 1865, it was necessary for him to issue a last general order to the soldiers still remaining in the hungry and depleted Confederate ranks. The order, drafted by his adjutant and approved and signed by Lee, began by saying that after four years of loyal service, the Army of Northern Virginia had been compelled to yield to overwhelming numbers and resources. "I need not tell the brave survivors of so many hard fought battles, who have remained steadfast to the last," it continued, "that I have consented to this result from no distrust of them; but feeling that valor and devotion could accomplish nothing that could compensate for the loss that must have attended the continuance of the contest, I determined to avoid the useless sacrifice of those whose past services have endeared them to their countrymen."

That is more or less the way I feel about
sailboats.

The decision to have a power cruiser built on a
workboat hull did not come out of a lack of admiration
for the virtues of sailing. It was reached in spite of them.
For it wasn't as if I had not given sailing a fair trial, or
did not appreciate its merits. On the contrary; it is my
belief that by any objective standard other than utilitarian
efficiency, sailing is to powerboating as a first-rate
Vouvray or Cabernet is to *vin ordinaire,* or a two-hit
shutout to a routine baseball game in which the winning
pitcher gives up several home runs and is replaced after
seven innings. Leaving out for now the subjective factors
involved, I gave up sailboats in favor of power because I
was not up to sailing, rather than the other way around.

The fact is that, after a six-year period of owning
sailboats, I made the decision to go back to what
dedicated sailors refer to as the "stinkpots" some months
before the idea of having a new boat built came to me. I
did so because I realized that, given my native clumsiness
and accumulating antiquity, I was not only never going
to be a reasonably competent sailor but indeed was,
physiologically at least, moving in the opposite direction.

Before concluding that it would be the better part
of valor to leave the ranks of those who cruise the waters
with the aid of wind rather than fossil fuel, I went

through five sailboats in all. I acquired the first only after a four-year hiatus during which the only boating I did was via small, trailerable runabouts made for fishing in lakes near my home in Chapel Hill, North Carolina. The period in question coincided with the college years of our two sons. From having myself taught at several kinds of institutions of higher learning, I was convinced that one gets the most for the education dollar at good—the adjective is important—small liberal arts colleges rather than at large universities, however prestigious. But the cost of such colleges runs very high. Between education and boating, therefore, it was either/or, and education came first. So my wife and I remortgaged our house, and I sold my power cruiser and did without the consolations of boating on salt water.

Once our older son graduated, our priorities could be readjusted, and borrowing money to acquire another boat was no longer beyond consideration. During the boatless years, however, OPEC had asserted itself, and oil prices had skyrocketed. The wave of the future, so far as pleasure boating was concerned, appeared to lie with sail power. Various of my friends were avid sailors, and they were constantly extolling its glories. Not only that, but our older son, who enjoyed sailing, was now back at home and working as a reporter on the local newspaper.

So sailboating it would be. I bought a fifteen-foot

---

day-sailer to learn the rudiments at a nearby lake. It took
me a while to get the hang of it; the contortions required
for changing directions were remarkable. The first time I
tried coming about all by myself, I ended up leaning as
far back as I could over the side, the tiller clutched with
one hand against my adam's apple and a length of the
jibsheet wrapped around my pipe while I worked
frantically at looping the rest of it around a winch.

Eventually I managed to learn how to tack, reach,
and keep to an approximate course without falling off
from the wind or jibing, whereupon I went in search of a
cabin craft. For reasons of stability and safety I was
determined to get one with a fixed keel rather than a
centerboard. A novelist friend and former student of
mine, John Barth, for whom sailing is as compulsive and
almost as accomplished an activity as writing, helped me
locate a reasonably priced twenty-two-foot Columbia
sloop in Annapolis, Maryland, which I bought and had
transported to a marina in Washington, North Carolina,
at the head of the Pamlico River.

The sloop was fin-keeled, and bore the name
HMS Groundhog. She was reasonably fast, stiff, and quite
seaworthy. The HMS business was a bit much, and I
painted out the initials, but I liked the name *Groundhog*
and retained it. To my surprise I found that she was far
easier to handle than the day-sailer had been; when

coming about, the boom generally stayed put and only the jib was shifted, and the operation in general was more forgiving of error and imprecision.

By the time I learned to take *Groundhog* out by myself, however, my son had departed the city for a job on a larger newspaper. I still didn't feel particularly comfortable single-handing a twenty-two-foot sailboat, so the following winter I sold *Groundhog* and bought a seventeen-foot O'Day day-sailer, which I kept in my yard on a trailer, intending to improve my skills for a while at a lake not far from home. What I found, however, was that getting her to the lake, stepping the mast and setting the stays, then shoving her off the trailer and into the water, only to have to repeat the process in reverse several hours later, was a formidable chore for one person, with the result that the O'Day wasn't getting used. After a year or so I sold it, too.

There was another half-year hiatus, but when spring drew near the vital juices began stirring. What was I doing without a boat? Moreover, my sailing son was back in town, having set aside journalism for the pursuit of a Ph.D. in literary study (just as I had done several decades earlier). So off to salt water I went again, in search of a sailboat. I wanted something with a cabin large enough to sleep aboard without undue discomfort, and an enclosed head. At a marina near New Bern, North

---

Carolina, I found what I thought I wanted, a twenty-two-foot Westerly Nomad, a twin-keeled, British-made sloop with an unusually small cockpit and an unusually large cabin. She was a heavy, ruggedly constructed affair, and slow in the water, but certainly on the safe side for a none-too-agile soul such as myself. We named her the *Diane,* after my younger son's wife, and installed her in a slip in a marina at Minnesott Beach, on the Neuse River in North Carolina.

The limitations of the *Diane* became fully apparent on a four-day cruise that my son and I made to Belhaven, North Carolina. It was not merely that the compromise made to provide her with a larger cabin meant that only two persons could occupy the cockpit at the same time, one of them sitting behind the tiller. It was also that, as noted, she was English-built and constructed to withstand the chilled winds and often heavy weather of the English Channel and the North Sea. It made her seaworthy, all right; she was even equipped with a storm stay. It also meant that the cabin windows did not open, and except for the hatches, interior ventilation was confined to what could be extracted through several small round ports forward.

We tied up one steamy evening alongside a dock at Hobucken, North Carolina, on the Intracoastal Waterway; the forecast called for a procession of cold fronts to converge on the area from the north and south, each with heavy weather. There was even a tornado alert. Fortunately the tornados did not materialize, but thunderstorms raged all night long. The wind blew at so sharp an angle that the tarpaulins we had rigged over the forward and companionway hatches so that we could keep them open were useless; we had to fasten the hatches all the way. The single small twelve-volt fan I had installed in the forward cabin was of little use. It was hot, sweaty, clammy, and miserable, with the rain shattering in sheets upon the cabin roof just above our heads, the lightning blasting away in continuing salvos, and the boat rocking and pitching against her lines. The *Diane* had V-berths forward, and these were decently roomy; since my son is six feet four inches tall he slept there. That left the main cabin berths for me, and not only were these very narrow, but to gain room they were designed to extend back underneath the cockpit for half their length. Needless to say, the resulting *cul-de-*sack was if anything less ventilated than the interior of the cabin. It was a long, uncomfortable night.

Compared with the contours of American hulls, the *Diane*'s traditional British shape did not make for blazing speed; as John Rousmaniere notes in *The Golden Pastime: A New History of Yachting,* the British boating fraternity encountered this truth as far back as 1851, when the *America* routed the best that the Queen's yachtsmen could throw again her at Cowes: "To [the English], a bow was not a knife but a blunt head of a codfish. The widest beam should be at the boat's shoulders, about one-third of the way aft from the stem, and from there to the narrow stern should be a long tweezers. No wonder that, after seeing *America* perform, the Earl of Anglesey commented that he had spent his lifetime sailing backwards."

Diane was built 119 years after that demonstration took place, yet she had the identical cod's-head conformation: blunt bow, tapering stern, a narrow beam, and a deep draft for stability. She was certainly not built with speed as her object; this was true not only for her considerable below-waterline acreage but her twin bilge keels, meant to enable her to sit firmly and level when the extreme tidal ranges of the English Channel left boats high and dry in harbors. That the twin keels produced extensive drag through the water was secondary to the stability and comfort they gave in strong winds and rough waters, and during breezy conditions *Diane* could sail along at an almost-level keel while nearby craft were heeled far over with railings awash.

Unfortunately, this also meant that in light airs *Diane* moved very slowly indeed, if at all. Jack Barth had warned me about this when I had consulted him before

buying her; boats like the Westerlys, he said, were fine in
blustery situations, but sailing conditions on the East
Coast of the United States, unlike those in English
waters, encompassed many days of balmy weather and
gentle breeze. And that was the problem: I didn't object
to *Diane*'s slow pace; her stability was a more than ample
trade-off. The difficulty was that there were too many
days when she moved along hardly at all, managing to do
little more than drift placidly while other sailboats,
although setting no speed records, were nonetheless
making their way across the water with sufficient celerity
to offer the sense of sailing to those aboard.

Why didn't I heed Jack Barth's all-too-accurate
warning? I think it was the *Diane*'s looks. She didn't *look*
like your ordinary sloop; with her curved-out rather than
undercut prow, her stubby mast, storm stay, long cabin,
round ports, stubby stern, and general absence of chrome
and brightwork, she seemed different, more down-
to-earth, more utilitarian—in short, not only more
old-fashioned but somehow more like a working
watercraft.

In any event, ultimately I began looking for
another, more satisfactory, sailboat. I put the *Diane* up
for sale, and set out to find a replacement that would sail
better in conditions of light air and would be adequately
ventilated on summer evenings, with wider and less

claustrophobic berth accommodations. It wasn't long before a broker friend of mine in Beaufort, John Nelson, turned up a 1963 Pearson Triton, twenty-eight and a half feet long, that completely took my fancy. There was ample cabin room, a spacious cockpit that could accommodate four persons without undue cramping, complete liveaboard facilities including a stereo radio, propane stove with three-burner oven, a refrigerator, a half-dozen ports that opened, and a ventilation hatch in the main cabin as well as a larger hatch forward. Her previous owner was a sailmaker, and not only did she come with an extensive inventory of sails in excellent condition, including a cruising spinnaker, but he had done much cruising aboard her, and she was equipped with Loran-C, and RDF, a knot-meter and depth-finder built into the cockpit, spare gas cans, storm covers over the cabin windows, an autopilot, and moreover was rigged for sail handling from the cockpit. Built for bluewater cruising, she was full-keeled, with a thirty horsepower Atomic 4 gasoline engine. Designed by Carl Alberg, the Triton had been the first production sailboat of her size, and her fiberglass hull was close to an inch thick. She was sturdy, stiff, seaworthy, had plenty of sail space for light airs, and she was *fast*—so much so, in fact, that she had done her share of racing and was equipped with stay tackle for bending her mast. She had, indeed, a great deal

of equipment that I would probably never be using, for I
had no plans for racing or bluewater cruising anytime
soon.

The survey turned up only two major flaws. At
one point in her career the Pearson Triton's forward deck
had become jammed underneath a pier, causing a portion
of her starboard deck to become spongy. The current
owner agreed to pay for having that repaired. The other
problem was the Atomic 4 engine—it was original
equipment, and had seen almost a quarter century of
service. It was still functioning, however, and I decided
that, since the owner was going to deliver the boat to the
marina, a twenty-mile journey about half of which would
be under power, it was likely that if she made it from
Beaufort to Minnesott Beach the engine would thereby
have proved itself in decent enough shape to be used for
a while longer—the more so because my son would go
along on the trip to observe its performance.

So I bought her, renaming her *Virginius* after a
longtime writer friend, Virginius Dabney.

My assumption about the engine proved wrong.
Apparently the run from Beaufort to Minnesott Beach
was its last gasp, because thereafter it began overheating,
the transmission began slipping, and I ended up having to
replace the engine with a rebuilt Atomic 4 that I located
in Irvington, Virginia. As a sailboat, however, both in

action and at the dock, the *Virginius* was everything I had hoped she would be. She handled beautifully, showed her heels to many a new craft of the same size, and was at her best in rough water.

Why, then, did I decide to sell her after only two years? The answer, alas, was that she proved to be too much sailboat for me to handle. As long as my older son could sail with me, all was fine. But by then he had gotten himself married, was holding down a part-time job while continuing his doctoral studies, and he had his own life to live, so that only occasionally could he take weekends off to go down the Neuse River with me.

Meanwhile I had turned sixty-five, and after much soul-searching, I was forced to come to the realization that sailboats were for the young, or in any event for persons whether young or old who were more agile and in better physical shape than I. Even with winches, the act of raising the *Virginius*'s sizeable sails was a demanding task. By the time I got her out of the entrance canal to the marina and raised the sails, I was out of breath, exhausted, with my heart pounding wildly. Once under way, in any kind of weather there was the constant need to be adjusting this or that, going up onto the narrow, pitching bow to change headsails, on each tack freeing one jibsheet and winching in the other tightly, and so on.

The sum of it was that I could not single-hand the *Virginius*. I found myself taking her out on the river only on days when breezes were light and seas gentle—yet anybody knows that by far the best sailing comes when the wind is brisk and a sailboat can heel over on a long run, her windward deck trailing barely above the surface of the water, and go streaking along at full speed, hell for leather. It is when the reaches are long and exhilarating that a sailboat like the *Virginius* becomes her true self, and amply justifies her existence.

I could swap the *Virginius* for a smaller boat, of course, but as anyone familiar with sailboats also knows, smaller size does not diminish the physical exertion and dexterity required. Raising the sails might be less demanding, since there was less canvas to hoist up, but there would be more frequent coming about, changing of headsails, adjustments and trimming.

Reluctantly, therefore, I had to concede that if I was going to continue to do much boating, I would have to return to powerboats. If only I had learned to sail when I was young, so that all the acts I found so arduous would long since have become second nature, accumulated skill and experience making up for waning physique. How old was Sir Francis Chichester when he sailed single-handed across the Atlantic? How old was Joshua Slocum when he rounded the tip of South

America aboard the *Spray?* How old was Ulysses when he set out for the Happy Isles (though he had help, to be sure)? Regretfully, that wasn't the point: I was too heavy, too flabby, had spent too many years at a typewriter or in front of a class and not enough on boats. I was a not-very-skilled weekend sailor—and that wasn't good enough.

In short, it was time to toss in the towel. In General Lee's words, overwhelming numbers and resources had forced me to yield. My all-too-brief sailing days were over.

A friend of mine once remarked that of all the various kinds of pleasure craft—power cruisers, sportsfishermen, skiffs, houseboats, canoes, kayaks, bassboats—sailboats receive the least amount of use by their owners. I have no statistics to support his contention, but my hunch is that it is true. Drive past any marina on the coast and you will find there a forest of bare masts, resembling so many telephone poles. If the weather is good and it is a weekend there may be some sails in view out on the river or bay, but in a proportion of, say, one for every ten bare masts at the docks.

Yet paradoxically, those who own sailboats are among the most enthusiastic and intensely engaged of boat people. Step into the office of someone who keeps a

sloop or a cutter on salt water, and there will be a
picture of the boat prominently displayed on the wall or
the desk. Your sailboat owner will passionately talk
sailing by the hour. He will own a collection of books
on the subject. Copies of the latest issues of boating
magazines will lie on his coffee table and next to his
couch. In a little book about fishing and fishermen that I
once wrote, I remarked that whereas bass fishermen are
literate, trout fishermen are literary. The same distinction
holds for powerboat owners and sailors. Sailing is not
merely a kind of boating; it is a stance, a face with which
to meet the world, an attitude toward life. You operate a
powerboat; you *are* a sailor. The sailboat aficionado
thinks, reads, dreams about sailing. He has taste; it is
impossible to imagine him naming his boat what I once
saw plastered in large letters across the stern of a costly
double-decked power cruiser: MENOPAUSE MAMA.

You can always recognize a sailboat person at a
marina or along a waterfront, because he will be clad in a
uniform, one that is no less standard for the fact that no
two such uniforms are exactly alike. It is characterized by
a kind of studied frowziness. There is a soft, flop-
brimmed canvas hat (in very cold weather a woolen
watch cap)—never a cap with a visor. Why no sailboat
people wear visored caps, while all powerboat people do,
is puzzling, since both are exposed to about the same
dosage of sunlight and wind. The full-time sailor

customarily sports a full, grizzled beard. The weekend sailor cannot usually manage that, but while on his boat he goes unshaven, and when he takes his summer vacation and is able to stay away from his office for several weeks at a time, he contrives to get himself sufficiently fuzzy to permit a snapshot to be taken showing him in proper form.

The shirt of the sailing uniform is worn wrinkled and unironed, and is preferably made of faded denim, although a horizontally striped jersey will do. No genuine sailboat person wears full-length trousers, or, if female, a skirt. Shorts—khaki, gray, or dirty white—are de rigueur, or, in cold weather, sweatpants. The belt is preferably of rope weave, though fabric is acceptable—but *never* patent leather. Sneakers or sandals may be worn, if they have gripper soles. In chilly or rainy weather the top half of a set of foul-weather gear, with hood thrown casually back from the neck, is absolutely mandatory; yellow is the approved color, but red or blue will do if this is the only way that a Henri Lloyd label can be displayed. Forest green, if properly shabby, can be tolerated without permanent loss of status. (Do not, by the way, ever refer to such garb as a "raincoat"; it is essential that it be called "foul-weather gear," if the proper image of bluewater seafaring is to be maintained.)

Worn properly, a sailing uniform closely

resembles the outfit that one might expect to see on a
beach bum in Tahiti or Key West. Yet for all its
hangdog look, one would never suspect the sailboat
person of actually being down and out. Perhaps it is the
waterproof gold Rolex or Omega wristwatch, perhaps the
class ring; perhaps it is the authority with which he
comports himself; but whatever the reason, your
appropriately clothed sailboat person is not likely to be
mistaken as belonging to the downtrodden and
underprivileged of this world. He is Work Ethic all the
way, with a smidgen of Lawrence-man thrown in for
flavoring.

I used to wonder sometimes why weekend sailors
are so dedicated to their art, and yet use their boats less
often than other boat owners. I decided that what is most
important to them, more even than the enjoyment of
sailing, is the symbolism involved in owning the boat.
The act of possession—being able to think in terms of
"my boat"—is what is crucial. Certainly on any kind of
economic scale, even that by which one justifies keeping a
boat, most weekend sailors would be far better off with
an inexpensive day-sailer, kept on a trailer rather than at
the dock, considering the amount of sailing they will
actually engage in. They could charter a decent-sized
cabin craft for the two or three weeks a year that they
will actually be able to travel anywhere on a boat. But

no, the sailboat must be owned. Chartering won't do,
except as a supplementary activity to be conducted down
in the Caribbean—in which case it can be a definite plus.

Is it the snobbery of the thing? Is the boat a
status symbol? To an extent, perhaps, depending on the
circumstances. But most sailboats aren't palatial affairs; if
conspicuous consumption is what is desired, expensive
power cruisers and trawler yachts are far more effective.
Moreover, the older the sailboat, the more primitive its
accoutrements, the greater the prestige and respect that the
owner commands among most sailboat people. Is it a
resurgence of the seafaring instinct, the assertion of
long-suppressed seafaring blood? Hardly. I have noticed
no particular correlation of sailboat ownership with
descent from the time-honored seafaring races. Besides, if
seagoing ancestry is responsible for the urge to own
sailboats, then why was I so taken with sailing that from
the mid-1970s until the sale of the *Virginius* I had owned
five different sailboats, ranging from fifteen to twenty-
eight and a half feet? So far as I can determine, my own
forebears have mainly been landlubbers for the past
several millennia; the only really notable seafarer of my
ethnic past was a certain fugitive who took passage on a
boat bound for Tarshish, was thrown overboard by the
crew during a storm, and was saved from drowning by
being swallowed by a whale.

The truth that lies behind sailboat fever is to be found neither in economics nor genetics, but in metaphysics. For the compulsion toward ownership of a sailboat is ultimately symbolic—but not in terms of status.

Consider that a sailboat depends for her propulsion not on machinery but on air. An engine may be appropriate for getting her away from her berth at the marina and out into the river or bay or ocean, but it is hardly an essential feature of the activity. People owned sailboats for pleasure long before Robert Fulton first thought of hooking up a steam engine to a set of paddle wheels. Once under way, a boat's sails are hoisted, and the wind takes her whither she is bound. The point is that it is an elemental situation—basic, primitive, literally dependent upon the elements. The sailor who takes his boat out on the water is surrounded by flowing water, and is doing no more than what the seagoing folk of earliest times did: using a thin sheet of fabric—woven mat, cotton, flax, silk, nylon, Kevlar, it is all the same—hoisted upon a pole to traverse that water. The boat may be constructed of reed grass, oxhide, cypress planking, steel plates, fiberglass; it is still a floating object.

The sailor, whether bound from a yacht harbor on the mainland to a point downriver or from Cadiz to Hispaniola, is setting out across a body of water, using only the wind to propel him, and how rapidly or comfortably he may attain his destination will depend upon such skill as he possesses in interpreting the tide and wind, selecting and adjusting the sails, handling the tiller, and keeping the bow properly aimed. He is, in short, engaged in bending nature to human purposes, and in a palpable and very direct way.

Nature is inextricably involved. The wind, the water, the sun are not only unmistakably present; there is no way that anyone can pretend that they do not matter and need not be reckoned with at all times. At home the sailboat person may drive to work in his automobile and not be overly concerned with whether it is raining or blowing or snowing. He lives in a sturdy house, safe from the elements. But once he ventures out in his sailboat he must pay vital heed to them, for not only his comfort but his safety depend on what is going on with wind and weather.

Sailing, therefore, is an experience—not the only kind, but one kind—that can allow one to exist and function under conditions that speak to one's basic situation as a human being. Aboard a sailboat the boatman consults, and seeks to use, wind and current. What he does—tightening or slackening off a sail, steering a course, allowing for tidal drift, staying alert to spot and take advantage of a gust of wind moving across

the water, pointing just off the wind, coming about—will
directly affect his progress. He moves along without
machinery; there is no engine grinding away, but only
flowing air and rushing water.

What owning a sailboat offers, I think, is a kind
of symbolic reunion with the natural world, a reassertion
of basics. No matter that in actuality the sailor will
venture no further from his boat's dock than a few dozen
miles, and then only on infrequent occasions. When he
casts off the lines and takes his sailboat out on the water,
he has placed himself in a situation that is about as
independent of the complex social involvement of
modern life as is possible. He can experience a
self-sufficiency, an elemental freedom, that is otherwise
lacking in his life.

It is scarcely coincidental that so many sailboat
owners live at a considerable distance from the marinas
where their boats are kept—which is of course why
sailboats are actually used comparatively rarely. It is
precisely *because* he is able to get to his boat only
occasionally that he must own the boat. His job, his
family, his community responsibilities, the regimen of his
daily life keep him caught up in their constant demands
on his time and energy. It is therefore of great symbolic
importance to him to be able to feel that, a hundred
miles away down on the coast or at the lake, his boat is

there, waiting for him, so that he can break away from
his routine and take it out on the water, away from land,
to deal with wind and wave and tide on his own—so
that he can be self-sufficient.

No, the pride of possession involved in owning a
sailboat is not so much conspicuous consumption,
sublimated sexual symbolism, and so on, as the assurance
that one can regain access—can flee, if you will—to what
is basically and inescapably natural and real. Subject to
the elemental restrictions of the natural world, and with
the aid of those natural forces of wind and tide, the sailor
can control his life, choose his destination.

But is this not also true of powerboats? Well, to
an extent—but ultimately it is not the same. One steers a
powerboat; one sails a sailboat. The involvement is far
greater. The sailboat will be able to move through the
water precisely in ratio to the skill with which the sails
are tended and the bow kept aligned. It is that very
primitiveness that is so attractive.

The sailor is thoroughly engaged with what he is
doing. He must constantly exert himself, stay alert and
observant. He must hold the tiller or wheel, keep on
course, constantly check the trim of the sails, the direction
of the wind, the action of the waves. Such daydreaming
as is possible must be tentative and wary; there is too
much reality around and above and underneath to permit

the attention to wander from the here and now for very long. Abstract theorizing, extended cogitation—these are for later, when the sailboat is at anchor or back at the dock and the sailor can relax on a berth in the cabin. While sailing one is always busy.

There is nothing in powerboating (which however has satisfactions of its own) that is really comparable, for example, to the act of tacking. True, when steering a powerboat in rough water one sometimes alters course to quarter the oncoming seas rather than meet them headlong, so as to reduce pounding. But when one tacks a sailboat one is using the very contrariness of the wind against itself. The sailor cannot proceed directly into the face of the wind, so he alters his course just enough to force that oncoming wind to propel him, however indirectly, toward its source. Depending on the direction from which the wind is blowing and the course that the sailor selects, he sometimes gives up actual forward progress in order to gain it back in greater measure, by sailing on a losing tack, so that he can then come about and get closer to his destination.

What a skilled sailor who knows the capabilities of his boat and the way of the wind and water can do to maximize his progress and minimize the adversities of the weather is remarkable. One need only watch the progress of two sailboats of approximately similar construction and sail area, one of them sailed by a tyro and the other by a skilled sailor, to see the difference. As they zigzag back and forth before the face of the wind, first on gaining and then on losing tacks, each will appear at times to be overhauling the other—and measured as one measures distances with a powerboat, straight ahead from point of departure to destination, each boat will at times be nearer to the destination than the other. But gradually it will become evident that with each action of tacking and coming about, the gap between the boats is widening.

Eventually, as the two boats repeatedly pass each other going in opposite directions, the one boat will be farther ahead, closer to the destination even though never actually sailing toward it. Ultimately, even at the extremity of its losing tack, the boat sailed by the skilled sailor will be farther along than the other boat is at the apogee of its gaining tack. A few hours later, the leading boat is out of sight, or at most a tiny object on the horizon.

He who would do good must do it in minute particulars, quoth the poet Blake, and that is exactly what the skilled sailor has done. Small decisions, seemingly insignificant in themselves—exactly when to come about, to tighten or loosen mainsheet or jibsheet just a trifle, to vary course a few points to take maximum advantage of an oncoming gust, to give a sail more belly or to set it a

little more tautly, to adjust the position of the slide on
the traveler, to increase or reduce heeling and exactly
how much—add up to a sizeable advantage.

In general one uses a powerboat to do something—go
fishing, take a trip, observe wildlife, look at scenery,
explore creeks, bays, islands, waterways. The chief use of
a sailboat, by contrast, is for its own sake, for sailing.
How often do you see a sailboat anchored somewhere so
that its occupants can fish? There is certainly no law
against fishing from a sailboat; and although such things
as stays, booms, and lifelines make it rather less
convenient to use a rod and reel than is true of an
open-decked powerboat, it can be managed with
reasonable competence. But very few people with
sailboats ever use them for fishing, for the simple reason
that the act of sailing the boat itself is all the recreation
and activity anyone needs.

Compared to what sailors must do and know,
powerboating is relatively undemanding. I do not mean,
of course, that in severe weather it does not require
considerable skill (which is why I take care to avoid
severe weather). But the fact is that so long as his engine
is functioning the powerboatman can cope, while without
it he is helpless—and the reliability of that engine does
not significantly depend on the skill with which he

operates it. Either it runs or it does not. By contrast, the sailboat not only admits of degrees of flying canvas—from full sail to storm trysail—but is designed to function in conditions of wind and wave that would soon swamp most powerboats of comparable size. It is not foolproof against all wind and wave action, but it can survive horrendous blows—if the sailor knows what he is about. It is no wonder that sailboat people, being human and therefore susceptible to the sin of pride, often tend to look down upon those who use powerboats as lesser creatures, and to employ such terms as "stinkpots" and "gassers" to designate the craft that such lesser breeds utilize. Human motives are rarely pure. I sometimes think that sailboat people are not guiltless of wanting to own and operate sailboats in order to feel themselves superior.

There is also a certain element of masochism involved in sailing, a positive taking of pleasure in doing things the hard way. How otherwise to account for the contempt with which no small number of sailboat people view such conveniences as roller reefing, electric-powered raising and lowering of mainsails, Loran-C, fiberglass hulls, even the use of Marconi rigging rather than the demonstrably less efficient gaff rigging? In this sense, perhaps, they resemble antique automobile enthusiasts; but the person who restores and drives a 1923 Maxwell or a 1932 Ford V-8 does not, so far as I know, affect a disdain for drivers of late-model cars. So while the joys of antiquarianism are involved in sailing, there is considerably more to it than that. Rather, it is a kind of primitivistic impulse, reminiscent of the impulse that led Henry David Thoreau to live alone in a shanty next to Walden Pond. And just as there is a good deal of ostentatious self-righteousness in *Walden,* so your sailor of sailboats sometimes tends toward the sin of pride.

On the other hand, sometimes he has a good deal to be prideful about.

I have to say that in my own brief sailing career, which the sale of the *Virginius* now formally brought to a close, I was not guilty of that particular sin, and for good reason—I was not much of a sailor, and I knew it only too well. For one thing, I came to it too late. However much I enjoyed my years of sailing, and drew pleasure and satisfaction from owning a sailboat out of all proportion to my expertise when aboard, it was getting so that keeping and maintaining the *Virginius* was becoming a charade—and a costly one at that, for old boats constantly require repairs, and long-used mechanical parts and fittings wear out.

So I gave my old sailboat up, and there can be no doubt that I was right to do so. Someday I may want to acquire a small day-sailer to go along with the new powerboat, but hereafter most of my boating will be conducted aboard boats driven by engines. And I shall enjoy it. But it will not be the same as sailing. Boating for me will be something like the situation in the closing lines of Robert Frost's poem entitled "The Oven Bird":

> *The question that he frames in all but words*
> *Is what to make of a diminished thing.*

I intend to make as much of it as I can.

Before I could think about acquiring a powerboat commensurate with what I wished to do with her—not merely go about the harbor and do some fishing—I would have to sell the *Virginius*. In truth I was not at all sure what kind of boat I would get. I knew that I wanted one with sufficiently spacious cabin accommodations to spend weekends aboard her in some comfort, and with an engine and mechanical equipment reliable enough to take trips—perhaps even down the Intracoastal Waterway to Charleston—without worrying about imminent breakdowns.

Meanwhile, however, the bottom had fallen out of the used-sailboat market. Production fiberglass boats had been built and marketed for thirty years, and the supply had outreached demand. Unlike wooden craft, the hulls of fiberglass boats, if properly constructed, do not wear out. New boats were replacing old boats, which, although often requiring repair and refurbishing, were still in usable condition. There were now too many of them. When I put the *Virginius* up for sale I looked at the used-boat listings in *Soundings,* a monthly publication which contains thousands of boat-for-sale advertisements, and discovered that no less than nine other Pearson Tritons were being offered to buyers.

I put the *Virginius* in the hands of the Minnesott Beach Yacht Basin brokerage service, planning to use her occasionally as a powerboat to do a little fishing until a buyer was found. The Neuse River, however, though an ideal place for sailing, had its drawbacks for fishing, and Minnesott Beach was far enough upstream from the entrance to Pamlico Sound that its water was brackish. If one wanted to catch fish, the North Carolina coast was the place to be—namely Morehead City, twenty miles away from Minnesott Beach by river and canal.

Late that spring, I was over in Morehead City visiting my friend Bob Simpson, an outdoors writer one of whose books my publishing company had published, and we had happened upon a thirty-year-old wooden, lapstrake-hulled Luhrs Sea-Skiff for sale at an extremely low price. She was powered by an ancient Chrysler Crown gasoline engine, which might well go bad at any time and have to be replaced or completely re-built. Even if that proved necessary, however, the total cost would not be too far out of line considering what one might expect to pay for a serviceable fishing boat of that size.

So I bought her, with the idea of using her in and about the waters near Beaufort and Morehead City that summer and fall, and then selling her once the *Virginius* was sold. In the meantime I would be able to enjoy a summer and fall of fishing.

The *Mary Simpson,* as I named her, after Bob's good wife, was berthed at a small marina in Peltier Creek. During June and July, with Bob's help, I built a roof over much of the cockpit, and installed folding benches and a VHF radio. She was ideal for use as a fishing boat, and had no deep keel to get hung up on the tricky bars, shoals, and tidal flats of the Beaufort–Morehead City harbor.

I did not for a moment consider using her for anything more demanding. Even if I were to replace her engine, she was too old, and she was not suited for cruising or for sleeping aboard. Her forward cabin was tiny and dark. To close in her open main cabin and make it sufficiently habitable to live on board for extended periods would have cost far more than she was worth. There were too many things that could go bad—the steering, the electrical system, and for all I knew even the old lapstrake hull itself.

Just as had happened with the *Virginius,* the

chance I had taken on her old engine behaving for a while was in vain. As is the way with old boats and old marine engines, it went bad without warning, the very first time I took her out for an extended run up the Waterway. For twenty minutes or so she ran perfectly, her oil pressure high, her cooling water temperature low, just as she had done for me and for the mechanic who had checked her out. Then she began to lose power.

Bill Simpson, Bob's brother, and his wife Susan were along with me for the run. Bill knew more than I did about gasoline engines, and we both assumed that there was merely something wrong with the fuel line. It turned out to be far more serious than that: there was water in the engine block itself. The cylinders had rusted through. What I then found out was that the notion that I could find another, later-model, engine in good condition for five or six hundred dollars or so, and drop it in to replace the ancient Chrysler Crown, was fallacious. It seems that all the more recent engines were built with the flywheel toward the stern, while that on the old Chrysler Crown was located in the front. The angle of the propeller shaft was therefore such that only another flywheel-forward engine could be installed.

At the time I bought the old boat I had paid an additional fifty dollars for an inoperative Chrysler Crown engine to be used for spare parts. Upon inspection by a mechanic, it appeared that the block of that engine was sound, and could be exchanged for the one now in the boat. But from long disuse and corrosion the cylinders of my fifty-dollar Chrysler Crown were frozen in place, and they would have to be drilled out, metal sleeves inserted in the holes, and the cylinders of the other engine used. It would also be necessary to remove a number of parts from the engine being replaced and fit them onto the replacement. In short, a formidable job, and one that would require many weeks to accomplish.

Thus for the time being any fishing I intended to do would have to be done from the good sailboat *Virginius*. But there too resided trouble, less serious to be sure, but equally if only temporarily incapacitating.

After having waited many months for the broker at Minnesott Beach Yacht Basin to turn up a buyer, I had asked my friend John Nelson in Beaufort, just across the river from Morehead City, whether he would handle it for me. He was quite willing to do so, but said he would be able to show her to many more prospective buyers if she were based nearby rather than at Minnesott Beach, which by land was a fifty-mile drive for him.

So my son and I had run the *Virginius* from her berth at Minnesott Beach Yacht Basin on the Neuse River up to the Waterway and then through a canal to Beaufort, North Carolina, across the harbor from

Morehead City. There it would be left at a dock on the waterfront and put up for sale.

An old boat is an old boat. Just as we reached the boat slip where the *Virginius* was to be berthed and were maneuvering to enter the slip against a strong tide, a pin holding together the coupler that joined the transmission to the propeller shaft dropped out, allowing the shaft and propeller to slide down onto the rudder. The rudder was thus locked into place, and the boat was without propulsion.

In other words, there I was with *two* boats, neither of which was in working condition.

I arranged with a boatyard to come and get the *Virginius* and repair the propeller shaft, and my son and I drove on home to Chapel Hill.

My wife, when she heard about the incident, was irate. "Sell them all!" she declared. "Sell both boats and for once in your life get yourself a boat that you can count on. Buy a new boat. For thirty years you've been messing around with old boats that are always breaking down, because you're afraid to spend enough to get something better. Most of the time you've ended up putting more money into fixing the old boat than a new one would have cost!"

"I know. You're right."

"Then why keep on doing it? We've got some

money now. You're sixty-five years old. You haven't got forever to use a boat. And besides, you're paying dockage on two boats. Sell them, and for heaven's sake get one boat that you'll be able to use when you want it! Get a new boat that won't break down."

Although the placing of the noun "boat," whether new or old, next to the verb phrase "won't break down" is what is known as a Contradiction in Terms, there was no denying her logic. A new or late-model boat *may* break down; an old boat *will* break down. The problem was that (a) old twenty-eight-and-a-half-foot sailboats like the *Virginius* are not for everybody, and there was no telling how long it would be before the broker found a purchaser; and (b) nobody was going to buy the *Mary Simpson* until it had an engine in operating condition. But my wife was right. Finally, in our mid-sixties, we had indeed reached a stage in our fiscal affairs at which I could afford to purchase a new boat—not one priced in the six figures, to be sure, or even close to that, but at least a new boat in the twenty-foot range—without unduly jeopardizing our future security.

Very well, then, I would do it. And when the new boat was ready I would take her down the Waterway all the way to the scene of the crime—to Charleston, and up the Ashley River to the point along the shore where, more than a half century earlier, my friend John Connolly and I had paddled the flimsy little boat we had made to the river's edge. Only this time I would not be looking *out* from the shore and marsh, at the river that was flowing past us toward the harbor and the ocean beyond, but *in,* toward the land and the place from which I had started out. I would then have come, as it were, full circle. The journey that I had wanted to make when young would have been completed.

3

THE SEARCH BEGUN

At any given time there are powerboats of all shapes, sizes, and degrees of costliness available in Morehead City, North Carolina. I looked at a few that were for sale, and was momentarily tempted by a new twenty-five-foot fiberglass skiff with a dead-rise hull and a high stand-up pilothouse forward. The skiff was powered by a two hundred horsepower outboard engine and was designed along the lines of the working launches of yore; it could be used either for work or pleasure. It was beyond a doubt a fast, well-built, efficient craft. I had been passed by such boats on the Waterway and had always admired their trim lines and workmanlike look.

The giant outboards manufactured today have reached a level of reliability, along with a degree of compactness, far beyond what was available twenty years or so ago, and my own recent experience with outboard motors had been quite satisfactory. Although they continue to be less fuel-efficient than inboard engines, they are readily and conveniently repairable; with a lighter engine on a stern bracket for trolling and emergency use, an outboard-powered skiff could be counted upon to go wherever I wished and to get back without incident or embarrassment. Considering the light use that she would get from me, there was much logic in acquiring the boat. A rational man, in my situation, would doubtless have opted for it. But if such a creature exists, it is not me, at least where boats are concerned. I wanted a boat that did not come out of a mold. I wanted one that was built of wood—built for me.

If you are going to have a boat built in my part of the country, you head for the Outer Banks. The guidebooks all refer to the enormous amount of boatbuilding from east of Morehead City and Beaufort to the tip of Carteret County, about forty miles to the northeast. The kind of boat known as a Core Sounder, recognizable by its flared bow and gracefully curving lines, is named for the long, shallow body of water lying between the mainland and the barrier islands. Modified to fit various needs, its shape has served for trawlers, head boats, power cruisers, and workboats of all kinds.

Harkers Island is known for building so many boats that the Core Sounder is frequently designated by

---

that name. Beyond Harkers Island, spaced at intervals along the highway that leads from Beaufort to the mainland terminus of the Cedar Island–Ocracoke ferry, are other small communities, each of which engaged in boatbuilding.

I had visited Harkers Island several times, but not in recent years. I called Ken Markel, who operates a marine repair service in the Morehead City area, and asked him about possible builders. The person who could tell me about such things, he said, was a man named Jerry Davis, who operated a boatbuilding works on Sleepy Creek Road in Marshallberg, just up the way from Harkers Island.

By telephone I got from Davis an estimate of approximately twenty-five thousand dollars for the kind of boat I had in mind, which was about what I had thought would be involved. He couldn't build the boat for me himself, he said, but he might be able to suggest someone. So on a Thursday afternoon in August I drove down to the coast. My plan was to go looking for a builder and then, if I could find an appropriate one and make some preliminary arrangements, to spend Saturday fishing in the harbor on the *Virginius,* which had been scheduled to be repaired the previous week.

I located Jerry Davis's shop easily enough. It was a tall, partly open building with a large, half-completed wooden cruiser inside; the cruiser was at least fifty feet long and there were two men hammering away up on the flying bridge. Davis was a small man of slight build with a thin black moustache. I explained my mission.

"I wish I could help you," he said, "but we don't build anything under forty-five feet anymore." We talked about boats and boatbuilding for a while. "There's almost nobody making small wooden boats now," Davis said. "It's all fiberglass, and that takes a big shop." He did know of one person who still turned them out, over on Harkers Island. His name was Jamie Lewis. "Just ask anybody on the island and they'll tell you where to find him." It was his understanding, however, that Lewis had orders that would keep him tied up for at least two years. Maybe Lewis could suggest someone else.

"How about in Atlantic? Is anybody building them there?" I asked, referring to a town twenty-five miles to the east.

"Nobody there, either. You'll find lots of people building boats in their backyards, but nobody's doing it commercially anymore."

I drove around Marshallberg, seeing only one other boatbuilder's establishment—that of M. W. Willis, whose fiberglass Willis-Craft sportsfishermen I had seen advertised in boating magazines. It was a large installation, with numerous automobiles parked outside

---

and the hulls of several large fiberglass boats nearby, obviously no place to go looking for someone to build the twenty-four-foot wooden workboat hull I had in mind.

Instead of heading for Jamie Lewis's place, I drove further eastward along Highway 70 toward the little towns that lay between Marshallberg and Atlantic. I hoped I would come upon a boatbuilder, despite what Jerry Davis had said, but primarily I wanted to have a look at the area that Claiborne S. Young, in his *Cruising Guide to North Carolina,* describes as affording "an idea of what life in coastal North Carolina was like when the area was isolated from the rest of society."

It was my favorite kind of country, with numerous creeks and enclaves of marshland close to the highway; wooden houses, mostly painted white, with gabled roofs, side porches, and shade trees; clusters of pine trees on points of land jutting out into the sound; and everywhere the signs of the proximity and importance of salt water—crab pots, nets, buoys, markers, otter boards, defunct rowboats in front yards converted into flower beds, piles of oyster shells.

As always when traveling through such country, I had a sense of anticipation. I thought about why this should be so, and decided that it was because of its resemblance to James Island, across the river from

---

Charleston. In my childhood days in the 1930s, when my
father drove us out to spend the day at Folly Beach, it
was through just such a low-lying place, with marshes,
creeks, bays, and numerous trawlers and workboats in
view close to the highway. No doubt some of the
excitement of going to the beach and the imminence of
viewing the ocean had become part of my association
with that savannahlike terrain. On the Folly Beach Road
there had been a succession of bridges, the last several of
them with elevated spans, and as we approached the final
wooden span and drove up the slope, I would know that
on the far side lay Folly Island itself and, several blocks
down the road, the beach and the ocean, and I would
await the moment when we would top the rise and the
goal would lie in sight just ahead. Now, driving along
the North Carolina coast, even though I had no particular
objective in mind and the bridges were level causeways, I
felt something of the same excitement.

At Williston I passed by a large corrugated tin
building with a sign on it that read: CUSTOM
SPORTSFISHERMEN. Although I felt sure that such an
establishment would not be interested in building the kind
of boat I wanted, I turned around and drove back. When
I stepped inside the shed I was rewarded with the heavy
bouquet of freshly cut cedar wood. Several young men
were at work on a splendidly crafted cruising hull, at

---

least forty feet in length with what must have been a fourteen-foot beam. Each narrow, one-by-one-inch strip of hull planking had been carefully nailed and glued into place, a labor that must have taken dozens of hours. No party boat or head boat this, but somebody's custom-constructed yacht, obviously costing its fortunate future owner six figures or more.

I asked the young man in charge whether he knew of anyone in the area who built small workboats, explaining why I was looking. Immediately he too named Jamie Lewis. He proceeded to write down the name for me on a piece of notepaper.

I remarked on the fragrance of the cedar. "You're so used to it that you probably don't notice it," I added.

"Not during the day," he said, "but every time I come into the shop the first thing in the morning I get a strong whiff of it."

He had several other orders to fill after the boat now being built was finished, he said, and so I thanked him for his help, and departed. I drove through the little towns of Davis, Stacy, and Sea Level, seeing numerous boats and several boatyards, but nothing to indicate that any wooden boatbuilding was going on. At Atlantic, an attractive little community, I passed by a number of small commercial buildings and more boatyards, and finally came to a dead end at a creek, along which were

numerous shrimp trawlers. Across the creek the road
appeared to resume, indicating that at one time there must
have been a bridge there. The docks on the far side
looked more interesting, so I turned my car around, took
a right turn at an intersection and then another several
blocks farther on, and after a few more blocks turned
back toward the sound, ending up on the road leading to
the creek from the east.

I parked my car, got out, and taking my camera
with me walked down to the water. There was a good
view of the creek, and I could see several dozen
workboats tied up at wharves along the banks. Nets,
trawl boards, floats, crab pots, and spools of wire and
rope were everywhere about. I felt the same sense of
mingled fascination and envy that I always knew at such
times, as if I were still a child looking at the workboats
at Adger's Wharf in Charleston, feeling myself an
intruder and wishing I were part of the activity.

I took a few pictures, then walked southward on
the dirt road paralleling the creek toward a high mound
of white sand at the end. I climbed it and looked out.
Before me for miles was the sound, with here and there
clumps of marshland and, several miles out, the low line
of the barrier islands. Far off to the east was the white
hull of a trawler. It was a warm, sparkling-clear
afternoon, and the green salt marsh seemed to glisten in
the sun. I could see the line of channel markers stretching

off across the sound toward Drum Inlet (how many
Drum Inlets, I wondered, must there be along the South
Atlantic Coast?).

To my right was a body of water known as
Styron Bay. The novelist William Styron's people
originally came from this area, though his father grew up
farther inland, in Goldsboro, and Bill himself was raised
in Newport News, Virginia, the Port Warwick of his
first two novels. Styron is one of the more common
names in southeastern North Carolina, along with Willis,
Midgett, Ballance, Gilliken, Stacy, Williams, Howard,
and a variety of names beginning with the letters
Ga—Garrish, Gaskill, Gaskins, etc. Look at any local
telephone directory in the area and there will be a
column or more of listings under each name. In the old
days, before the highways and the bridges and ferries
came, the Outer Banks was isolated country, with much
inbreeding. No doubt Bill Styron has numerous blood
relatives throughout the Outer Banks, still pronouncing
certain words with the unique intonations of the area:
"There'll be a hoigh toide raound the Saound." I
wondered whether the name Styron was pronounced
Stoiyron out here. Bill Styron himself has traveled a long
way from coastal North Carolina, and spends his summers
on Martha's Vineyard, likewise close to the ocean but in
considerably more high-powered literary company.

It was getting on toward late afternoon, and I

---

decided to resume my search in the morning, so I got
back into my car and headed back toward Morehead
City. En route I stopped by the Beaufort waterfront to
see whether the *Virginius* was back at her berth as
promised. She wasn't. It turned out that after the repair
had been completed and the engine tested at the dock, the
Town Creek Marina manager had set out for the
waterfront with her, only to find that when he put the
gear into reverse the propeller shaft slipped down once
again. They were going to work on it that evening, and I
could probably take the *Virginius* back to her berth the
following day.

What was wrong with the *Virginius* was really
fairly minor, yet it rendered the boat quite unusable, and
obviously she could not be shown to prospective buyers
until repaired. The difficulty with every repair shop I
have ever known, whether for automobiles or boats, is
that each must recapitulate for itself all the steps that have
already been taken to correct a problem before attempting
anything new. I had told the shop that since the
connecting pin on the coupler holding the shaft and the
transmission together kept dropping out, the coupler itself
must be the culprit; but before the repairmen were
willing to install a new coupler they had to try merely
replacing the pin, only to have it fall out again. Now
they were finally proceeding with replacing the coupler.

* * *

In the morning, before I set out for Harkers Island, I
stopped in at the Town Creek Marina and got another
report on the *Virginius*. They expected to have her
repaired by early afternoon. They were machining the
coupler, they said, so that the pin would no longer fall
out.

Jamie Lewis's shop on Harkers Island was a neatly
kept, white-painted shed, two stories high. Through the
open doorway I could see yet another large wooden
workboat hull under way. "Boatbuilding runs in spells,"
Lewis said, in a rich Outer Banks accent. "You do several
large boats, then you might have a string of small ones."
At present he had two more large craft to build after this
one was done, and then two orders for smaller boats, so
that his schedule was filled at least for another year. He
showed me photographs of several boats he had recently
completed, and they were handsome vessels indeed.

There was someone else on Harkers Island, Jamie
Lewis said, who could probably build the boat for me.
His name was Clem Willis, and he was retired from
boatbuilding, but he had mentioned recently that he
would be interested in taking on a small boat if Lewis
received any orders that he could not fill. However,
Lewis cautioned, Clem Willis was an elderly man and
would probably take longer to complete the boat than a
younger builder might.

"How old is he?" I asked.

"Oh, he's at least sixty-five."

For some reason, sixty-five did not seem prohibitively ancient to me. For this boat I *wanted* someone who would take his time building it, preferably someone who had been building Core Sounders for a long time and would go about the job in time-honored ways. As far as I was concerned, the builder could work on it through the winter, delivering it to me in the spring.

I found Clem Willis's establishment with no trouble. It was located on the main street of Harkers Island, in a corrugated tin boat shed next to a wooden bungalow with a wide screened porch, and surrounded by shade trees. There was a sign on a tree at the edge of the highway:

> CLEM'S BOAT WORKS

Clem Willis was at work with a grass trimmer around the trees in his front yard when I arrived about noontime. He was a bony-faced man of medium height, who spoke in a low voice and with a deep accent. At first I had trouble making out his words. I wear hearing aids in both ears, and I removed one to turn it up a little, whereupon Clem Willis did likewise. If he were to end up building the boat, I thought, we would make a first-rate communications team by long-distance telephone.

He was not sixty-five years old, he said, but seventy-four. He had been building boats all his life; he had lost track of how many he had built. I handed him a sketch I had made of the boat I had in mind, with a list of what I wanted the builder to do and what I would do myself. He took his time reading it. We went over the general dimensions of the boat I had in mind; the particular specifications could wait. "How much will a boat like this set me back?" I asked.

"I'll have to figure it," Clem Willis said. "I'll have to see what the engine will cost, too. There's a man out here, Larry Myers, who installs them. No way I could say now."

He took me into the shed and showed me the boat now on the trailer there. It had a small cabin and a modified planing hull. He had built it seventeen years earlier, and the owner had recently had him rework the interior and put a seventy-five horsepower diesel in place of the original gasoline engine. He had done so, but the owner had decided that it needed still more power, so he had taken it out and installed a 120 horsepower diesel. That had been six months ago; the owner had paid him for his work and left the boat sitting in his shop ever since. The shop did not appear to have been used recently. There were very few tools lying about, and no wood.

"Look her over while I go into the house for a minute," he said. I peered through the side ports; the interior was much like what I had in mind, and except for the fact that the main cabin was not fully enclosed, the boat was close to my specifications. It occurred to me that I could probably buy her quite cheaply, if I wanted. But no, I told myself, that was out of the question. I didn't want yet another boat; I wanted a *new* boat, built for *me,* and one that I could complete with my own hands. This boat—which might well turn out to be my last boat; who could say?—was going to be *exactly* what I wanted, all the way, from stem to stern, keel to anchor light.

Clem Willis returned with two large leatherbound scrapbooks, containing photographs of the boats he had built. There were dozens and dozens of boats, ranging from crabbing skiffs to trawlers, runabouts to cruisers, to buy boats that were more than seventy feet long. The earlier photos were in black-and-white, and some were faded. These showed a much younger Clem Willis, black-haired and wiry, standing with pride alongside his products.

"If you build the boat for me," I asked, "when do you think you'd have her ready?"

"Depends on when we start. If we start this fall, it ought to be ready by spring. I used to turn them out in six or seven weeks, but I can't work at that clip anymore."

We agreed that he would prepare an estimate of costs, and I would telephone him in ten days or so. We shook hands. I returned to my car, backed out of the driveway onto the street, and drove off. I decided that I rather liked Clem Willis, though he was on the taciturn side. No doubt he had had long experience with outlanders coming to see him, talking expansively about having boats built, after which he heard no more from them. What I appreciated was that he had made no effort either to ingratiate himself or to play hard-to-get, although he was obviously eager to receive a commission to build another boat and had said readily that he could do it.

On the way I noticed another boat works, also owned by someone named Willis, and I told myself that I ought not to decide on Clem Willis without at least checking into what else might be available. I pulled in, and saw that a large power cruiser was under construction. The proprietor said he could build me the boat I wanted, but not for at least a year. Once he started on it, however, the boat would be ready in six weeks' time. I told him about having talked with Clem Willis, and was informed that if I wanted a boat built this winter that was my best bet. Clem Willis, he said, built good boats.

I drove back to Beaufort, hoping to be able to run the *Virginius* to her berth on the waterfront, and then pick up some bait and go fishing. The sailboat was not yet ready, however. The repairmen were planning to work on her that afternoon and I could take her back over to the waterfront the next morning.

Saturday morning was cloud-free. After breakfast I drove over to Town Creek Marina. The *Virginius* was ready to go, the marina manager said. They had repaired the coupler, installed it, and then repeatedly thrown the gear in and out of reverse, with no adverse effect. So the manager and I drove over to the waterfront in two cars, left mine there, and returned to Town Creek. I started the engine and we cast off.

The highway bridge at Beaufort opens every hour on the half hour to let boats through. Arriving at the bridge with ten minutes to wait, we circled around for a while. Several other sailboats also showed up, so we got in line to go through when the span opened. I placed the engine in neutral, and then, when we began drifting out of line a little, into reverse gear. There was a clank, and once again the coupler failed and the propeller shaft slid down, thrusting the blades into the rudder and immobilizing the tiller.

All we could do was to drop anchor before we drifted into shallow water. A tugboat, the *Sampit,* was tied up close to us, and the marina manager called over and asked someone aboard to telephone for help. Presently a marine employee showed up in an inflatable dinghy. The plan was to lash the dinghy alongside the sailboat and return to the dock on the dinghy's outboard power. The sailboat's rudder, however, was jammed at right angles to the keel, and getting the boat to move in a reasonably straight line would be extremely difficult. So the dinghy was dispatched to pick up a mechanic.

When the mechanic arrived, the marina manager discarded his shirt, shoes, and the contents of his pockets, and clad only in shorts went overboard and underneath the boat. After much trial and error he was able to knock the propeller shaft back into position. Using some kind of jerry-built pin the mechanic reaffixed the shaft to the coupler, and we hauled in the anchor and set out for the marina. This time I was careful not to place the engine in reverse gear, and we made it back without further incident. The marina manager vowed that he was going to install a brand-new coupler and in addition drill a second hole in the coupler and shaft, place pins in both, then wire them together so that they could not possibly come loose.

One way or the other I was still determined to
go fishing. So I drove through Morehead City and across
the Bogue Sound bridge to Atlantic Beach, bought a
package of frozen squid, then drove out to Fort Macon,
at the western rim of the Morehead City–Beaufort
harbor. I parked my car and lugged my tackle over the
dunes to the beach at the edge of the channel. For an
hour I cast out into the strongly flowing current without
so much as a strike, meanwhile observing a procession of
powerboats as they cruised by along the channel, bound
for assorted fishing spots. And there I was, sole owner
and proprietor of two boats, looking on from the shore
and trying to catch fish in the surf, even while planning
to have yet another boat built. In my own small and far
less disastrous way, my case was something like that of
Melville's Captain Ahab:

> Now, in his heart, Ahab had some glimpse
> of this, namely: all my means are sane, my
> motive and my object mad. Yet without
> power to kill, or change, or shun the fact;
> he likewise knew that to mankind he did
> long dissemble; in some sort, did still. But
> that thing of his dissembling was only
> subject to his perceptibility, not to his
> will determinate.

Some people never learn, I thought sadly—people with obsessions, people who spend their money and their adult lives attempting to relive their childhood. After a few more minutes, I tossed the remainder of the frozen squid out into the water for the delectation of the resident gulls, gathered up my fishing tackle, and headed for the car and home.

4

THE DEED DONE,
TOGETHER WITH
MEMORIES OF ANOTHER

Clem Willis reported that he could build the boat I
wanted, so far as carpentry, timber, and supplies went, for
ten thousand dollars. For that amount he would build a
twenty-four-foot boat on a workboat hull, with a
stand-up forward cabin, a berth, a pilothouse–main cabin
with an engine box, an enclosed head, a forward hatch,
and a five-foot-deep stern cockpit. All other equipment,
including engine and transmission, fuel and water tanks,
controls, shaft, propeller, rudder, keel cooler, ports,
window glass, electrical system, storage batteries, lights,
cleats and mooring bitt, mattress cushion, sink, the head
itself, holding tank, bilge pump, hardware—everything,
that is, that had to be installed rather than built would be
my responsibility. Depending upon what I wanted, he
estimated that the boat, in the water and ready to go,
would cost between eighteen and twenty-five thousand

---

dollars. He was ready to begin whenever I gave the word, he said.

Faced with the decision to commit myself to having the boat built, I temporized. What I hoped was that during the weeks that followed my visit to Harkers Island, John Nelson would find a buyer for the *Virginius.*

It was about then that Hurricane Hugo decided to put in an appearance on the Caribbean weather map. After devastating the Virgin Islands, it proceeded northwestward and for several days seemed intent upon coming ashore somewhere on the North Carolina coast. Needless to say, nobody nearby was thinking about buying boats.

During my childhood I had lived through hurricanes in Charleston, and as an adult had several times dodged them while vacationing on the coast. But Hugo was by all accounts going to be an extraordinarily powerful affair, and the *Virginius,* her defective propeller-shaft coupler finally replaced, was now tied up at a dock on the Beaufort waterfront, with nothing between her and the Atlantic Ocean but a low, uninhabited barrier island.

My older son and I drove down to Beaufort, bought an additional supply of rope and bumpers, and did what we could to secure her, doubling all the lines, rigging additional springs, wrapping cloth around the lines where they led through the chocks, placing bumpers along the hull, and the like. As we were working away on the lines, a waterman on a nearby boat called over, "You got a camera?"

We nodded. "You better take a picture of her," the waterman said, "because if that hurricane comes along it's the last you'll ever see of her."

The approved procedure when a hurricane is imminent is to take a boat such as the *Virginius* up a protected creek, where it will be shielded from the ocean, tie the bow securely to a tree trunk or two, lay out anchors from the stern, batten down everything as tightly as possible, then stay inside the cabin and wait it out. I had no intention of doing that, however; it would be dangerous, since there was no telling how long it would be before Hugo showed up. Also, I could not stay there indefinitely while waiting to see what happened. I would take my chances; if worse came to worst, I did have full insurance coverage.

As it turned out, Hugo decided to come ashore two hundred miles to the southwest, and instead of wreaking havoc on eastern North Carolina, it chose Charleston and the South Carolina coast as its landing site. The hurricane arrived at high tide, drawing with it an enormous tidal surge, and as I watched in appalled fascination on cable television, my native city was

---

devastated to an extent that far surpassed anything in living memory. Compared to its fury, the hurricanes of my childhood were mere summer squalls. Moreover, once it came ashore Hugo did not dissipate into manageable proportions, as lesser hurricanes are wont to do. Instead it ripped through South Carolina like a planetary bulldozer, and its winds were still raging at upwards of eighty miles an hour when it struck the city of Charlotte, North Carolina, just over the border.

So if Hugo *had* chosen to come ashore anywhere near Beaufort, North Carolina, it would have done no good whatever to have taken the *Virginius* to a sheltered creek to ride it out—unless the creek in question were located several hundred miles away and well inland. For a blow of such magnitude the customary precautions would not have worked, as numerous boatmen in South Carolina discovered. Hugo's 142-mile-an-hour winds would have pulled my boat loose from any such anchorage and smashed her to pieces, along with anybody who was aboard at the time.

Even though Hugo had hit well to the south, the *Virginius* did sustain damage. Despite all our doubling of lines and rigging of bumpers, the high tide and wind combined to push her up against the dock, and a vertical streak several inches across was rubbed off her hull paint. Had the impact lasted much longer the damage could have been far worse, for when I went down to check on her I found that several of the triple-strand nylon docklines had worn through to a single strand. I replaced the worn docklines and rigged an additional assortment of bumpers and foam-rubber padding at the point where the hull had rubbed against the dock. Meanwhile the *Virginius* continued to go unsold, and I could not bring myself to order the new boat built.

It was clear even to me that even if I was unable to sell the sailboat, I could, for once in my life, afford the outlay without undue inconvenience. What was I waiting for? Why did I not call up Clem Willis and tell him to go ahead with the new boat?

When I was growing up in Charleston in the 1930s, my family lived on a fixed income. We were not well off, but neither could we be said to be poor. We lived in a new house on an acre of land in a good neighborhood, we ate well, and we did not lack for anything necessary to our welfare.

My parents had few needs. They neither drank nor smoked, they never traveled or went on vacations, they went out seldom, and they needed few clothes. All the family's extra money over and above household expenses went toward improving the house and the garden. It was dinned into me that spending money for pleasure was wasteful, sinful.

The constant admonition did not succeed in making me frugal. What it did was it made me feel guilty for wanting to spend money.

In other words, more than half a century later I was hesitant to go ahead and commit myself to having a new boat built, despite the fact that I was quite able to do so.

What it came down to was that I felt guilty because I wanted the boat.

As it turned out, events caught up with me. Several days after Clem Willis had called to give me his estimate on the cost of the boat, I received a telephone call from Larry Myers, who Clem Willis had said would be providing and installing the engine for the boat.

We talked about boats and engines at some length. My best bet, he told me, considering what I wanted to use the boat for, would be a small rebuilt diesel engine. The difficulty was that very few used diesels were available for rebuilding in the size I needed, so that I would probably have to buy a new engine—which along with transmission would probably cost me in the neighborhood of six thousand dollars or so. Was I prepared to spend such an amount?

What he really wanted to know, of course, was whether I could afford it. I told him that the figure he had cited did not seem out of line to me—*if* I decided to go ahead with the new boat.

Then, shortly after the scare from Hurricane Hugo, Larry Myers called again. He had just acquired an eighty-two horsepower Mazda diesel engine, which he was now rebuilding. The engine was in prime condition, and from what I had told him of my plans, it would be exactly what I needed, an excellent alternative to buying a new small diesel. He had recently bought up, at cost, some twenty new marine engine transmissions from a bankrupt dealer, and still had four of them in the shop. I could have the rebuilt diesel engine and the new transmission for $3,650.

I told Larry Myers that I hadn't sold the sailboat yet and I wanted to think about it, and would call him back in a couple of weeks. That was all right with him, Larry said, but there was little likelihood of the engine in question remaining in his shop for a week without being sold. "I'm not trying to pressure you into buying it," he told me, "but for what you want to do, your chances of finding another rebuilt engine like this one won't be good. I don't come across them very often."

It was entirely possible, of course, that Larry Myers, being a businessman, was exaggerating the supposed scarcity of rebuilt engines of that size. On the other hand, I had been watching the advertisements for used marine engines in a commercial waterman's publication, *Boats and Harbors,* and I knew that the

---

chances of doing very much better than Larry's price were minimal. If I did not take advantage of this development I might very likely end up paying about the same amount for a new engine with only half the power of this one, or else spending several thousand dollars more for comparable power.

How about accepting a deposit and holding it for me for a month? I asked. Larry agreed to do so.

So now I was committed, even though the deposit would be refundable if I changed my mind. As I thought more about it over the next several days, I realized that I *wanted* to be committed. In effect Larry's call, and the deposit I had made on the engine, had served to ease me into it, so that I hadn't been forced to declare, out of a clear blue sky, "Yes, I will spend twenty to twenty-five thousand dollars to have a new boat built."

I mailed my check for the deposit to Larry Myers, telephoned Clem Willis, told him I was ready to go ahead, and sent him a deposit by mail. I would drive down on Friday to settle the details.

October afternoons are when the Carolina coast is at its absolute loveliest. Barring, of course, the possibility of a hurricane—and though the hurricane season is still alive then, today's satellite tracking and early warning systems

give the alert days and weeks ahead of time—by the
middle of the month the heavy sunshine of summertime
has gone, there are no longer thunderheads building
toward the southwest almost every afternoon, and the
temperate air seems to lie upon the land and water like a
transparent lens that brings into sharp focus all surfaces,
edges, and objects. The foliage has not yet begun to lose
its color; the tidal marsh is still bright green. There is
always a light breeze, just enough to arrange the surface
of the water into line and grain so that the sunlight is
caught opaquely and reflected back.

Driving toward Harkers Island from Beaufort I
crossed the long causeway spanning the North River,
from where I could see across several miles of water. The
area beyond the long expanse of shallow water, known as
the Rachel Carson Coastal Reserve, looked like a distant
unbroken marshland, though I knew that in actuality it
was made up of several dozen islands of assorted sizes and
was threaded throughout by creeks and channels.

To get from Beaufort to Harkers Island one must
drive north for five miles, turn eastward along another
five-mile stretch to cross the North River and Ward
Creek, then go southward toward the ocean. After a
four-mile drive on the mainland one reaches the Straits
and proceeds across a causeway and a bascule bridge to
Harkers Point, on the island's northernmost edge. The

island is shaped like a briar pipe, with the bowl to the
west, aimed upward, and the shank and stem pointed
west-east, parallel with the long barrier island of
Shackleford Banks. Harkers Island is not an old
community; before the 1930s most of its inhabitants lived
on Shackleford Banks, until a hurricane cut a channel
between there and Cape Lookout, stripping the remaining
land of trees and protection; after that, everyone moved
over to Harkers Island.

One enters the island at the top of what would
be the bowl of the pipe and drives a half mile southward
until one is close to the water's edge. Then one turns left,
and moves along the three-mile shank and pipestem.
There are houses all along the road, and beyond those on
the south side are fishing docks, piers, wharves, and
pilings jutting unevenly out into the sound like an old
garden rake with some of the prongs gone. The island is
thickly wooded with pines, oaks, and maples, and the
brightly painted wooden homes with their wide porches
are flanked with oleanders, crepe myrtles, and other
shrubs. There can be no question about where the ocean
lies, because most of the shrubs and smaller trees have
grown away from it, and are bent toward the north, their
branches and foliage averted from the sea winds.

Clem Willis's place, a bungalow with a boat shed
to one side, is well down the island. The principal

difference between a boat shed and a garage is that the
former is both wider and considerably taller, and has no
swinging doors. Clem Willis's shed is deep enough to
allow a boat as long as forty feet to be built inside.
Overhead there is a network of steel H-beams with
hoisting tackle.

There is nothing of the production line in
Harkers Island–style boatbuilding. At the same time,
modern power tools, glues, resins, and the like are used;
no sense of the self-consciously antiquarian characterizes
the effort, no pretending that the builder is adhering with
a religious purity to Traditional Boatbuilding Methods. I
have always felt a little uneasy about the kind of willed
antiquarianism that goes on in such places as Colonial
Williamsburg and, with boats, along the Maine coast.
Each to his own, of course, but it is not the actual
materials and tools used that are the missing ingredients in
modern assembly-line, plastic-and-chrome boatbuilding.
Adzes, caulking irons, drawknives, handsaws, augers,
braces and bits, chamfer planes, steam boxes, and so on do
not of themselves confer blessings upon the boat they are
used to build. What is really "traditional" is that
everything is prepared individually, and laid up by hand.
It is the care taken in turning out the product that makes
the difference.

The boatbuilders on Harkers Island are not

Upholders of Tradition in any intellectual or
self-conscious way; they do what they do because it
comes naturally. If the latest polymers will hold better
and tighter than the older glues, they do not hesitate to
employ them. If a three-quarter-inch power drill will
make a hole for a keel-bolt faster and more efficiently
than a brace and bit, they use the drill. What matters is
the care taken with each item glued, each hole drilled.
The Clem Willises and Jamie Lewises *are* the tradition.

When I arrived at Clem Willis's place he was in
the boat shed doing something with a flat-bottomed
wooden skiff on a trailer. He had just been clamming
with the skiff on the tidal flats along Back Sound.
"Clams are selling for seventeen cents each now," he
explained. The skiff was powered by a forty horsepower
Evinrude outboard mounted on the transom, and was
obviously meant to be steered standing up, because in
place of a wheel and console there was a large stick
mounted perpendicularly amidship. It was fastened by a
single bolt at the bottom and attached to a system of
ropes and pulleys, so that if the stick was shoved sideways
the engine was made to pivot in the opposite direction.

It used to be that not only workboats were
steered this way, usually with the stick mounted at the
side rather than in the center of the boat, but numerous
bassboats as well. When in the 1960s manufacturers began

building fiberglass boats specifically for bass fishing on lakes, they used a stick system, except that the stick and controls were made to push cables. As outboard-engine horsepower increased, however, and instead of running on 25 or 40 horsepower, bassboats were equipped with motors that produced 90, 100, 150, and even 200 horsepower or more, the use of lever steering became very dangerous. After some fatal accidents caused by boaters stumbling and falling onto the stick while moving at high speeds, boat manufacturers began building boats with steering wheels, which turned the outboard motor more gradually. But for a waterman working the tidal flats—tending crab pots, flounder-graining, or even seine-hauling in an open boat—it is not only less expensive but far more convenient to be able to change direction by pulling or pushing on a lever, especially if he is standing up at the time.

We drove over to Larry Myers's place to see the diesel engine and pay him the balance owed on my purchase. Myers was a large, pleasant, talkative individual; he and an assistant were at work crating up a GM 6-71 when we arrived. The moment I saw the rebuilt eighty-two horsepower Mazda I had bought, I felt sure that I had made the right purchase. It was in beautiful shape and clean as a whistle, with glossy baked-on black enamel and new chrome. All-new working parts had been installed. It had new bearings, liners, and piston rings, the valves had been ground and resealed, a marine manifold and cooling system installed, and the generator had been replaced by an alternator. The transmission, with two-and-a-half-to-one reduction gear, was brand-new, and the shift lever clicked nicely into place.

This was the kind of engine I should have had in my previous boats—a diesel in first-class shape, certain to run well and not break down for years to come. The only other diesel boat engine I had ever owned was the ancient GM 3-71 that had powered my first large boat, the *Bill James;* it had been noisy and smelly, but it had given no trouble whatever despite its quarter century of use. The transmission, not the engine, had been the *Bill James*'s Achilles' heel. *This* transmission was obviously going to give no such trouble.

So it was done—and I was eminently satisfied at having done it. As I drove back toward Beaufort I had no second thoughts, none of the post-decision qualms that ordinarily accompanied all such decisions. At the same time, I felt little or nothing of the exhilaration that usually went along with buying a new boat. No doubt I had bought and sold too many boats in my time for much of that anymore. What I now felt instead was the comfortable conviction that *this* boat, with its rebuilt diesel engine, was going to be reliable and sound as

almost no larger boat I had ever known had been. I
would be able to go anywhere on her, weather
permitting, and know that I would get there and back
without trouble. I had had my fill and more of old boats
with things that went wrong—the *Bill James*'s
transmission, the *Little Eva*'s O-rings and overheating
engines, the *Virginius*'s ailing Atomic 4 engine and shaft
coupling, the *Mary Simpson*'s worn-through engine block,
and so on, the memory of man running not to the
contrary. Finally I would have a new boat, and not one
of those elaborate mass-produced cruisers, but a craft with
a simple workboat hull, clean lines, and only the basic,
tried-and-true gears and steering system, properly done.

(A small voice whispered, *"Fooling yourself again,
eh? Some folks just will never learn."*) Well, we would see.

On the way home from Harkers Island I got to thinking
about the *Bill James,* and wondering whether she was still
afloat somewhere. The new diesel engine had reminded
me of her. She was a Chesapeake Bay oyster boat that
had been converted into a cabin cruiser, and she was
thirty-six feet long. I named her after an older friend of
mine who came from the Rappahannock River area,
where the boat was built. Long and narrow, she rode low
in the water, and was powered by a World War
II–surplus GM 3-71 diesel engine.

I bought her in Hampton, Virginia, in 1969, and with the help of the previous owner took her over to a boatyard at Gloucester Point on the York River, a few miles from where my in-laws had a summer place, and where she was right at home among the numerous Bay-built workboats, crabbers, and buy boats. She was made of juniper, her planking was an inch thick, and in rough water she was stable and solid. Her dead-rise hull tapered to a sharp, knifelike, straight up-and-down prow, and she parted the waves rather than leaped over them. She could only do nine miles an hour at full throttle, and many a teak-and-chrome cruiser with twin engines swept by her at twice her speed and more as she churned along. But at the close of a day's run her tank would require eighteen or twenty gallons of diesel fuel, while the superpowered chariots next to her at the gas dock would be loading up with seventy to a hundred gallons.

I purchased her in the late spring, used her no more than once or twice, and then had to leave for Massachusetts, where I had agreed to teach two classes at Harvard University. For a man with his first real boat, as distinguished from outboard motor runabouts, it was a frustrating summer. I had left my family at home in North Carolina, which was a mistake to begin with, and the weekends that I flew home were not long enough to permit trips up to Virginia and the boat. I spent a

considerable amount of time down along the Charles
River and on the Boston waterfront, looking on
enviously as others came and went on their boats and
watching with admiration as the snubnosed harbor tugs,
with their sturdy hemp bumpers, nosed up to huge cargo
ships and maneuvered them alongside docks.

Several weeks before the summer term was
scheduled to end, I had an idea. Why not enhance the
Bill James's workboat appearance by purchasing a hemp
rope bumper for her prow? I drove down to the only
two marine stores on the Boston waterfront and tried to
find a bumper, but none were for sale. So I telephoned
one of the tugboat companies and asked where it
purchased its bumpers. The Boston Welding Company, in
East Boston over near Logan Airport, made them for all
the harbor tugs, I was told. I telephoned the company
and arranged to have a tugboat bumper made to order. It
was to be approximately three feet long, and fit over and
around the prow of my thirty-six-foot boat. The price
was fifty dollars, and it would be ready in ten days'
time—giving me four days' margin before I would be
leaving for home.

On the appointed day I drove from Cambridge to
Boston, through the Callahan Tunnel and into East
Boston, and located the Boston Welding Company. My
tugboat bumper was ready, I was informed. As indeed it

---

was: it was woven of gold-brown hemp, and at the moment had chains attached to the loops at both ends pulling them back tightly around a post. This was in order to "break it," it was explained, so that the hemp would bend around my boat's prow.

Just as I had ordered, it was three feet long. There was, however, one problem. What I had in mind was something about six inches in width. The Boston Welding Company, thinking in terms of what was appropriate for harbor tugs thirty-six feet in length, had produced a bumper with a circumference of forty-eight inches, weighing a minimum of ninety pounds.

The bumper was loaded into the trunk of my automobile, and I drove back to Cambridge. When four days later I headed southward, my books and suitcases were on the rear seat of the car; the tugboat bumper took up all the room in the trunk.

A few days afterward we were at my in-laws' place on the York River, and I drove down at once to see the *Bill James*. There she was, all right, waiting at the dock and ready to go. The following morning my wife and I together managed to lift the tugboat bumper out of the trunk of the car and drag it down to the dock. After much exertion we were able to hoist it onto the bow. It was all too clear, however, that to use it as I had intended was out of the question. Even if we had been able to get it around the narrow prow without dropping it into the water, it would have been nearly impossible to affix it there; in any kind of a sea it would soon slip down and, its ninety pounds of hemp soaked through with water and doubled in weight, flop around with each oncoming wave until it either fell all the way off or else stove in the bow.

So regretfully we lowered the bumper down onto the dock and dragged it ashore, where it lay on the grass like some enormous sea lion taking a noonday nap.

While I stood there, looking at the bumper and wondering what to do with it, the owner of the boatyard, Leonard Jordan, came walking by. In his dealings over the years with boat owners, both of commercial and pleasure craft, he had doubtless witnessed many strange things, and was not easily awed. But what he saw now was beyond previous experience.

"My goodness, Mr. Rubin," he said after looking at the heap on the grass for a long moment, "you got a bumper there big enough for a tugboat!"

There were aspects of operating the old ex-workboat that I had to learn the hard way. All my previous boating under power had been confined to outboard craft of various sizes; I had no experience with rudders that were separate from propellers, and propellers that did not swing

---

sideways when the steering wheel was turned. The creek on which the *Bill James*'s slip was situated was narrow, and to get her out of it, it was necessary to back most of the way across the creek. Unfortunately, she would not back in more than one direction, as all the outboard motorboats I had used did. No matter where I placed the rudder, the direction of her choice was invariably downstream from the dock, which left her pointed the wrong way. I then had to spend long minutes inching forward as far as I could go, then drifting back, then inching forward again, until finally I could get the prow pointed down the creek. When the wind was blowing and the tide setting strongly, the problem was intensified, and there were times when it was all I could do to keep from putting the stern aground.

This went on for a week. Then, one night, I happened to be reading a boating book. Single-screw boats, it explained, do not maneuver like automobiles; when power is applied, the stern swings before the boat's forward motion commences. To turn a boat in close quarters, the thing to do is to start with the boat dead in the water, then throw the wheel all the way over, place the transmission in forward gear, and give the engine a quick burst of power, throttling down immediately afterward. This would cause the stern to swing in whichever direction was desired.

The next morning I tried the new technique and it worked like a charm. The *Bill James* backed out of the slip, swung her stern around nicely, and headed down the creek. I wondered what nearby boatmen, observing those lengthy forward-and-reverse, forward-and-reverse sessions I had been staging, must have thought. How many other things were still to be learned before I would be reasonably competent at her helm?

Several weeks after my return from Cambridge, I decided I was ready to travel somewhere aboard my boat. It was eight miles downstream from the creek where the *Bill James* was to the mouth of the York River, and about fifty miles or so up the Chesapeake Bay to Tangier Island on the eastern shore. It seemed simple enough; I had worked out all the compass bearings on the charts. We—my wife and our two boys, Bill and Robert, ages eight and eleven, were going along—would spend one night at Tangier Island, go over to Crisfield, Maryland, for the second night, then head back down the Bay for home.

We set out from the dock in the morning. The day was bright, the temperature was in the eighties, and the forecast called for good weather all the way. The breeze rustled the tops of the trees that walled in the creek as we made our way along it; we cruised past the

York River Yacht Haven docks with their dozens of expensive cruisers and trawler yachts, and on out into the York River. Finally I was doing what I had for so long wished to do: *go* somewhere aboard my boat, to harbors I had not seen, across water that was new to me.

Out on the York River the gentle breeze began to get less gentle. The *Bill James* was moving along nicely, but there was a decided rise and fall as the bow cleaved the waves. The river was four miles across at that point, and the ship channel we were in seemed a long way from shore. For the first time it began to occur to me that the surface of the Bay might not be quite so serene as that of the York River. By the time we were drawing abreast of the lighthouse at the river's mouth, the wind was coming out of the northwest, across Mobjack Bay, at a decidedly brisk clip. A quarter mile away from us a crab buy boat was headed into the river. She was sixty feet or so long—twice our length at least—with her cabin at the stern and her mast and boom forward, and her bow was lifting and falling heavily and throwing sheets of spray as she made her way along. And when the bow of the *Bill James* smacked into oncoming waves we were taking some spray, too.

We rounded the buoy marking the northern edge of the river mouth, and I changed direction, heading northeastward up and across the Bay along the course I had marked on the chart. Once we did this there was a marked difference in the way the *Bill James* rode the water. The waves were now meeting us squarely abeam, and the boat rocked from side to side as she bounced along. I found myself swinging the wheel vigorously in an effort to stay in the troughs and keep from veering into the wave crests. When I nosed into a wave a formidable sheet of spray would surge over the bow and rattle against the front cabin windows.

Meanwhile my wife and the two boys were happily installed out on the stern, enjoying the breeze and the boat ride with no notion whatever of the trepidation I was experiencing. They were watching the waves, the gulls, the shoreline, the boats in view far across the water. The rollercoasterlike maneuvers when we dropped down the sides of oncoming waves and then rode up again were highly pleasurable to them.

As for myself, the thought that we were going to have to proceed this way for fifty miles, and that the farther we traveled away from the western shore and toward the open expanse of the Bay itself, the rougher it was going to get, became ever more dismaying. What if the engine were to quit? I had no idea whatever of how to repair it. Suppose my calculations were wrong, and the estimate I had made for being set off our course by the tide and the current was inadequate? With every wave

---

that sent spray dashing against the cabin windows I became more anxious. What was I getting us into? Before long my throat had turned dry and my innards were stirring.

I began to apprehend just what I was doing. Here I was, a landlubber who had until very recently never handled anything larger than an outboard motorboat, proposing to take a thirty-six-foot craft fifty miles up and across the Chesapeake Bay, with my wife and two little boys aboard, and with nobody along who could be of any real help if we got into trouble.

Suppose—as is so common on the Chesapeake in late summer—a thunderhead began building and a full-fledged storm, with fifty-mile-an-hour winds, caught up with us out in the middle of the Bay? I knew so little about handling rough wind and weather. What kind of foolhardiness had led me to think that all I had to do to take a trip up the Bay was to pencil in a compass course on a chart and steer in the right direction, as if little more than driving an automobile along a highway were involved?

At length I could take it no longer. After an especially formidable wave broke over the bow of the *Bill James* and thoroughly drenched the windows with salt spray, I announced that we were turning back. "It's getting too rough," I said. "I don't think we can get across the Bay."

Minutes later we had reversed direction and were
headed due southwest, back to the York River.

My family was disappointed. Here we were, all
set for an excursion in the new boat, and I was turning
back. We retraced our course and drew somewhat closer
to the shelter of the land—whereupon I began
second-guessing myself. I had given up too easily. A little
wave action, a little rocking of the boat, a little spray
across the bow and I had chickened out, disappointing my
wife and children, and most of all myself. I felt
humiliated at my failure of nerve.

As we neared the buoy at the mouth of the river,
a Coast Guard cutter, white with a slanting red stripe
along the side, was headed outward, sheets of spray
flaring from her bow as she swung along. *They* were not
inhibited by the wind and waves; they were real sailors,
real seamen.

"Hey, look, it's flying a red pennant!" my older
boy announced.

I looked. So it was. A small-craft warning
pennant.

So it wasn't just my innate timidity. The weather
had taken a turn for the worse; the wind was blowing
hard out of the northwest, and we were not supposed to
be out there in the middle of the Chesapeake Bay in a
thirty-six-foot boat. I felt much relieved.

As we moved upriver to where we were not
directly exposed to the wind blowing across open water,
the waves abated considerably. No longer were we being
rocked by a beam sea. By early afternoon we were back
in the creek, its surface scarcely rippled by the breeze.

So ended my first planned excursion on the *Bill James.*
Later, after I came to know more about boating and
cruising, I realized that part of my mistake had been in
sticking to my charted course and steering northeast, once
I found that the wind was out of the southwest. Instead
of taking the sea abeam, I should have continued eastward
until we were clear of shoals along the western shore,
then swung straight northward and headed up the western
side of the Bay, taking the waves on the port quarter.
This would have eliminated the need to negotiate the
troughs of the waves, making the steering easier and
greatly diminishing the rolling and pitching. Yet the truth
was that indeed I had no business planning and setting
out on such a trip at all, but instead should have waited
until I was considerably more familiar with the ways of
boats in general, and my thirty-six-foot converted oyster
boat in particular.

I kept the *Bill James* for two years, taking her down the
Intracoastal Waterway when summer was over and

berthing her at Southport, North Carolina, three hours
away from my home. All went well until one December
day, when, just as I was docking her, her transmission
gave out. The succeeding six months were spent trying to
find a replacement and, when I finally located one,
getting it installed. The marina at Southport did not have
a diesel mechanic, and the only thing the proprietor of
the marina could think to do was to send for one from
Wilmington, twenty-five miles away—adding a surcharge
for time and distance, of course, on top of the fee for the
actual work done. Before I was done I had paid out close
to a thousand dollars in repair bills, and the transmission
still didn't function properly. What was particularly
annoying—I was still a novice at dealing with boat-repair
yards—was that neither the mechanic nor the marina
operator at Southport seemed to feel any responsibility
whatever when the repair job did not succeed in
remedying the problem. Another trip from Wilmington
to Southport was in order, with another charge for time,
distance, and work done, plus the marina's percentage,
which I was expected to pay.

Finally I located an ancient and profane waterman
in Southport named Pappy Stubbs, who fixed the
transmission for me for fifty dollars. At one point, he
showed me a set of thin brass shims which he said had
simply been left lying loose inside the transmission.

"That's a fucking master mechanic they got over there at Wilmington," he said. I was so grateful for his good work that I gave him an additional fifty dollars. By then I had had enough, however, and I sold the old boat.

I came to regret it. Her plebeian nature, her workboat origins had a meaning for me that I was years in understanding. She wasn't a Fancy Dan; she didn't presume to be other than what she so obviously and sturdily was: a working craft built to go about her business in wind and weather, without fuss or show. She *belonged.* She was twenty-five years old when I acquired her, and if still in commission now she would be nearing the half century mark. Unless some subsequent owner piled her up on a rock, my guess is that she is afloat and earning her keep somewhere, though doubtless with her original engine long since replaced. God bless her and keep her, wherever she may be.

5

ALL SYSTEMS — WELL,
ALMOST ALL — ARE GO

It was Indian Summer in Chapel Hill and across the North Carolina piedmont—temperature in the sixties, clear sky, light winds, the leaves turned red and gold, a mildness over everything. But as my son Robert and I drove eastward toward the coast the sky began clouding over, and after a while there was a thunderstorm in the offing. By the time we reached the outskirts of Morehead City rain was falling. It didn't last long, however; five minutes later we were at the Harbor Master boatyard, and the rain had ceased.

The *Mary Simpson,* the thirty-year-old Luhrs Sea-Skiff that I had bought the past spring, was alongside a dock, and George Alletsee, the mechanic, was applying the final touches to his work. There was the reassuring sound of a Chrysler Crown droning away as we drew near. Working evenings and weekends, he had needed six

weeks to achieve that result. The day after he took over
the project from Ken Markel's marine service, he had
gashed one hand to the bone with a Skilsaw, and it was
two weeks before he could begin the work.

By now he had removed the original engine from
the boat and had replaced the worn-out block with the
one from the old Chrysler Crown that I had bought for
spare parts. Since the pistons in the replacement engine
were frozen in place, he had drilled them out, rebored the
chambers, inserted metal sleeves in them, salvaged five
pistons from the defunct engine and located a sixth, then
installed them in the rebored block. From the defunct
engine he had removed cylinder heads, rocker arms, water
pump, carburetor, fuel pump, manifolds, alternator,
transmission, and other parts and appurtenances, and
installed them, too. Using the motor mounts on the
rebored block he had placed the rebuilt engine in the
engine compartment. He had joined the transmission to
the propeller shaft, hooked up the gas line and the water
hoses, wired the engine to the battery and starter, and
started up the engine. Then he had lined up engine,
transmission, and shaft, until all was turning smoothly and
with minimum vibration. When we arrived he was
applying the last of several coats of gray engine paint,
and the once-useless engine was ready for duty again.

George Alletsee was a master at his craft. Several

persons had told me that he knew more about Chrysler
Crown engines than just about anyone else in the
business, and I could believe it. His New York accent
came through clearly as he discoursed on the ways of
such engines, which he insisted were the best marine
propulsion units ever built. He had been raised on Long
Island and had gone to high school there, but he dropped
out before graduating because he wanted to learn
mechanics and related practical matters, not the history
and literature and other such recondite subjects they
insisted on teaching him. He had begun working on boats
while a teenager, then gone to the Maine coast for a
while, then to Smith Mountain Lake in Virginia, and five
years ago had moved to the Carolina coast.

We untied the mooring lines, and after three long
and frustrating months of enforced idleness, the *Mary
Simpson* was under way again. George, Robert, and I
headed down Peltier Creek toward the narrow entrance,
with George listening intently to the engine while I
steered. Just inside the creek mouth we passed Bob
Simpson's boat, the *Sylvia II;* she was moored at her
dock, awaiting the return of Bob and Mary from the
High Country of Montana and the Dakotas. Then we
moved out into Bogue Sound. I edged the throttle to
1,200 RPMs as we proceeded along the entrance channel,
and then, after we had rounded the last marker and

turned eastward, opened her up to 2,000 RPMs. The old boat surged along, her engine rumbling happily.

George kept a close eye on the engine, occasionally making small adjustments. The water-temperature gauge was showing just under 130°; George worked at it until it was near the 140° mark, where he wanted it. After several minutes he came up to the wheel and shoved the throttle all the way forward. The engine's drone became a subdued roar, the RPM needle rose to 2,600, and the *Mary Simpson* churned along the channel with an élan that belied her thirty years of existence.

"What's the best cruising speed?" I asked.

"You just have to find out from the way she runs," George said. "Usually it's about ten percent under maximum power." I did a quick calculation, and dropped her down to 2,100, to be on the safe side. She lowered her husky roar a trifle and moved comfortably ahead.

When George had finished his ministrations I swung the *Mary Simpson* around in a tight arc and headed back toward Peltier. Although she sounded fine to me, George declared that there must be some barnacles on the propeller, because she was vibrating more than was appropriate. En route we passed a trio of large power cruisers, each tossing up a formidable wake. The *Mary Simpson* rocked and dipped as I turned her bow into the waves, but she did not falter.

We found a vacant slip at Taylor Boat Works, where George had arranged to have the boat hauled out the next day if it proved necessary, and we tied her up. The proprietor, John McCallum, a large man with a thick red beard, came along. "I think she's got some barnacles on her propeller," George told him.

"When did you last have her bottom painted?" McCallum asked me.

"In March, when I bought her."

"She probably won't need painting, then," McCallum said. "We'll just clean off any barnacles and put her back in the water."

So the *Mary Simpson* was back in service.

While we were walking back to the Harbor Master boatyard to get our cars, George Alletsee told Robert and me a lengthy story about a man who bought a farm. It seems that with the farm came a sow, and the new owner decided to raise piglets. A farmer nearby had a male pig, so the new owner loaded his sow into a wheelbarrow and took her over to be serviced. The farmer warned him that it might take five or six such servicings before it took.

"How will I know?" the owner asked the farmer.

"When you get up in the morning, if she's rolling in the mud, that means that it took. If she's eating grain, it didn't, so load her in the wheelbarrow and bring her on back and we'll try again."

The next morning the sow was eating grain, so the owner loaded her in the wheelbarrow and took her back for more. This continued for several days. Then one morning the owner got up and asked his wife to look out the window and tell him what the sow was doing. "Nothing," his wife reported after looking.

"What do you mean, nothing? Is she eating grain, or is she rolling in the mud?"

"Neither one," his wife replied. "She's sitting in the wheelbarrow."

Before George departed for his home and we left for Harkers Island, I arranged to meet him some weekend soon and have him go over the actual workings of the *Mary Simpson*'s engine from beginning to end. After years of owning and operating gasoline-powered boats I still had no real idea of how the engines worked. I thought of George's complaint that in high school he had been unable to get the practical studies he wanted, but had had to study history, literature, and the like. Well, history and literature had been the "practical," "vocational" courses for me. Even so it wouldn't have hurt, somewhere along the way, to have been taught something about the basic functioning of an internal combustion engine.

Before George took on the engine rebuilding job, I had asked him whether he thought it was worth doing, and he had answered no. I had explained to him that I wanted to sell the boat, and that to do so the engine would have to be in working condition. Moreover, I would now be able to use the *Mary Simpson* about the Morehead City harbor until the new boat was completed. With her rebuilt engine she was actually in better shape than she had been for many years, and I should be able to count on her—provided nothing else went wrong. It would be ironic indeed, now that I had finally mustered the nerve to take on a new boat, if this old Sea-Skiff turned out to be completely reliable.

It was Sunday afternoon, and the main street of Harkers Island was more crowded than during my last visit. There were a number of small boats being towed on trailers, and the parking areas at the commercial ramps contained numerous pickup trucks, campers, and automobiles, all with empty trailers attached. It was prime fishing weather off Cape Lookout and in the protected bight behind it, and hundreds of boats were out there trolling for fish.

Clem Willis was not at home. Robert and I went into the tall galvanized boat shed, its entrance half closed off by a canvas. Again, as I had done when I first went looking for a builder and entered a shop, I caught the

---

aroma of cedar, or juniper, as it was called, only this time it was for *my boat.*

She was already a recognizable nautical creature, though upside down. The keel and stem were made of four-by-four timbers glued atop one another—clamps were pressing them tightly together—and the lowest transom board and frames were in place, spaced carefully underneath according to penciled marks on the keel. The hole for the rudder was already drilled, though not the one for the propeller shaft. The chine planks were fastened to the ends of the frames with copper nails from stem to stern, so that the curved outline of the boat bottom was evident. There were temporary supports underneath to elevate the construction several feet from the ground, and a hole had been dug to accommodate the tip of the stem. She was going to be a wide-beamed lady; the longest frames were a good twelve feet. The solid, four-inch-wide keel would protrude twelve inches beneath the hull, and was already notched at the stern for the propeller and rudder. Construction throughout was solid, even massive; there would be nothing flimsy or tender about this boat. Nearby on the ground was the lumber that would go into her ribs, planking, and floor, all of it sturdy juniper.

My son and I took photographs of the construction from almost every conceivable angle. When we were done, Clem Willis had not yet returned, so we left. At least one of the visits I would make would be on a weekday, when he would be at work on the boat, so that I could ask him about the details of the carpentry. This was one boat that I intended to be familiar with and informed about in every particular, and truly make into *my* boat.

Everything seemed to be going well that day. The *Mary Simpson*'s engine had been installed and was running splendidly. The new boat was actually under construction. On the way back to Chapel Hill, however, we stopped at the Beaufort waterfront, where the *Virginius* was berthed. When we looked into the cabin, we saw that a piece of paneling was hanging halfway off under the port berth. A closer look revealed that the head's flexible holding tank, underneath the berth, had expanded and had forced it off. There was supposed to be nothing whatever in the holding tank, because, again supposedly, it had never been used. Yet it was greatly inflated, and if not pumped out soon might well come apart and discharge its contents into the cabin.

I had been told that there were no facilities in the Beaufort area for pumping out holding tanks. All I could do was hope that the tank would hold long enough for the carburetor to be repaired and replaced. On my next trip to the coast I would take the *Virginius* out to some place where we could safely empty the tank, while also hoping that when we did so, the contents would indeed go overboard and not into the cabin. Until this was attended to, of course, the chances of selling the *Virginius* were considerably decreased.

"Sometimes," said my son as we drove off for home, "that damn boat is a pain in the ass."

Two weeks later, on a Sunday evening, I drove down to the coast again, checked into a motel, and the next morning headed for Harkers Island for another look at the new boat. The carburetor on the *Virginius* had now been repaired, but George Alletsee—who, having replaced the *Mary Simpson*'s engine, had agreed to take a look at the old sailboat—wanted to work on the starter. So I still could not do anything about pumping out the holding tank.

At Harkers Island, when I entered the boat shed, I found that Clem Willis had turned the hull of the new boat topside up. The long, pointed ribs had been partly covered over with one-by-one-inch strips of siding, each cut to exact fit, glued, and clamped tightly in place, and tapering gracefully forward in a flared curve to the tall wooden stem. The broad transom was all but complete, and inside the shell of the hull the ribs and members were bolted into place. The bottom planking had not yet been installed, but the floor timbers were fitted in place atop the heavy keel, and the deadwood was already bored for the propeller shaft and the rudder hole drilled through.

I had not realized just how massive a twenty-four-foot workboat hull could look when out of the water. "She's deep," Clem Willis commented as I looked it over. With the high ribs arching upward and outward several feet above the uncompleted sides like the teeth of a garden rake, the boat-to-be had an almost ferocious appearance, as if it were vaunting its solid strength of construction. It was the width of the hull that seemed most impressive; this was to be nobody's narrow, sleek, bulletlike affair, but a wide-bodied, fat-fannied craft that would come and go in comfort.

After he had completed the siding, Clem said, he would turn the hull bottom up to begin installing the bottom planking. When that was complete, it would be time to begin the interior of the hull, followed by the cabin frame and the deck. There were numbers and marks scrawled in pencil all over the timbers of the boat, and an assortment of plumb bobs suspended down on cords, but I could see no signs of any drawings or templates anywhere in the shop. "Do you draw plans to work from?" I asked.

For answer, Clem pointed to a shelf in one corner of the rear of the shop, on which were piled several

---

dozen shingles. Taking a shingle down, he blew the dust off it and showed it to me. On it was penciled a line, with a number of crossbars and numbers inscribed at various places. The crossbars indicated the bottom frames, and the numbers between them showed the width of the spaces between the frames. He had shingles with similar diagrams for boats ranging from fifteen to forty-five feet, he said; that was all that he used in the way of plans. "I know where everything goes," he explained—as apparently he did, for there was a uniform precision to the way the frames and planks led out at sharply registered right angles from the perpendicular plumb lines. It was indeed "traditional" boatbuilding.

I got my cameras and began photographing the hull work and framing. Of all the boats I had ever owned, except for that little wooden skiff I had built when I was thirteen, this would be the first that I had seen take shape from the keel up, and become herself before my eyes. Oddly enough, I felt no particular eagerness for the new boat to be completed as quickly as possible. This was because I was thinking of her in terms of the coming of spring, and it was still mid-autumn now, the formal onset of winter more than a month away. I remembered something that a friend had once said. "In the spring, some men fall in love, or leave their wives, or take off to far places, or begin planting

gardens," he said. "You buy a boat." There was truth to
it. When I got cabin fever during the dreary indoor
months of January and February, the form it always took
was a craving for a cabin that was mounted atop a hull.
Besides, thus far there had been no time at all to use the
Mary Simpson. All during the late summer and early fall,
when I had expected to enjoy her, she had been laid up
with that interminable engine-swapping. Now she was
ready to go, at my disposal—and I was within a few
months of replacing her.

I said goodbye to Clem Willis, telling him I hoped to be
back the following weekend, and drove to Morehead
City. It was shortly after noon, and I stopped at Williams
Hardware and bought some supplies, then proceeded to
the *Mary Simpson* at Gillikin's Boat Basin. I needed to
install something that would prevent the battery-
compartment hatch board from sliding against the
flywheel of the engine, and to place several ledges under
the board to support it better. It took me some time to
do all this, and afterwards I ran the VHF radio power
lines down the inside of the cabin wall, then under the
deck, and connected them to the battery. Getting the two
wires down behind the interior-wall stripping proved to
be quite a job; I had to take a wire coat hanger,
straighten it out and place a loop at one end, then force

---

the tip of the hanger up to where I could thread the
wires through the loop and pull them down to where I
could get at them. Finally the job was completed, and I
turned on the radio and listened to the marine forecast. It
called for fair, warm weather for the next several days
and nights—perfect conditions for running down the
sound to the harbor entrance and trolling for blues or
mackerel just offshore.

Unfortunately, I could not wait around to do it; I
had to get back to my office for an appointment early the
next morning. I switched on the rebuilt Chrysler Crown
engine and listened for some minutes as it churned away.
Then I turned it off, rigged a new blue plastic tarpaulin
over the stern cockpit area, and departed for Chapel Hill.

The weekend following, the *Virginius* got in her licks
once again, with some help from me. My friend Bob
Simpson, back from his annual late-summer-and-early-fall
hunting, fishing, camping, and picture-taking expedition
along the Continental Divide, agreed to help me move
the sailboat from the Beaufort waterfront to the Town
Creek Marina, where the vertical streak rubbed off the
hull paint by Hurricane Hugo was to be repainted. It also
turned out that Town Creek had a pump-out station after
all, so it would not be necessary to run the *Virginius*
three miles offshore to empty her holding tank.

I drove down on Saturday morning, picked up Bob at his place on Peltier Creek in Morehead City, and we headed for Beaufort. The temperature was in the low fifties, the sky was leaden gray, and the wind was at something like twenty knots. There was a powerful incoming tide flowing along the waterfront, which made getting the *Virginius* out of her narrow slip more than ordinarily difficult. George Alletsee had informed me earlier in the week that the starter had been repaired, but that the gears were slipping and needed overhauling. When Bob and I finally managed to get the *Virginius* free of the docks and all her lines cast off, I found out what George meant. She would stay in gear only at very low speed; when I attempted to give her more throttle the gear popped out.

What had caused the gears to go bad, when the *Virginius* had not been moved from her berth for some weeks? Why was it, as George had several times remarked, that it is when boats are left idle, and not when they are being used, that things happen to them? Almost all my experience bore out the fact. The mishap with the *Virginius*'s shaft coupler earlier in the summer was the exception, not the rule. Whatever the mystique of old boats, they have a way of behaving in acceptable fashion for as long as they are being taken out frequently, and then going bad and costing lots of money when left to themselves at the dock. Hell Hath No Fury, etc.

It is a strange business. One would think that if a gear intended to wear itself out, òr a bolt drop out of a tiller, or an armature brush cease functioning within an alternator, or whatever, it would do so when in use and under strain. But it almost never happens then. Rather, the flawed or worn part waits until the boat owner departs for home, and then sometime before the next outing, it undergoes a private crisis and gives up the ghost. The owner doesn't find out until he shows up several weekends later, typically with invited guests along, ready for several days of happy boating. He prepares to leave the dock, perhaps even gets under way and travels fifty yards or so—and then perceives that something is very wrong.

On such occasions there is no hope of summoning a repairman to remedy the trouble, no matter how simple the job, so that owner and guests can enjoy at least a portion of the weekend out on the water. It seems to be an inviolable law that repair shops at marinas must shut down on weekends, even though that is when nine-tenths of the customers at the marina use their boats, and when almost all of the troubles are discovered. One can only apologize to the guests, leave a work order at the marina office, and drive back home. Wouldn't it make more sense to have the engine mechanics and other shop employees take their days off on Mondays and Tuesdays, say, even if their salaries had to be increased and repair

---

rates raised a bit to make up for the inconvenience? One would think so, but I have yet to discover a marina anywhere that arranges for its repair staff to be on duty on the days when the marina's customers most need their services.

It isn't that the boat owner arbitrarily chooses to use his boat on Saturdays and Sundays. In most cases he holds down a job Monday through Friday—how else could he afford to own and maintain the boat?—so if he wishes to use his boat it must be done on weekends or not at all. Given how seldom the average boat owner gets to enjoy his boat anyway—say eight or ten weekends plus two weeks of vacation time a year at most—the least that the marina could do would be to plan its operations with that in mind. But then, what marina was ever conducted with the needs of its clientele as a major consideration? I have encountered none.

In any event, beyond question the gears on the *Virginius* were slipping. Fortunately we would have only a short distance to go. We circled around until the Highway 70 bridge opened, then proceeded through. As we passed by the tugboat *Sampit,* just beyond the bridge, Bob began telling me a fascinating story about how another Morehead City–Beaufort tug, the *Winchester,* had sunk in heavy seas just off Cape Lookout earlier in the week. Meanwhile we neared the green channel marker, and I turned in toward the Town Creek Marina two hundred yards away. A minute later there was a bump, and the *Virginius*'s forward progress ceased.

We were aground. I had been so engrossed in Bob's story that I had neglected to turn on the depth-finder, and instead of looking at the chart to make sure, had assumed that I should keep the green marker on the port side. What I had forgotten was that the markers were placed so as to indicate the channel southward into Beaufort from the Waterway, and not out of Beaufort northward into Town Creek. Thus the maxim "Red Right Returning," meaning that one should always keep red markers on the starboard side and green markers on the port side, did not apply, because in this instance "returning" was going into Beaufort, not away from it.

If the *Virginius* could have produced anything resembling full power we could probably have backed off, but as it was we got nowhere. I was about to call in to the marina on the radio for help, when a sports-fisherman with twin outboards happened along and her owner offered us aid. We handed over a line and the sportsfisherman backed off and began tugging, while Bob rocked the boat and I gunned the reverse gear as best I could. After a minute we eased off the shoal into deeper water, thanked our rescuer, and headed for the Waterway marker.

In the process something had happened to the *Virginius*'s engine, so that now it was giving power only in brief spurts. What was disturbing was that the uneven power came even when the engine was in neutral. I shuddered to think of the possibility that there might be salt water in the rebuilt Atomic 4 engine. Bob's guess, which turned out to be correct, was that some mud had gotten into the engine and that it could be cleaned out without excessive trouble.

We made it into the Town Creek Marina dock only with difficulty. Bob Simpson's brother Bill was waiting for us there with an automobile. I left a repair order at the marina office, and we drove back over to the waterfront to collect my car. From there we headed for Harkers Island.

In the five days since I had last seen the new boat, Clem Willis had completed most of the siding strips, though the tips of the ribs were still showing. Bob was much taken with her construction. A professional outdoors photographer, he had brought along his camera, and after commandeering a nearby stepladder he proceeded to photograph her from various angles, while I concentrated on close-ups of the siding joinery. Before my boat hit the water it would surely be one of the most photographed craft in the history of the Carolina coast.

* * *

Bob Simpson and I were set to go fishing the following day. In the morning the sky was still clouded over, however, the temperature was down in the forties, and the wind was blowing steadily from the north. I loaded my fishing gear onto the *Mary Simpson,* though the prospect of trolling outside the mouth of the harbor in fairly rough water with a cold wind knifing at us was not especially inviting. Still, I was determined to take my boat out this time, whatever the conditions. So I cast off the lines and edged the *Mary Simpson* out into the creek branch.

I maneuvered alongside Bob's venerable *Sylvia II* at its dock near the creek mouth and gave a toot on the air horn. A minute later Bob appeared on the dock, stepped onto his boat and out onto the gunwale, then onto the stern of the *Mary Simpson.* He was wearing a heavy mackinaw over a sweater and a cap with earflaps, and he had brought with him a thermos of hot coffee. He gave the *Mary Simpson* a push to get her stern clear of *Sylvia II,* and we set off.

As we emerged into Bogue Sound and proceeded along the channel leading out of the creek I began to realize just how nervous I was. Except for the trial run with George Alletsee I had not taken the boat out on my own since the day in July when, with Bill and Susan Simpson along, she had begun losing power and I had

---

found out that the engine had to be rebuilt. And that had been the *only* time I had taken her out. Add the two excursions aboard the *Virginius*—the run from Minnesott to Beaufort when her coupler had given way just as we were docking her, and yesterday's fiasco—and the truth was that each and every time I had attempted to use a boat all summer and fall, something had gone wrong. Even for me, the run of bad luck had been extraordinary.

A large tugboat pushing a pair of laden barges was coming along, a quarter mile to our west, as we swung past the entrance marker. I shoved the throttle forward. The rebuilt Chrysler Crown responded with a husky roar and the *Mary Simpson* picked up speed. Ahead of us, a mile to the east up the Waterway, was the high span of the recently completed Atlantic Beach highway bridge, and beyond it we could make out what appeared to be Navy craft of some sort.

I nudged the throttle all the way up, until the gauge showed 2,800 RPMs, then eased it back to a steady 2,150 cruising speed. I looked at the oil pressure; it was high and steady. The ammeter showed a light charge, and the water temperature was just under 140°. The engine ran smoothly.

As we drew nearer the bridge I throttled down and moved closer to the southern edge of the Waterway channel to allow the tug and barges, which had been following steadily, to pass us, so that we could follow them under the bridge span rather than the other way around. The tug went by us at a steady eight and a half knots, as called for by regulations, and I turned into her wake to take advantage of the slick surface. When running canals and rivers along the Waterway it is advisable not to follow too closely behind tugs, because their huge propellers have a way of churning up the bottom and dislodging waterlogged tree trunks and other objects. It was probably deep enough where we were not to worry about such things happening, but I kept a prudent distance anyway.

Beyond the bridge the two Navy vessels, which turned out to be landing craft manned by reservists, were practicing laying their bows on a shoal. Giving them a wide berth, we followed on behind the tug, and I edged the throttle forward until we appeared to be moving at the same speed, neither gaining nor falling farther behind. The RPM needle showed 2,150, which indicated that eight and a half knots was what the *Mary Simpson* made at cruising speed.

East of the bridge a dredged channel leads to an area of docks alongside the causeway, and moving down it toward the Waterway was a whole procession of large sportsfishermen and cruisers. One after another they were pulling into the main channel, as if on parade. Several of them reached the channel in advance of us, and the others followed off our stern, so that the *Mary Simpson* became in effect part of the procession.

Directly ahead was a handsome sportsfisherman, the *Fast Company,* home port Havelock, North Carolina, and behind us was another classy-looking cruiser with an enclosed flying bridge and a tuna tower above that. There were eight boats in all, and each must have cost its owner a minimum of a hundred thousand dollars. The *Mary Simpson* was in fast company indeed. What the owners of these luxurious vessels thought of my little twenty-five-foot wooden Sea-Skiff venturing to become part of their processional I had no idea. Had we been in open water, of course, they would have gunned their twin engines to planing speed and shot past us. As it was, all they could do for now was to keep in line behind us in the channel and await their chance.

"Do you feel like trying the fishing?" I asked Bob.

"It's all right with me either way," he replied, "but it's going to be mighty cold and rough out there near the mouth of the harbor, with this wind like it is."

"That's what I'm afraid of," I told him. "Let's take a look, and if it doesn't look good we'll skip it." The truth was that what I wanted to do was to operate the boat; the fishing had been mostly an excuse.

We passed by the State Ports Authority docks and went into the turning basin, then pulled out of the parade, doubtless much to the relief of the participants, who turned northward into the Newport River. The mouth of the harbor was in clear view. The north wind was blowing steadily and vigorously from the inner harbor toward the ocean against the incoming tide, and the surface of the water was very choppy. Except for a couple of outboard runabouts anchored inside the protected mouth of the Coast Guard station at Fort Macon, no other boats were in sight. The outlook for fishing was not encouraging.

"To hell with it," I said, and turned the *Mary Simpson* northward and portward in a wide circle. Regaining the relative shelter of the Ports Authority docks we headed west, then turned into the entrance to the Morehead City waterfront channel. We swung by a large cargo vessel—the *Globe Trader,* home port Monrovia—which was alongside a dock where huge cranes were at work on her cargo, then by a trio of oceangoing tugs, and continued westward up the waterfront. We passed several marinas, a phalanx of deep-sea fishing charter boats, an assortment of workboats and sailboats, and a wreck—a long black-painted hull, her sides half gone, which Bob Simpson said was what was left of a hundred-year-old schooner. We passed the

Sanitary Restaurant and DeeGee's Books and Gifts, a pair of white-painted Stacy shrimp trawlers and a half-dozen others, and so on along the waterfront.

Winter was i-cumen in; no doubt about that. Bob Simpson poured cups of hot coffee from his thermos for us, and the steaming brew was comforting. I guided the *Mary Simpson* westward, back up Core Sound toward the bridge. The rebuilt Chrysler Crown was emitting a steady, healthy growl as it propelled us along. We passed several cruisers and a very handsome trawler yacht, then crossed under the bridge. Another tug pushing a string of barges was headed toward us, these apparently hauling liquid cargo, probably chemicals. We gave it a wide berth, keeping to the deep water close to the shore, and continued on.

"Do you know that those tugs don't use depth-finders?" Bob remarked, and when I expressed surprise, he explained that inasmuch as the barges ahead of the tug drew the same depth of water as the tug itself, the latter could go anywhere they did. If shallow water was involved, by the time a depth-finder on the bridge of the tug began indicating shoal water, the lead barge would be hard aground.

We reached the entrance to Peltier Creek, turned in between the markers, and moved along the entrance channel at reduced speed to the creek mouth. Once inside

I cut the *Mary Simpson*'s speed to where the boat was barely moving forward, then placed the gear in neutral and let the incoming tide bear our bow up close to the side of the *Sylvia II.* Bob Simpson stepped aboard his own boat, and I placed the *Mary Simpson* in reverse and backed off into the creek. As I swung the wheel all the way to port and gave the throttle a brief burst to turn the boat, Bob flashed me the thumbs-up sign, as if to say, *All systems are Go!*

As indeed they seemed at last to be.

6

TUGBOAT CAPTAINS, RIVER PILOTS, AND THE CRAFT OF FICTION

And let me in this place movingly admonish you, ye ship-owners of Nantucket! Beware of enlisting in your vigilant fisheries any lad with lean brow and hollow eye; given to unseasonable meditativeness; and who offers to ship with the Phaedon instead of Bowditch in his head.

—Melville, *Moby-Dick*

By day or night, the tugboats that Bob Simpson and I encountered on the *Mary Simpson*'s jaunt along Bogue Sound to the harbor and back are familiar presences on the Intracoastal Waterway—to be exact, they are push boats rather than tugs, since customarily they do not pull barges behind them but push them ahead as they go. They are large affairs, with high pilothouses, for the man at the wheel must possess a clear view not only of the barges but of the Waterway beyond, the channel and the banks on both sides, and the presence of any and all approaching craft. During the course of, say, a five-hour run one is likely to encounter a half-dozen such strings of barges, a few of them of them so lengthy that there are tugs with propulsion units both fore and aft.

Depending on the portion of the Waterway being traversed, meeting up with barge traffic can involve considerable perturbation. To come upon a barge just as one is rounding a sharp bend in a narrow cut tends to be disconcerting. Theoretically there is room for two-way traffic, but the barge is not likely to be hugging one side of the Waterway, and the sight of a vast, blunt rectangular bow, several times the height of your own small vessel, gliding ominously and relentlessly toward you can be daunting. What you do is to edge over in the channel and let the barge pass by, while hoping that the side you choose isn't shoaling and that you won't run aground.

Yet, all things considered, I would rather meet a tug and barges than overtake and pass them. When you do manage to draw even with them and begin to pass, if your boat has a slow, displacement-type hull like mine, a goodly amount of time will be needed to traverse the length of the tow and get into the clear. Moving along a narrow channel with only a couple of dozen feet separating you from a huge barge that towers far above your own boat can be unnerving. What if another boat shows up, coming toward you from the opposite direction? What if you suddenly encounter a half-submerged log just ahead, and must swerve to avoid it? The barge can't move over to let you past.

Still, when dealing with barges on the Waterway there is the comforting knowledge that the captain of the tug knows exactly what he is doing, and that if anything goes wrong it isn't likely to be the result of his actions. For the ability to guide a string of barges along a narrow, winding channel, without running aground and with due consideration for wind, current, tide, and traffic, is no ordinary skill. No prudent proprietor of a barge-transportation company is going to entrust half a million dollars or more worth of tugboat, barges, and cargo to anyone without a great deal of experience. Barges, after all, must be operated at night as well as in daylight; with the aid of a spotlight of several million candlepower the man at the wheel must feel his way along shoaling channels, across inlets with tricky currents, paying close heed to the coded, blinking lights of Waterway markers and never mistaking one marker for another.

Consider the judgment and skill required of a tugboat captain who from a quarter mile away must aim a string of barges forty feet wide at the gap in a drawbridge that is no more than twice that width, through which a strong current is swirling, while a twenty-knot wind is blowing steady on the beam off the nearby ocean. He knows all too well that it would require half a mile or more to bring the tow to a halt, and that a bit too much lateral drift now, translated and expanded over the course of a quarter mile, will send the bow of the barge ramming into the pilings of the bridge, very likely tearing up the span and sinking the barge. As he aims his tow at the passageway, he spots, on the far side of the bridge, a large yacht speeding along the Waterway toward him, throwing up a sizeable wake, and very likely slated to reach the opening in the bridge at about the same time that his lead barge will do so. Meanwhile several runabouts are anchored in the channel near the bridge, their occupants intently fishing away. And all the while a foolhardy youth on a jet waterscooter is racing back and forth across the channel a couple of hundred feet ahead, playing at imitating a porpoise but without the porpoise's ability to dive to safety. Clearly it is no place for a novice to be at the wheel of the tug.

Anyone who has seen barge traffic on the Mississippi River, of course, knows that the size of the operations there dwarfs that on the Waterway. It is not uncommon to see a string of a dozen long barges, tied two and sometimes three abreast, negotiating the big river, with a single tugboat furnishing the propulsion. By comparison, the narrowness of the Intracoastal Waterway and its numerous sharp bends and turns would render any such massive arrangement of barges impossible.

It would be interesting to hear a Mississippi River and a Waterway skipper comparing trade notes. The riverman would in most instances have a great deal more room to maneuver his tow, and so would not have to keep an eye constantly on the chart to make sure he was not in danger of running aground. On the other hand, the Waterway skipper would face nothing remotely comparable to the enormous force and volume of the Mississippi River current; and surely the consequences of a grounding along a tidal Waterway channel would be slight indeed compared to the havoc that would ensue if a Mississippi skipper were to misgauge the direction and pattern of the river flow while rounding a wide bend, and have his string of barges swing out broadside to the current. In any event, the skill required for either operation must be considerable.

When I see a tugboat conducting its string of barges along the Waterway, I often think of that most renowned of all Mississippi River pilots, Mark Twain. Which thought leads me in turn to consider another kind of craft—the craft of language. What follows will have chiefly to do with stringing together sentences rather than barges.

For some four years, until the outbreak of the Civil War brought a hiatus to passenger traffic on the Mississippi River, Samuel Langhorne Clemens earned his livelihood as a steamboat pilot. In later life he sometimes referred to

---

the period as the most satisfying of his lifetime, and several times declared that he would put aside his literary vocation and go back to it in an instant "if madam would stand it." He knew better, of course, and so did Olivia Clemens, but it was a pleasant enough fantasy for a middle-aged man living in a luxurious mansion in Hartford, Connecticut, to indulge.

In the days when the young Sam Clemens was on the river, piloting was an extremely risky business. There was no vigilant U.S. Army Corps of Engineers to set out markers and beacons to indicate the edges of the channel and warn of shoals, or to remove snags and impediments. The river was constantly shifting its borders, and there was no warning service alerting pilots to changes in channels, fluctuations in water levels, or potential sources of danger. Powerful electric searchlights were not yet available to illuminate the water ahead, nor were there carefully updated hydrographic charts to indicate every turn, bend, shoal, and irregularity of the waterway. The shores of the river were still largely unpopulated; a pilot at the wheel of a river steamboat had to negotiate in effect a trackless wilderness, relying almost totally upon his memory of previous trips and his skill at reading the signs of current, shoreline, and sky to make his way in safety.

I have wondered sometimes why it was that, if

---

piloting a steamboat on the Mississippi was such a glorious epoch for Clemens, to be looked back at ever afterward with fondness and pride, he never chose to write about it. For he did not; he wrote about learning how to be a river pilot, and he wrote about revisiting the river many years later as a passenger aboard a boat, and taking the wheel for a spell. He wrote about Huckleberry Finn and Jim drifting down the river on a raft. He wrote about ocean steamship travel, and even about barge travel in Europe. But at no time did he ever compose an extended work, whether fiction or nonfiction, showing what it was like as a grown man—and Sam Clemens was in his mid-twenties during his piloting days—to be earning a living at the wheel of a steamboat.

The section of *Life on the Mississippi* devoted to the education of a cub pilot was originally published in *The Atlantic Monthly,* in 1875, as a series of articles, and then in England as a book under the title *Old Times on the Mississippi.* In writing about his apprenticeship as a cub pilot Clemens tailored the material of real-life memory to the literary requirements of the story he was telling. When he decided to apprentice himself to Horace Bixby in order to learn how to run the river, he was no callow youth first starting out in the world; he had already been away from home and on his own for four years, working as a journeyman typesetter in St. Louis,

Cincinnati, Philadelphia, and New York City. But
Clemens wanted to present the naiveté and innocence of
the cub as he comes up against the disciplined
requirements of piloting a steamboat, so to develop his
story better he made his cub pilot a stripling of no more
than seventeen years. What this did was to lead Clemens
to try to visualize the experience as it would have been
seen by a person significantly younger and more naive
than he had been at the time, so that in effect he began
writing autobiographical fiction rather than a humorous
but essentially factual memoir. The cub pilot's experiences
on the river are doubtless based on Clemens's, but they
are shaped to the imaginative demands of a tale of a
youth's education and growth.

In order to learn how to be a river pilot, the cub
must not only learn to read the river accurately, and to
remember what each and every mile of the river and
shoreline looked like by night and day; he must also learn
to rely upon his own knowledge, and in so doing trust to
his judgment and resolve, rather than get by on courage
borrowed from the proven pilot who is teaching him the
river. He must, in short, *grow up,* change from a boy into
a man. *Old Times on the Mississippi* is an "initiation"
story, and learning to pilot a steamboat becomes a
metaphor, as it were, for learning to confront the adult
world.

* * *

There is a famous passage in *Old Times on the Mississippi**
in which Clemens contrasts the way that a river scene
might look to a tourist with the way it would appear to
someone experienced in reading the signs of the water.
He prefaces the passage with a lengthy comparison of
running the Mississippi to reading a book, one with a
new story to tell each day. In twelve hundred miles, he
says, there was not a page devoid of interest or one that
could be skipped over; no man could possibly write so
wonderful a book as the river itself. Then he describes an
especially beautiful sunset he had observed when he was
still new to the river. It is a conventional scenic
presentation modeled on the standard travel description of
the nineteenth century, with elaborately ornate and
prettified figures of speech such as "the surface was
broken by boiling, tumbling rings, that were as
many-tinted as an opal," or "high above the forest wall a
clean-stemmed dead tree waved a single leafy bough that
glowed like a flame in the unobstructed splendor that was
flowing from the sun." And so on. "I stood like one
bewitched," he effloresces. "I drank it in, in a speechless
rapture."

*The chapters in question are those numbered 4 through 15 in *Life on the
Mississippi*. They are also conveniently available as a unit in Walter
Blair's edition of *Selected Shorter Writings of Mark Twain* (Boston: River-
side Editions A58, Houghton Mifflin Company, 1962).

Once he had learned to read the river in terms of piloting a steamboat on it, however, what he saw was no longer scenically elevating: "all the grace, the beauty, the poetry had gone out of the majestic river!" He proceeds to interpret the earlier scene as it would have been read by a skilled pilot. The sun means there will be wind tomorrow; the floating log means the river is rising; a slanting mark is the sign of a dangerous bluff reef developing; the "tumbling boils" indicate a dissolving bar and a shifting channel, and so on. "That silver streak in the shadow of the forest is the 'break' from a new snag, and he has located himself in the very best place he could have found to fish for steamboats; that tall dead tree, with a single living branch, is not going to last long, and then how is a body ever going to get through this blind place at night without the friendly old landmark?" What this all means, Clemens reiterates, is that "the romance and beauty were all gone from the river. All the value any feature of it had for me now was the amount of usefulness it could furnish toward compassing the safe piloting of a steamboat."

Now that, of course, was nonsense, because what has caught up the reader in Clemens's cub-pilot tale has not been any of the conventionally poetic tourist prose depicting the "speechless rapture" at "boiling, tumbling rings . . . as many-tinted as an opal" or the leafy boughs glowing "like a flame in the unobstructed splendor that was flowing from the sun." Rather, the fascination for us is precisely the vividness and authenticity with which Clemens has been showing us what he saw and what he learned on the river *as a cub pilot,* in the kind of everyday vernacular diction—intensified, to be sure, through Mark Twain's literary artistry—that he used to see and learn it. The kind of writing that Clemens contends, or doubtless pretends, would be suitable for reproducing "the grace, the beauty, the poetry" of the river offers only high-sounding but empty generalizations and abstractions, while the writing that shows what the cub pilot actually sees and does is filled with concrete detail, and alive with excitement. In reality the passage describing the river as it appears to an experienced pilot engaged in running the river is every bit as literary as the tourist's-eye passage, in the sense of being imaginatively evocative and well written. What it is not is elaborately decorative and self-consciously Poetic.

The notion that *using* something, rather than merely contemplating it, destroys its imaginative dimensions would imply that there can be no artistic involvement, no emotional satisfaction in observing and contemplating anything that happens to be of much imaginative importance to us in the world. Running the river, Clemens seems to be arguing, can be emotionally satisfying to us only if we are ignorant of its real workings. Once accurate knowledge in depth is involved, all apparent beauty departs. One might just as logically contend that only a non-musician can find a piano sonata beautiful, for once one learns to play the piano, the music is merely being *used*. The truth, of course, is just the other way around; the *more* one grasps the intricacies within a complex work of the musical imagination, such as a Beethoven sonata, the greater its fascination. A concert pianist can perform the *Waldstein* Sonata again and again, year after year, without boredom or surfeit.

Look at the matter this way. Do I, steering my own boat down the Intracoastal Waterway, derive greater aesthetic pleasure and emotional satisfaction from doing so than the captain of the push-boat tug who guides his string of barges regularly along the same stretch of water repeatedly, month after month, year after year? It depends in part, of course, on the relative capacities for same of myself and the particular captain. But it would be foolish indeed to claim that *because* I am only an amateur boatman I am therefore more capable of enjoying "the grace, the beauty, the poetry," as Clemens would seem to be arguing. The tugboat captain may not think of what he does in terms of those particular qualities, yet surely the circumstance that it is his vocation rather than his avocation, and that he has studied and knows that stretch of Waterway with a concentration and an eye for significant detail far surpassing my own, does not restrict the imaginative satisfaction he takes in his work. What he gives up in superficial spectacle is more than made up in the depth and complexity of his involvement. The fact that he has negotiated the Waterway again and again does not reduce the quality of the experience; it *expands* it.

Where, for example, I might observe a bend in the Waterway, a stretch of green-yellow marshland, a green channel marker, an opening in the marsh leading to a creek, he sees the set of the current, the direction of the flow, the stage of the tide at that point. Lighter water indicates the presence of a shoal just inside the marker, the crests of waves and the movement of the reed grass indicate the effect of the breeze, and so on. He does not see these things *instead of* what I see; he sees them *in,* and *as part of,* what I see. Doubtless he does not say to himself, "Isn't this stretch of marshland beautiful?" as I might think to do at the novelty of the sight; but it is not the fact that I think to describe it to myself that way that makes the marshland beautiful, so much as the emotional experience itself.

What I *might* be able to do better than the tugboat captain, if I worked hard enough and long enough at it and if he did not happen to be named Sam Clemens, would be to write about the stretch of Waterway in such a way as to recreate my experience of traveling upon it in language, so that others could share that experience. For that is my line of work rather than his. To do it, however, I should have to study it with considerable thoroughness of detail, for the more I know about it, the more authentic and vivid my description is likely to be. A brief impressionistic depiction would scarcely do.

If I were to set out to write such a description, I would surely use as my organizing principle not the geographical location of the Waterway as such but my involvement with it. I would try to convey to my readers my personal experience of the Waterway through language, which would include the process whereby I learned it, my feelings while doing so, the pleasure I took and take in boats, some of the adventures I had as I learned it, the mishaps, and so on. To do this properly would involve not only careful observation but a great deal of study, reflection, and remembrance.

To write well—to communicate my emotional experience to someone else through language—I should also have to think about it not only as the rendering of an experience but as a piece of writing, a story. For what I write must encompass, within the range of a few hours of reading time, the essence of what would have taken me long months and even years to learn. I could not possibly imitate the experience as it happened; I would have to find a way of shaping and directing what I write so that I captured its fundamental details, including not only factual but emotional experience as well. In order to give my description of the learning process greater focus and vividness, I might want, for example, to present myself as more naive and less informed about boats and the Waterway than I actually was (if that is possible). I might even find it appropriate to borrow aspects of other people's experiences and incorporate them as if they had been my own, in order to convey what I feel and know about the Waterway more intensively.

Needless to say, too, I would omit a great deal as being irrelevant or repetitious. I would not want to be like those characters that Sam Clemens wrote about, who were incapable of omitting any item in their memories, no matter how unimportant or peripheral, from the story they were telling. For whatever literature, or any other kind of art, may be, it is not direct, unmediated "real life" experience, but language shaped to give the reader the sense of "real life" while providing the order, development, and meaning that could only be extrapolated from life over a period of years. In short, I would try to go about the matter pretty much as Mark Twain does in *Old Times on the Mississippi*.

7

A TALE OF TWO
LAPSTRAKE BOATS

The forecast for Thanksgiving weekend predicted clear and cold weather. I called several friends to invite them to go fishing aboard the *Mary Simpson* with me, but they were all younger than I, and their family responsibilities were not conducive to taking off that weekend. As for Bob Simpson, who lived on Peltier Creek, he was to be away on a photographing assignment. Well, I had lots of work to do at the office, with the sales conference for our spring books only two weeks away and a stack of manuscripts to read. So I would stay home that weekend. The fish would just have to wait.

Friday was a holiday, and nobody else would be at the office, making the working conditions perfect. I put in a long and productive day's work. That evening I just happened to tune in the coastal weather forecast. The temperature would be in the high fifties, with light

---

clouds only, and what wind there was would be coming from the southwest, at five knots or less. What the hell. The next morning I packed my cameras and my binoculars into the car—the fishing tackle was already there—and took off for the coast.

At Gillikin's Boat Basin the *Mary Simpson* was waiting. I started the engine, and it roared satisfyingly into action. I cast off the lines, eased her out into the creek, and steered for the entrance. At Bob Simpson's dock I passed the *Sylvia II,* looking lovely as ever, and headed out into Bogue Sound.

Conditions were near to ideal; the forecast had been absolutely accurate, and moreover there were almost no other craft in sight. I edged the throttle up to 2,150 and proceeded eastward, under and past the bridge, then toward the Morehead City waterfront. A few small boats were anchored off the State Ports Authority docks and along the edges of the turning basin, bottom-fishing. I steered the *Mary Simpson* southeastward, past the Coast Guard station on the starboard. I thought about turning inside Shackleford Point and going behind the barrier island, where there was a deep hole. I could see a half-dozen boats anchored there. More than once I had taken some nice blues there on Hopkins jig spoons.

But I didn't want to anchor and fish. I wanted to run my boat, my so recently idled old lapstrake Sea-Skiff

whose Chrysler Crown was now rumbling happily away.
I checked the gauges; all was well. So I kept going, past
buoy No. 15, toward the entrance to the harbor. On the
beach and the jetty abutting Fort Macon there were
dozens of people fishing, casting out into the channel,
precisely as I had done that day earlier in the fall with
both my boats out of commission, watching gloomily as
powerboats cruised past. No longer.

I rounded buoy No. 11, and steered due south
along Beaufort Inlet channel, out into the Atlantic Ocean.
It was a magnificent early afternoon in late autumn. The
ocean was quiet, with only low rolling waves. The sun
was halfway down in the clear southwestern sky.
Southward the line of buoys stretched two miles out to
sea. To the west, a long distance away, I could make out
the rectangular shape of a menhaden factory boat. A few
cruisers and sailboats were scattered about the water, none
of them very near. On either side of the harbor mouth
the white sand beach led east and west, the Bogue Banks
lined with beach homes, the Shackleford Banks deserted
except for a few wild ponies grazing along a ridge of
dunes.

I continued seaward another half mile or so to the
No. 7 buoy, to be clear of the shoals along the channel
edge, then placed the *Mary Simpson* in neutral and began
rigging my rod and reel. I put a six-inch length of wire

on the end of a trolling sinker in case there were bluefish around; their sharp teeth could easily bite through gut leader. Then I attached a Hopkins jig spoon, freed the reel spool, and cast the jig off the stern. I hurried back to the controls, put the *Mary Simpson* into forward gear, throttled the engine back to its lowest operating speed, and began trolling.

When you troll for fish in coastal waters, what you look for are gulls working. If they are circling in posses, occasionally dipping down to the surface, it means that there are schools of small fish, and that larger fish—blues, mackerel—may be hitting them from below and knocking some out of the water where the gulls can grab them. There were a few gulls hovering over the water now, but they did not seem very excited. Even so I steered in their general direction.

The *Mary Simpson* had been built as a sportsfisherman, with a shallow, open main cabin and a large stern cockpit. In roofing over much of her cockpit earlier in the summer, I had made her into a more comfortable boat for cruising or for bottom-fishing on hot days, but I had also severely compromised her suitability for single-person trolling. From the control console to the open area at the stern there was now ten feet of roofed-in cabin, so that I could neither lift the tip of the trolling rod vertically, nor extend it out over the side of the boat. I had more or less to hold it so that it pointed semisternward, and hope that if and when a fish hit, I would have time to throw the engine into neutral and get back onto the stern before the fish threw the hook. Of course I could have looped a rope around the rod butt and let it rest against the transom, with the clicker on to signal a strike, but with the *Mary Simpson*'s engine rumbling away happily but loudly under the engine box, and being half deaf as I am, I would probably never hear it.

It turned out not to make any difference, because in an hour and a half of trolling all over the area, from the sea buoy to close to the beach, I got not a single strike. If there were any fish around, they must have been running deep, and operating single-handed as I was, I could not very well manage a deep-running plug with a planer from deep inside the cabin. The several other boats that were trolling around in the area seemed to be doing no better than I was, and the gulls remained passive.

The only way I was likely to catch any fish would be if I went back and anchored behind Shackleford Banks, then threw Hopkins spoons or green grubs with a casting rod, to attract blues or gray trout. But it was much too pleasant out there even to think of leaving merely in order to catch fish. I had caught fish before, and I would do so again, but today I was taking too much pleasure in guiding the *Mary Simpson* over the lightly rolling ocean, gazing around at the seascape, and watching what was now a recurring procession of charter boats returning from the Gulf Stream and the Continental Shelf.

Truth to tell, not only was there satisfaction in so doing, but reassurance as well. For not only was my boat's engine *running,* smoothly and steadily and free of trouble, but this was the first time that I had taken a boat offshore by myself in a half-dozen years or more. The sailing I had been doing had been on rivers and sounds. I had not owned a powerboat large enough to venture beyond the mouth of a harbor since the mid-1970s. To be sure, there is little risk involved in piloting a boat a few miles out into the ocean on a day when there is a minimum of wind or current; one might almost be afloat on a millpond. But this *wasn't* a millpond; it was the Atlantic—the ocean that I had seen as a child in Charleston, had watched from land as the seagoing ships and the Clyde-Mallory passenger liners left the harbor, bound for distant ports. *"I never see a sail afloat but in my heart's a song . . ."* Later, in the early 1970s, with the *Bill James* and her successor the *Little Eva,* I had done considerable fishing out of various ocean inlets. Since then there had been lakes, rivers, sounds—but nothing bounded on one side by beach and on the other by Africa and

Europe. Now I had made it out here again. A small
victory, but my own.

A beautiful gaff-rigged schooner had rounded the
sea buoy and was sailing harborward, and I trolled over
toward the channel to take a photograph or two. As I
did so I realized that the sun was now fairly far down in
the sky. It was well after three o'clock; I had been out
here for over two hours, and it was a good hour's run
back to Peltier Creek. Afternoons in late November were
short; it was getting closer and closer to the shortest day
of the year—*in solstitio brumali.* A cold time I would
shortly be having of it. Now it was time to go back, the
more so because the *Mary Simpson*'s running lights were
not hooked up. I hauled in the trolling lure, shoved up
the throttle, and headed for the mouth of the harbor.

Unlike the outward-bound trip, there was
company this time, in the form of assorted deep-sea and
charter craft that swung past the *Mary Simpson* and
showed their transoms to us. They could easily double
our eight and a half knots. Let them pass; we, my old
wooden Sea-Skiff and I, were in no particular hurry.

There was one difficulty. When the other boats
did go by they threw up a formidable wake, which set
the *Mary Simpson* to rocking briskly. I didn't mind the
rocking itself, but it caused a horrendous rattling aboard
the boat, as if a couple of duckpin balls were rolling

loose in the hull. I was fairly sure it wasn't the engine or gears, which were performing flawlessly, or anything else really serious. It occurred to me that perhaps the radio antenna had come down and was rolling on the roof, but when I held a mirror out the window to check, the antenna was standing as upright as ever. Maybe there were some old lengths of galvanized pipe somewhere down below the deck—though the noise seemed to be coming from above.

Once we reached the turning basin and headed down the sound, past the entrance to the Morehead City waterfront, there were no more fast-flying charter craft and sportsfishermen to come swooping past, hence no more rocking and no more noise. Up ahead was a sailing craft under power, headed in the same direction I was and at not a much slower pace. It was not until past the Atlantic Beach bridge that I drew abreast of her; she was a lovely rounded-stern motor sailer, with a roomy cabin that canted forward. She was headed southward down the Waterway at a steady six knots or so, no doubt bound for southern Florida and the Leeward Islands, and in no rush to get there. There was a Dutch look to her, as if she were built by deVries Lentsch. She was about fifty feet long and without the chrome and glitter of conspicuous consumption about her, yet she must have cost her owner a minimum of a quarter of a million dollars. Such a boat could obviously travel anywhere on the seven seas, in just about any kind of weather. I had never seen a more attractive boat. When the *Mary Simpson* had pulled ahead enough to allow me to leave the wheel in safety, I threw the gear into neutral and hurried back to the stern cockpit to get a couple of photos.

I had turned into the entrance channel to Peltier Creek and had cut speed and was moving along it, when out of the creek came another boat, an old wooden cruiser, lapstrake-built like the *Mary Simpson,* but with a much longer forward cabin and a small cockpit cabin set well astern. She was painted blue and gray, with white trim, and there was a 1960s look to her lines. Somehow she seemed very familiar. Where had I seen her before?

Suddenly I thought, the *Little Eva!* Either she was an identical twin, or else the selfsame Chris-Craft cruiser I had owned years ago. A year or so back, a friend had reported seeing the *Little Eva* tied up in a creek off the North River, near the Virginia–North Carolina line. What was she doing down here in southeastern North Carolina?

As the two lapstrake-hulled wooden boats passed each other I got a close look at her, and decided that she wasn't the *Little Eva* after all. The forward-cabin windows were different. This one had separate windows, whereas the *Little Eva* had a single expanse of sliding glass. She was probably a couple of years older than my ex-boat, which had been a 1958 model, but she was in excellent condition.

As I guided the *Mary Simpson* inside the creek mouth and on toward her berth, I thought about my onetime boat, and recalled in particular a certain day, not long after I had acquired her, which had been the most rending I have ever experienced as a boat owner.

The spring after I had sold my old converted Chesapeake Bay workboat, the *Bill James,* out of exasperation with the long ordeal of getting her ancient transmission replaced, I began to rue having done so. I went looking to see what was available, and at McCotter's Marina, on the Pamlico River in Washington, North Carolina, one of the employees suggested that I have a look at a Chris-Craft cabin cruiser now lying at one of the covered docks. He had recently checked her over thoroughly, he said, and at four thousand dollars she was as good a buy in an older boat as he had ever encountered.

The upshot was that I bought her. She was thirteen years old, thirty feet long, of wooden lapstrake construction, and she was powered by twin two hundred horsepower Ford V-8 engines. She was in spic-and-span

---

condition throughout, had V-berths forward, a settee and dinette that converted into berths in the main cabin, an enclosed head, a clothes closet, and a galley. She came with full twin-engine controls, marine radio, compass, bilge sniffer, and shore power; there was a forward cabin, a long trunk cabin, and a cockpit with sliding windows and a roll-down vinyl drop cloth that could enclose it completely. She was painted white and blue, and had a wide mahogany-colored transom on which I affixed the letters of her new name, LITTLE EVA, in honor of my wife.

I had never operated a boat with twin controls before, and the ease with which she could be turned by placing one engine in forward gear and the other in reverse was remarkable. She took the waves well, and when I moved the throttles up to three-quarter speed she planed along at eighteen knots.

The one feature that gave me pause was the gas consumption; I had been accustomed to the *Bill James*'s single GM 3-71 diesel, which might consume twenty gallons of diesel fuel during a sixty-mile run. The *Little Eva*'s twin two hundred horsepower V-8s, by contrast, drank just over a gallon of leaded gasoline per mile at three-quarter speed. It was true that by proceeding at the nine-knot pace of the displacement-hulled *Bill James* I could reduce that voracious appetite, but the *Little Eva*

did not operate comfortably when not at planing speed,
and with the capacity for more speed there, the
temptation to use it was too great.

There were various things I intended to do to the
Little Eva—install an automatic battery charger, an
automatic float switch for her bilge pump and a
hand-crank pump for possible emergency use, a spotlight,
fishing rod racks, and so on, but these could wait until
later in the summer, when I had finished teaching my
summer-school classes. My plan was to take the family up
the Intracoastal Waterway to Norfolk and then out into
the Chesapeake Bay to the York River, where I would
berth *Little Eva* at the York River Yacht Haven at
Gloucester Point for three weeks while we stayed at my
wife's parents' house further upstream.

On a day in late July we departed Little
Washington. The first day's excursion involved only a
thirty-mile run to where the Pamlico River becomes
Pamlico Sound and joins the Intracoastal Waterway, then
another ten miles up the Pungo River to Belhaven,
where we would dock for the night at the River Forest
Inn and Marina and enjoy its seafood buffet. The next
day we would make a seventy-nine-mile journey: up the
Pungo Canal and into the Alligator River, across
Albemarle Sound, and on up the Pasquotank River,
arriving at Elizabeth City, North Carolina. This would

leave a fifty-one-mile day's run farther up the Pasquotank to the Dismal Swamp Canal and on to Norfolk. From there to Gloucester Point and the York River Yacht Haven was another fifty-seven miles. The only spots en route where the weather might involve a layover were Albemarle Sound—which had a well-earned reputation for being the roughest stretch on the Waterway from Norfolk to Florida when the wind blew west to east or vice versa—and of course the Chesapeake Bay itself. Barring holdups at either place, with the *Little Eva*'s twin engines and planing hull we should be able to make the trip comfortably in four days' time.

The trip to Belhaven was uneventful; the *Little Eva* sped nicely along, her engines purring in fine style. The seafood buffet at the River Forest Inn was its usual spectacular self, and our two boys, ages fourteen and eleven, not only returned for enlarged second installments but polished off a pair of desserts each. The next morning, after an ample breakfast, we cast off and headed past the Belhaven breakwater and into the Pungo River, northward bound.

Whereupon the trouble began. The water-temperature gauge for the starboard engine swiftly rose to the boiling point. I cut off the engine, and running on the other one we returned to the dock at the River Forest. A mechanic was summoned, and after an hour or so he arrived and inspected the culprit engine. He proclaimed the trouble to be a broken O-ring in the transmission, and said it was causing the transmission fluid to leak out. He did not have a replacement ring of the proper size, and the nearest place where one might be purchased was back in Little Washington, twenty-five miles away by highway.

By this time the morning sun was blazing down from a clear sky, and the temperature was already in the nineties and still climbing. I rigged the canopy over the stern cockpit, and, leaving my wife and two boys aboard, drove to Little Washington with the mechanic. There I bought a replacement O-ring of the proper size and several spares as well, and returned to the marina, where, sweltering under the canopy, my wife and sons were waiting.

The O-ring was installed, and we set out once again. This time the water-temperature needle stayed at the proper level. We headed up the Pungo River, entered the canal, negotiated its twenty-mile length, and emerged at the Alligator River. By now it was well into the afternoon, so I pushed the throttles up and we roared along at close to top speed. Even so, it was after six o'clock before we passed under the sixty-five-foot clearance span of the Wilkerson Bridge near the mouth of the river and approached Albemarle Sound.

The sound appeared to be reasonably smooth, but beyond its three-mile width lay another fifteen-mile run up the Pasquotank River to Elizabeth City. It had been a long and mostly exasperating day, and the prospect of having to negotiate the unfamiliar last lap in gathering darkness was not appealing. The Waterway chart showed a small marina at the base of the western terminus of the bridge, with seven feet of depth at low tide. So we decided to put in there for the night, and cross the sound in the morning. With an early start we should still be able to reach Norfolk by late afternoon.

The marina was located in a cove surrounded on three sides by a grove of tall pine trees. As marinas went, it was not much: a single dock along a canal with a few boats tied alongside, and a marina office which was also a small grocery store and filling station. Although the hour was late the temperature was still in the nineties, and the pines cut off any breeze whatever. There was a smoky haze over the sky. Earlier that week I had read in the newspapers that a layer of smog covered much of the East Coast, and it was quite visible now.

The prospect of the four of us spending the night aboard the *Little Eva* was not inviting. Moreover, the nearest restaurant, which was connected to a motel, was in the town of Columbia, North Carolina, ten miles up the highway to the west. We decided to leave the *Little*

Eva at the marina, call the motel and have them send a courtesy car for us, and spend the night in air-conditioned comfort. So I moved the *Little Eva* from the fuel dock to a place farther along the wharf, tied her up, and we unloaded our suitcases and waited for transportation to the motel. There we had dinner and settled in for the night. It had been an exhausting day's travel, and the cool motel room was welcome.

"Where's the *Little Eva?*" our older boy asked when we arrived at the marina the next morning. There was no sign of her. I walked over to the edge of the seawall above the wharf. Our boat was there, all right, but with only her cockpit protruding above the surface of the water. Somehow, in some way, she had sunk during the night. Inside the cockpit floated an assortment of life cushions and other objects.

What had happened? Had we struck a submerged log or some other object the previous day during that dash down the Alligator River at full speed, and opened up a seam? If not that, then what? I had no clue whatever.

When I bought the *Little Eva* I had taken out full hull insurance on her with an agency in Washington; I had not even been billed yet for the premium. I went into the office, called the agent long-distance, and explained our plight. The agent consulted a directory and gave me the name of a boatyard in Elizabeth City which had a tugboat, so I called there and arranged to have someone come, raise the *Little Eva,* and tow her there for repairs. The tugboat, I was told, would arrive sometime in the early afternoon.

Our automobile was in Little Washington, seventy-five miles away, so I called McCotter's Marina and arranged for someone to bring it to me. It arrived about eleven o'clock, and I drove the young man from McCotter's back—my second trip to Little Washington since leaving two days earlier—and returned alone with the car. The tugboat had not yet shown up. There was nothing else to do except wait for her, which meant sitting around in the only shady place anywhere, the marina office. The afternoon was every bit as hot as its predecessor, and the office–grocery store was infested with flies. The boys played outside for a while, until it grew too hot even for them. Periodically I went outside to look out across the water, hoping to spy the tugboat coming. Occasionally a yacht or a tug and barge moved by, out on the river. Automobiles went by regularly, bound for Manteo and the Outer Banks. The grocery store did not even have a magazine rack; there was nothing to read except the Raleigh *News & Observer* and a telephone directory. It was not until after five o'clock that the tugboat from Elizabeth City put in its appearance.

Raising the *Little Eva* was accomplished quickly

---

enough. The tugboat operator, a highly profane man named Captain Suggs, ran hoses from large gasoline-powered salvage pumps into the cockpit, arranged the *Little Eva*'s seat cushions around the open stern to deter water from entering, then began pumping. Within ten minutes the boat was afloat once again, and in another five minutes most of the water had been removed from inside her. The interior was a soggy, appalling mess. We retrieved whatever seemed salvageable, Captain Suggs lashed her to the side of his tugboat, and, with a single pump left aboard to keep her afloat, tugboat and *Little Eva* departed for Elizabeth City.

As for us, fatigued by the heat and the long wait, we loaded our suitcases in the automobile and headed for home, 170 miles away. My wife, who had spent most of the long hot day swatting flies in the marina office and keeping the boys in line, was at the point of mental and physical exhaustion. If anything the two-day ordeal had been harder on her than on me, since I at least had been able to do something—drive to Little Washington with the mechanic and get the O-ring, drive there again to drop off the young man who had fetched our car—while she could only wait around in the stifling heat. We stopped for dinner at a Holiday Inn in Williamston, North Carolina. The wiser course of action would have been to remain there, get a decent night's sleep, and proceed on to Chapel Hill the next morning. But I was

---

at nerve's edge and not thinking rationally; all I could think of was to get home. So on we drove through the night.

It was a gruesome, nightmarish drive. To save a few miles I left the four-lane highway in favor of a state road that bypassed the city of Raleigh. The road was narrow and hilly, and previously I had driven on it only during the daytime. By night it was considerably less comfortable. Out of pure exhaustion my wife began sobbing every time we passed a car, which seemed to occur whenever we neared the crest of a hill. It was after midnight before we arrived home.

Two days later I received a call from a marine-claims investigator, sent by the insurance company to inspect the *Little Eva* in Elizabeth City. He reported that— apparently during our run from Belhaven to the marina at the edge of Albemarle Sound—a flange had been knocked loose from one of the engine exhaust ports. Once the forward motion of the boat ceased, water had begun flowing in around the exhaust pipe. Eventually enough water entered the hull so that the through-hull port of the bilge pump was below the surface of the water. Acting as a reverse syphon, the pump hose had joined in to allow more water inside, and the *Little Eva* had gone to the bottom.

Everything aboard would either have to be

cleaned or replaced, and the engines would have to be thoroughly overhauled and the interior completely repainted. The boatyard estimated the cost at about three thousand dollars—of which all except a three-hundred-dollar deductible charge would be covered by the insurance policy.

If only we had not given in to the heat and retreated to the air-conditioned motel, instead of spending the night aboard, I would have noticed what was going on, turned on the bilge pump and removed the water, and would probably have been able to locate the leak around the flange and stuff enough rags into it to get us to Elizabeth City the next morning without further trouble. Or if I had only gotten around to installing the float switch on the pump, there would have been sufficient charge in the large twin batteries to keep the boat pumped out through the night. If.

Two weeks later the reconditioned and refurbished *Little Eva* was ready for duty again, and we completed our interrupted journey to Virginia. Our troubles, however, were not yet over. Apparently her lapstrake hull had loosened up some during the sinking, for she had developed a slow leak. The float switch to the bilge pump had meanwhile been installed, and it seemed to be functioning well. But on the day that we were to set out for home we arrived at the dock to find some six inches of water in the bilge. After pumping it out I inspected the float switch and found that a wire had come loose. I repaired it, and we went on our way.

When we tied up at the Willoughby Bay Marina in Norfolk that afternoon, severe thunderstorms were forecast for the area, so I engaged a room at a nearby motel for my wife and younger son, while my older son and I stayed aboard. That evening the lightning flashed, the thunder roared, and the rain poured down, as one line of storms after another came through. It was uneasy sleeping; I lay awake for a long time, waiting to hear the reassuring sound of the bilge pump periodically cutting on to empty the hull. Finally I fell asleep.

A little after three o'clock that morning I had a nightmare. I was in our cabin aboard the *Christoforo Colombo,* an ocean liner we had once taken to Italy, and suddenly the voice of the captain came over the public-address system. "Ladies and-a Gentlemen, please-a to bring-a you life jackets and report to you lifeboat stations! This is-a not a drill. Our ship is-a sinking!"

Startled, I woke up, grabbed the lantern I had placed in the corner of my berth, clicked it on, climbed out of the berth, lifted up a floorboard, and checked the bilge. It was rapidly filling with water. I hurried into the cockpit, turned on the pump manually, then aroused my

son. He held the lantern for me and I checked the float
switch. The wiring had come loose again. I wired it back
together, wrapped the connection with a heavy covering
of plastic tape, and after I was satisfied that the switch
was once more functioning, told my son to go back to
sleep.

As for myself, I slept no more that night. I lay in
my berth reading, and listening for the sound of the
pump as it periodically cut on. The next morning was
bright and clear as we cruised up the Elizabeth River,
entered the Dismal Swamp Canal, and made our way
southward to Elizabeth City. We tied up at the boatyard,
where I left an order not only for the *Little Eva*'s hull to
be carefully checked and recaulked until every vestige of
a leak was sealed, but for a heavy-duty Jabsco bilge pump
to be installed—one with a built-in float switch that did
not require wires leading to an external switch.

Never again in the years since have I had a boat
sink on me. Yet even today, fifteen years afterward, when
I am driving down to a boat I begin to feel a nervous
unease as I draw near. Not until I see my boat afloat and
riding at the dock is my anxiety dispelled.

The denouement to the dreary adventure was
provided several days later by my wife. She said that on
the fateful evening when the boat had sunk at the dock,
as we were leaving the *Little Eva* at the marina for the
motel, our younger son had reported to her that he could

hear the sound of flowing water. "Well, don't say anything about it to Daddy," my wife cautioned him. "He's had enough to worry about today as it is."

During the two succeeding years that I owned the *Little Eva* I had no more trouble with leaks and bilge pumps. From time to time the transmission to the starboard engine acted up, but now that I knew how to replace the O-ring, this was only a minor inconvenience. In all other respects the lapstrake Chris-Craft performed impeccably.

In the late summer of 1974 my older son and I took her up the Waterway again from Wrightsville Beach, North Carolina, to the Chesapeake Bay. On several occasions that summer I had read newspaper stories describing temporary shortages of gasoline supplies in the Northeast. There were also magazine articles pointing out that such shortages were the result of insufficient transport facilities and our increasing dependence on oil from the Middle East. Gasoline prices, the article predicted, were bound to rise above the current fifty-cents-a-gallon average. If the nations that formed the OPEC cartel decided to raise the price per barrel, as seemed likely, it was even possible that the cost of gasoline at the pump might rise as high as a dollar a gallon within the next several years.

A dollar a gallon for gasoline? It seemed fantastic. If that were ever to happen, it would mean that fuel for even a single day's offshore fishing outing on the *Little Eva,* with her two very thirsty two-hundred horsepower V-8 engines, might cost upwards of forty dollars! And in less than two years our older son would be going off to college, which would involve a great deal of money, money that we did not have and would undoubtedly have to borrow by remortgaging our house.

Clearly the *Little Eva* would have to go—and if so, the time to sell it was now, before gasoline prices began skyrocketing and those two gas-guzzling V-8s severely handicapped her sales potential. So I traded the *Little Eva* for a trailerable fiberglass runabout. And that was the end of my dealings with a certain blue-and-white lapstrake-hulled Chris-Craft cruiser.

Now, fifteen years later, I was again the possessor of a lapstrake-hulled gasoline-powered wooden boat. But the *Mary Simpson* was no gas-devourer; her single Chrysler Crown engine was distinctly modest in appetite. The eighty-two horsepower Mazda diesel on the new boat would be even less thirsty. When I reached the dock at Gillikin's and began securing the *Mary Simpson*'s lines, I discovered what had been causing the disconcerting noise every time she was rocked by a passing boat's wake. Her unsecured aluminum boat hook had been rolling about on top of the cabin.

I went fishing aboard her again two weeks later, this time with a friend. By now it was early December, but the temperature was in the sixties and there was little wind, so we were quite comfortable. On this occasion we did not go outside the harbor mouth and troll; instead we proceeded to the deep hole beyond Shackleford Banks and anchored. For the next two hours we took one gray trout after another on Hopkins jig spoons. By 3:30 P.M. it was time to head back, and by the time we tied up at Peltier Creek the sun had dropped below the horizon and it was becoming dark and distinctly chilly. Barring an unusual run of good weather, the fall fishing season was just about over.

So a summer and autumn of frustration ended in at least a modified success. I finally had a boat with an engine that worked, I had gone out into the ocean at least once, and had even caught a few fish. Meanwhile my twenty-eight-and-a-half-foot Triton sailboat, the *Virginius,* was back in commission, with the storm-worn bare spot on her hull repainted. Moored on the Beaufort waterfront, she now awaited a purchaser, and would probably still be waiting until springtime came. Not until the weather warmed up again would prospective purchasers get the urge to be out on the water, and begin looking around for boats.

By that time, too, the new boat would be almost

---

ready for launching. I paid a call at Clem Willis's boat
shed on Harkers Island, and saw that the sides and
transom of the new boat were fully fastened, the keel and
members were securely in place, and the rudder and
propeller-shaft slots were drilled out. The flared Core
Sounder bow was clearly visible, although bottom, deck,
bulkheads, and cabin remained to be done. When the new
boat was ready, I would no longer have any need for the
Mary Simpson, even though she was now running so well,
and I would have to put her up for sale. Oddly enough,
I felt a little guilt at the prospect.

Which was ridiculous, of course. It was not as if
the boat were a bird dog that I would be discarding, or a
horse, or some other sensate being, but only a
manufactured, wooden lapstrake boat, without an emotion
or the capacity for one. Still, boats do have a way of
insinuating themselves into one's affections, and holding
on for dear life.

8

CARIBBEAN INTERLUDE

Do you know that land where the lemon flowers,
The golden orange glows on the dark bower,
The light wind blows from heaven's blue sky,
The still myrtles, the laurels standing high?
                                                  —*Goethe*

There comes a time in life when the children have
finished college and become approximately
self-supporting, while the physical indignities of the
so-called Golden Years have not importantly manifested
themselves. For the first time ever, money is available for
things hitherto only wistfully contemplated. A few years
ago during the Christmas break my wife and I found
ourselves sailing from New Orleans to Key West and the
Yucatán aboard the *Bermuda Star,* a 24,000-ton liner that
in an earlier incarnation had been the Holland–America
Line's *Veendam.*

It was something I had long wanted to do. In the
1960s I had twice journeyed to Europe aboard ocean
liners to lecture, and had formed my expectations of what
cruising would be like from those experiences. The
cuisine was what I remembered most fondly of all. I

anticipated ending dinner with a splendiferous dessert, followed by a tray of magnificent cheeses—Fontina, Bel Paese, Edam, Gouda, and the like. So when the first night out aboard the *Bermuda Star* I noted "assorted cheeses" on the menu, I ordered these forthwith, only to find that the cheeses offered consisted of pimento, domestic Swiss, Philadelphia Cream, and Velveeta.

The cruise itself, however, was delightful. We discovered the joys of reclining in a deck chair in midwinter, gazing idly at blue water, with the temperature well up into the eighties and nineties. At the ports where we stopped, excursions were available to view Aztec ruins, swim in tropical lagoons, and go snorkeling off reefs. My wife went on several of these trips, but I stayed aboard, chose a shady spot on the deck, and spent the time reading and observing the activities in port, the fishing boats, the workboats, the gulls and pelicans, the jade water over a sandy bottom, the towering cumulus formations of the tropics, the swiftly building mid-afternoon thunderheads that briefly poured rain and as quickly went on their way.

At Cancún I sat on the deck after dinner, and tuned in my pocket radio to try to pick up a news broadcast. Far off somewhere in the frozen North, a newscaster was describing a blizzard—deep snow accumulating, the mercury dropping into the low

---

twenties and still falling, the traffic at a standstill, the city all but paralyzed. Was it Boston? Minneapolis? Denver? Meanwhile here I was, on a ship tied up to a wharf on the Yucatán coast, in shirt sleeves, cigar lit, feeling at one with the famed southgoers of literature: Santayana in Rome, Stendhal at Civitavecchia, the Brownings at Livorno, Hemingway at the Finca, Wallace Stevens at Key West . . . *Do you know that land?* Yes indeed.

The city suffering the ice and snow turned out to be neither Boston nor Denver nor Minneapolis, but instead Houston, Texas, for an unprecedented cold wave was moving into the Deep South, with record lows forecast. When it reached the shores of the Gulf of Mexico it kept right on coming. Thus when the *Bermuda Star* departed Cancún a day later, rounded the tip of the Yucatán peninsula and turned northward, she moved directly and inexorably into the face of a descending cold front.

First it was breezy; then it turned windy; then it grew colder. It was too rough to stay out on deck. Not until close to midnight did the *Bermuda Star* move into the mouth of the Mississippi for the 110-mile run up the river to New Orleans. The next day, on a windless, clear, lemon-bright January morning, the outdoors temperature was at eighteen degrees Fahrenheit as the *Bermuda Star* rounded Patterson Point and moved toward her berth

alongside the Trade Center on the New Orleans
waterfront. Now I understood why it was that almost all
of the winter cruise ships departed from Miami, five
hundred miles further south.

We were, however, hooked. With cruise liners as
with most things you get what you pay for. The *Bermuda
Star* had been a bargain-fare cruise, and the cuisine
reflected it. We did not make that mistake again. The
December following we flew to Miami and then on to
Barbados, where we boarded the *Ocean Islander,* a
splendid little liner that took us not only to several island
ports but almost two hundred miles up the Orinoco
River. In succeeding years we cruised the eastern
Caribbean aboard the Holland–America Line's *Noordam,* a
magnificent ship with superb cuisine and service, based at
Fort Lauderdale, and again on the *Nieuw Amsterdam,* out
of Tampa. The latter, identical in appearance to the
Noordam, was less well run, and it seemed to cater to the
geriatric crowd. Though in our mid-sixties, we felt
ourselves to be decidedly on the juvenile side of the age
median.

In 1989 we were due to cruise aboard the P&O
Line's *Sky Princess,* which was scheduled to leave from
Acapulco, traverse the Panama Canal, and then touch at
Caracas, Venezuela, and Curaçao in the southwestern
Caribbean before sailing on to San Juan, Puerto Rico. A

week before it was to begin, however, President Bush
sent in the troops to rescue the Republic of Panama from
Señor Noriega, and at the last minute the *Sky Princess*
was rerouted via Fort Lauderdale and thence into the
eastern Caribbean.

Our cruising experience had revived in me what
had once been a passionately pursued hobby: photography.
Back when I had been a young man, I had spent much
time and energy photographing railroad trains. I ceased
doing it in the early 1960s, after the steam locomotives
were totally sidelined by unphotogenic, look-alike diesels.
On our first cruise, aboard the *Bermuda Star,* I had
brought along my old Pentax-Honeywell 35 mm camera,
and whenever I saw a ship or a boat of any consequence
I photographed her. It was not until we became
acquainted with the ports of the eastern Caribbean,
however, that the full photographic possibilities of
cruising dawned on me.

What I discovered was that the harbors of the
various islands in the West Indies were home ports for all
manner of fascinating workboats, tugs, island freighters,
and other vessels. The combination of generally
benevolent weather conditions and the disadvantaged
economy of the Antilles made feasible the continued
service of all kinds of craft that in American and
European ports would long since have been retired.

A three hundred-ton coastal freighter might have given decades of cargo-carrying service along the often-stormy coasts of Norway, Sweden, and Denmark, until the deteriorating condition of her rebuilt engine and her steel plates, together with obsolescent rigging and cargo facilities, inevitably caused her replacement by more up-to-date vessels.

If not scrapped for steel, she might have somehow made her way down to St. Lucia or Antigua or Grenada, where she could be acquired by a local merchant or fisherman at comparatively little cost. She might get a coat of paint and a name change, or she might not. Thereafter, whenever there was work for her to do she would do it, and otherwise she would remain at anchor or tied to a wharf in one of the small seaports.

Except during hurricane season, the tropic sea is normally placid, so that a steel hull with plates too rusted and worn to risk anyone's life inside in a North Sea gale could make it back and forth between small Caribbean islands in reasonable safety. An ancient Sulzer diesel, having been rebuilt several times until its behavior in the stormy waters off Heligoland had become too unreliable to justify yet another repair, might still be patched up to provide the power needed to negotiate the sixty miles between Castries and Kingstown. And if halfway across St. Vincent's Passage the engine did give out, the conditions of wind and wave were unlikely to render heaving-to perilous until some imaginative combination of scrap parts, bailing wire, well-taped lengths of old hose, and discarded plastic cartons could get it pumping again.

Thus many a photogenic antique is to be found still in service in Caribbean waters—and powered not only by gasoline or diesel engines but by sails as well, for if time is of no great urgency and trade winds are predictable, then canvas sails, however often mended, can traverse island waters at no cost in fuel whatever. With the occasional application of anti-fouling bottom paint to inhibit the marine growth that forms so rapidly in tropical waters, an old cargo craft can get along with minimum maintenance costs for a long time.

In sum, the harbors of the West Indies contain a host of picturesque ships and workboats—freighters, reefers, oilers, tugs, shrimpers, decommissioned naval craft, skiffs, yawls, ketches, sloops, schooners, whatever—sail- or engine-powered, round- or flat-bottomed, built of steel or wood. Plus, of course, newer vessels built especially for island service, many with ramped bows or sterns for convenient drive-on and -off handling of container cargo, and in shapes and configurations that might make them dangerously top-heavy and unseaworthy in more stormy waters but that are eminently practical in the island trade.

---

* * *

Which is not to say that I turn up my nose at photographing cruise ships. In Caribbean ports one is likely to encounter an array of liners of all shapes and sizes, ranging from the 70,000-ton SS *Norway,* three decades old and, at 1,035 feet, the longest passenger vessel in the world, to small ships such as the Cunard Lines' several new *Sea Goddesses,* 4,000-ton yachtlike beauties offering deluxe cruising at deluxe prices. Once, on a cruise aboard the *Nieuw Amsterdam,* we found docked at St. Thomas, Virgin Islands, alone, the huge *Sovereign of the Seas,* the 11,000-ton *Ocean Princess* (1967), and the 25,000-ton *Dawn Princess* (1957); our own ship's twin sister, the 34,000-ton *Noordam* (1984), was anchored inside the harbor and the *Norway* was outside. During the course of the afternoon the 28,000-ton *Royal Viking Sky* (1973) also showed up. As might be expected, the narrow streets of Charlotte Amalie were jammed with visitors.

Because the harbors of many of the island ports are small and prone to silting in, the newer craft all have bow thrusters—propellers mounted in a ship's bow which can shove her away from or toward a dock, so that in most instances the liner is no longer dependent upon a fleet of tugboats to get her snuggled up alongside a wharf or turned around and pointed seaward. Except in unusual cases, one or at most two tugs will be needed, or even no tugs at all.

The lack of bow thrusters can cause problems. I once saw a cruise ship at St. Lucia send a boat five hundred yards across the harbor to attach a line to a bollard, completely blocking entrance and exit to the harbor, in order to maneuver herself away from the dock, turn, and point seaward. Our own ship, equipped with thrusters, simply turned in place and went on its way.

In addition to the cruise liners and the numerous working craft, the ports of the eastern Caribbean are a mecca for viewing and photographing pleasure craft. Some of the most palatial vessels ever to grace the Lloyd's of London yacht registry can be found moored in the harbors of such ports as Martinique, St. Maarten, Tortola, St. Thomas, Kingstown, and the like. The amount of Conspicuous Consumption on display would gladden the heart of a Donald Trump.

Yet it is not the two hundred-foot privately owned floating palaces that I find most intriguing. Surely what anyone watching from the decks of a cruise liner—anyone, at least, who has ever enjoyed sailing—must admire and envy profoundly are the small bluewater craft—the sloops, cutters, ketches, yawls, and motor sailers from American and Canadian ports, or from France, England, the Low Countries, and Scandinavia. To survey the wintertime harbors of St. Thomas, Martinique, St. Maarten, Tortola, and other such protected waters is to see hundreds of such sailing craft anchored for lengthy visits, someone's laundry hung out to dry in the sun, the boat's inflatable tied to the stern for getting ashore and back.

Most of these small craft got to these harbors under their own canvas, sailing across long stretches of open ocean, relying upon their own navigation and their ability to put wind and wave to use. By no means are all of them posh, six- or seven-figure state-of-the-art sailing craft; there are numerous older and lesser boats, clearly the possessions of relatively impecunious free spirits who have opted for a live-aboard existence. Several times I have spotted Pearson Tritons, reminiscent of my own *Virginius,* anchored among them, and the last Triton was built in the 1960s. Indeed, the person from whom I bought the *Virginius* had once taken her down to the Caribbean for an extended stay.

When I see small craft like these in Caribbean ports I feel remorse for never having had the nerve to do what their owners have done. When I was younger I was never sufficiently tempted by the lure of sailing my own boat to faraway ports to be willing to say To Hell With It, throw over my work, buy a boat, and steer for the West Indies. Indeed, it never so much as occurred to me to do so. For one thing, I have always enjoyed my work too

---

much to leave it. I have no doubt, too, that the spectre of the Great Depression—an era I remember very well—and my parents' constant dinning into me the need for solvency and security, had their effect.

That the experience of those years had its impact upon me I know only too well. There is a recurrent dream that I have, especially at times when I am worried about finances. I am someplace—a newspaper office, usually—where I had thought I would now be working, but I find that something has gone wrong. The people there are friendly and are glad to see me, but there is no job for me. I walk through the building, looking around, and everything seems strange. Somehow I have made the mistake of giving up my previous job without making sure that the job I expected to have was to be mine. Now I have no job, no income. I am not panicked, only disconcerted. At that point I awake, and realize with relief that it has been only a dream and that I have not resigned my present position.

It is an odd business. Not for thirty years and more have I felt the slightest anxiety about employment, and now that I have retired from my professorship I not only have a decent retirement income but a salary as a book publisher. Yet during all these decades, throughout my adult life, the dream has recurred. I doubt that it will ever go away permanently.

We do not ever eradicate the early patterns of our experience; they remain with us all our lives. What we can hope is to be able to learn to identify such patterns when they occur, and to understand why they exist and what they mean, so that we will not be at the mercy of forces whose existence we do not recognize, and so be unable to prevent those forces from distorting our perception of reality.

Now it is true that when the new boat is completed and thoroughly broken in, conceivably I could even yet make a voyage to the islands. With a little application I could learn how to repair the diesel engine. Assuming that the eighty-two horsepower Mazda will use about a gallon of fuel every two miles, the fifty-gallon tank I am having installed will be good for about a hundred miles. I could doubtless have additional tanks, totaling another fifty gallons, installed along the gunwales, and fit another twenty-five-gallon tank forward, under the floorboards, so that I would have a cruising range of more than two hundred and fifty miles. From southern Florida to Bimini, then via the islands south to Hispaniola, and thence east into the Leewards there is no leg of the journey that need be longer than two hundred miles between fueling stops.

The trick, of course, would be the weather. I would have to travel only on days when the seas were of no more than four or five feet. And that would mean lengthy waits—I would have to cultivate the patience to wait day after day, no matter how barren and uninteresting the port, until conditions were overwhelmingly favorable. The abundance of weather information now available by radio is such that there would be little risk of being caught in weather that I could not handle. And with Loran-C the navigation would not be difficult.

Of course I would have to do a little modification to the boat. It would need storm ports and windows, for one thing, additional fresh-water carrying capacity, probably a third storage battery, a backup sonar, a solar charger, refrigeration, and more and larger scuppers in the cockpit. The cockpit itself would be small enough as presently designed so that there would be no danger of swamping.

The main consideration is that I would need lots of time—not merely weeks, but months. March would be the proper time to leave. It would take three or four weeks to go down the Intracoastal Waterway, and I would spend several weeks more in Florida getting ready, and waiting for the proper weather conditions. I would start out for the Bahamas in late April; to get to the Virgin Islands might take a month. Six weeks or so there, and then the return trip before the hurricane season

---

arrives, another month. That would put me back in Florida about the middle of August.

There is about as much chance of my ever doing such a thing as there would be of my journeying to Mars or Venus on the next space probe. And if I did somehow try it, make it down the Waterway to Palm Beach or Fort Lauderdale, then set out across the Gulf Stream, I would no doubt get about as far as Freeport, or Nassau, or at most Eleuthera, whereupon the engine would blow up or the hull spring a leak, or I would run up onto a coral reef, or the mosquitoes would drive me half-mad, and I would end up disposing of the boat for a tenth of her value and flying home. Still, who can say for sure?

One of the many reasons for owning a boat, I suppose, is that you can think in the above fashion. To descend to a less exalted level of discourse, owning a boat is, psychologically, something like staying overnight in a room with a bath. For some years I have had to spend a number of nights each year in hotels and motels. The rooms in which I stay always come equipped with baths. On the few occasions, mostly in Europe, in which, for one reason or another, it was necessary to accept a room with a washroom but no shower or tub, I have felt distinctly uncomfortable. Yet by no means do I invariably take a shower or bath each night that I stay in a hotel or

---

motel; sometimes I do, sometimes I don't. As long as the facilities are available, I experience no discomfort when not making use of them. But let them *not* be available, and it is another matter altogether.

In the same way, having a boat means that whenever I wish I can use her (assuming that the engine is operative, which, given my recent record, is something of an assumption). She awaits my pleasure, down on the coast. The syllogism runs something like this:

Major Premise: In order to sail to the Caribbean islands, it is necessary to own a boat capable of doing so.

Minor Premise: I own a boat capable of doing so.

Conclusion: Q.E.D., I can sail to the Caribbean islands.

Now, on the plane on which we live our daily lives, which is to say, the practical "real life" plane on which wars, fortunes, and elections are won and lost, there happens to be what the logicians call a Faulty Enthymeme (or two or three) in that particular syllogism, which I rather imagine anyone skilled in boats and boating rather than abstract logic can readily spot. But on the metaphysical—or perhaps psychological—plane, the one on which we buy boats, dream, hallucinate, build cloud castles, locate the foot of the rainbow, discover the mythical Kingdom of Prester John, and otherwise make corrections to whatever is imperfect in our lives, there is no flaw in it, no Ailing Enthymeme or Undistributed Middle whatever to the above logic. And my hunch is that most persons involved in boats and boating can understand that, too. For it is on just such metaphysical reasoning that half the boats sold each year are purchased. Without the prevalence of my kind of logic, boat brokers would have to close up shop and become carnival barkers or poets, or both.

The hold that boats exercise upon my imagination is not merely a matter of having grown up in a city bordered on three sides by salt water, and being made constantly aware of the existence of boats. The truth is that as a youth I had other interests that played a far greater role in my life—baseball, for one thing, which I yearned to play well, and, not ever being able to do so with other than varying degrees of incompetence, which was a source of enormous frustration to me. Yet I never have dreams about baseball; my failure to play it well presumably did not and does not symbolize anything beyond itself. The meaning that boats and boating hold and, I must assume, held for me, however, clearly involves something much more substantial and urgent. In part this book is being written in order to try to find out just what.

Yet if, when I gaze upon the small craft tethered in the harbor at St. Thomas, Martinique, St. Maarten,

Bridgetown, or wherever, I feel regret over opportunities unpursued, paths not taken, or loins ungirded, it is not for long. For merely by being there on the promenade deck of a liner and looking down at the boats and the harbor, I have already acted out a fantasy and fulfilled a dream of formidable proportions. For as already noted several times in this discourse, when in my younger days I stood on the Battery or alongside the Clyde–Mallory Line docks in Charleston and watched the ships put out to sea, I imagined how it would be to go along, and sail into the far-off ports where they were bound.

In Mark Twain's *Life on the Mississippi* there is a comic scene at the very outset in which the narrator describes the envy he felt when young, when the steam packet bound for Keokuk put in briefly at Hannibal, Missouri. A certain local youth who was now a junior crewman aboard her always made a point of lolling about the deck, in full view of the assembled hometown juveniles. "He would always manage to have a rusty bolt to scrub while his boat tarried at our town, and he would sit on the inside guard and scrub it, where we all could see him and envy him and loathe him."

A few years later, the narrator, finding himself in Cincinnati and not wanting to go home, took passage on a packet bound down the Ohio and Mississippi Rivers for New Orleans. *He* was now a traveler: "I was in such a glorified condition that all ignoble feelings departed out of me, and I was able to look down and pity the untravelled with a compassion that had hardly a trace of contempt in it. Still, when we stopped at villages and wood-yards, I could not help lolling carelessly upon the railings of the boiler deck to enjoy the envy of the country boys on the bank. If they did not seem to discover me, I presently sneezed to attract their attention, or moved to a position where they could not help seeing me."

In something of the same way, I too am now *on* a ship, and have finally made it to ports such as those to which the departing ships of my childhood were bound. When I was a boy the words "West Indies" had always seemed to me to be romantic and mysterious, with images of tramp steamers, white sand beaches, palms, coral, sultry heat, towering cloud masses, exotic plants, and skua birds with long extended wings. Now I am *there,* and what I had longed to see is spread out before me.

To make the trip to a Caribbean island by air, stay at a resort hotel, and see the harbor from the land would not be nearly as gratifying. It is seeing the harbor and the port *from* the ship that is of greatest importance. It is not the scenery, but the ship, that matters most.

To my taste there are few conditions more satisfying to the body and soul, the more so now that I am in my late sixties, than being installed in a comfortable deck chair in the shade, in company with a good book and a good cigar, aboard a cruise liner anchored in the harbor or alongside a pier at a tropical port on a winter day—St. Lucia, Grenada, Guadeloupe, St. Maarten, Bridgetown, any Caribbean port will do. There is a breeze blowing (there is always a breeze blowing), the temperature is in the seventies or eighties, and the harbor lies there before me.

The sailboats and the yachts and the other small craft come and go. Occasionally an ancient island freighter, or a government launch, or a pilot boat, perhaps, moves past. I lay down my book, pick up the binoculars, and take a good look. If I decide that the passing boat is one that I wish to add to my collection, I take the camera, get up and walk over to the rail, bring the boat into focus, and take a couple of shots at different exposures. Then I regain the horizontal position, and resume my reading. It does no harm to think that back home the temperature is in the thirties, and it is probably sleeting.

In a few days' time I will be back in North Carolina in mid-winter weather, taking care to dress warmly and to wear an overcoat and boots when I am outside, far from Lotus Land. But for now it is Snug Harbor in the Happy Isles.

9

PROJECTS AND
PROBLEMS:
Or, The Mary Simpson
Strikes Again

John Nelson had found a buyer for the *Virginius*. It seems
that another yacht broker had a client who was looking
for just that kind of sailboat—old but serviceable, fast
enough for club racing, and comfortably equipped for
cruising. The final offer was several thousand dollars
lower than I had planned to go, but my old Triton
sailboat had been up for sale for almost a year without
any takers, while costing a hundred dollars a month for
dockage alone. In addition, I had had to get the
propeller-shaft coupler repaired, the clutch plates replaced,
the starter rewired, and an area of the hull repainted
following the damage from Hurricane Hugo. So it
seemed the better part of valor to take what I could get
for her now, and concentrate on getting the new boat
ready.

As luck would have it, within a few days of my

having signed the sales agreement, another buyer turned
up with a bona fide offer that was a thousand dollars
higher. The agreement had given the first buyer ten days
to make up his mind to pay for the boat, so now I found
myself in the odd position of hoping that he would
default on his deposit. Nothing doing; on the appointed
day he handed over a check for the balance. I was happy
to get it. It would soon be time to place the *Mary
Simpson* on the market as well, but now that she was
running so well I wanted to hold off as long as I could,
so that I would have her to use until the new boat was
launched and ready to go.

In late January I drove down to the coast to keep abreast
of the progress that Clem Willis was making. Although a
formidable snowfall had piled two feet of snow on
Harkers Island and kept everybody housebound for
several days, the hull was now completed, and the bow
definitely showed that special Harkers Island workboat
flare that was so effective at throwing the spray from
oncoming waves sideways.

Clem had been building boats since his childhood,
he said, except for a period during World War II.
Exempted from the draft because of a physical disability,
he had worked during those years as a carpenter
constructing government buildings at Fort Fisher, near

Wilmington. He had begun his apprenticeship with his uncle, the now legendary Brady Lewis, who fifty years back had been the first to build a flared bow on a workboat. Lewis's innovation had at once been copied by other builders, and was now a trademark for Harkers Island construction.

Like all local shipwrights, Brady Lewis had worked by the eyeball method. He also loved to race the boats he built. "We'd go fishing," Clem said, "and we'd come back by way of Beaufort, and Hal Simpson would have his boat, and there'd be a race." Brady Lewis could build boats that were so well balanced that the merest shift of weight aboard could affect their performance. Clem confirmed a story that I had been told by several people. It seems that Brady Lewis was engaged in an all-out race with someone, and the two boats were so evenly matched that neither could gain an inch on the other. At length Brady Lewis filled a galvanized washbucket with water and placed it at a strategic position on the deck. The additional weight, at just that spot, enabled him to pull ahead of his rival and win.

In the days before World War II, money had been hard to come by on the Outer Banks. A new forty-foot workboat went for six hundred dollars. "We built boats, and we fished, and shrimped, and clammed—anything we could do to scrape by," Clem

---

told me. He had built or helped build, by his estimate, well over a thousand boats during his lifetime, from crabbing skiffs to large commercial craft. Although it was much more difficult now to get first-class juniper planking for hulls, the development of epoxies, polyurethanes, resins, and other sealants meant that the boats being built nowadays were put together better than those of a few decades back. "It used to be," he said, "that you'd build a boat, put her overboard, and wait for the wood to swell so that the seams would stop leaking. Now we build them so that they won't leak in the first place."

The joinery work on the new boat's hull was a thing of beauty. One-inch strips had been cut from eight-inch boards, then each numbered so that they would fit snugly together. The strips were put into place, glued, then fastened to the side timbers with silicon bronze nails, and to each other, vertically, by a pair of nails between each set of timbers. The ends of the strips were not merely butted against each other but cut diagonally and wedged together, with a nail driven through each joint.

I had assumed that timbers were steamed and bent. Instead, the curves were all cut into the proper shape from larger planks. The area that curved upward and inward to attach to the stem, known as the "loggin," was intricately shaped and fitted: first the garbit plank, then the second plank, and so on to the chine. Far from being evenly rectangular at that point, the planks were cut into multiple angles and curves; then they were cemented and fastened in much the same manner as one of those Chinese block puzzles composed of interlocking segments that fit together into an apparently solid ball. Unlike the side planking, the bottom was glued not with resin but with a rubber adhesive compound so that the planks would give with the action of the water against the hull. In a way it would be a shame to cover over all that beautiful cedar with white paint.

The long wormshoe underneath the keel, running from the base of the stem all the way back to the rudder post and protected by a three-eighths-inch stainless steel strip, was a work of art. A strip of tarpaper was placed between it and the keel to prevent marine borers from penetrating up into the keel itself. The deck around the gunwale would be of plywood sheathed in fiberglass.

I had made the decision to have the interior of the boat tailored in accordance with my own particular needs. The new boat, I was resolved, was going to be conveniently usable by and for one person—and not a lithe young man, either, but a paunchy, not-very-agile chap in his late sixties, of sedentary habits and disposition.

When I slept aboard on weekends, it would

usually be alone; my wife insisted that her boating days were over. There was no point in installing the customary V-berths in the forward cabin, when the space could be put to better advantage. What I wanted was room, so that I would not feel as if I were packed into the cabin of a space capsule. The forward cabin would have a single berth of ample width on one side, and an enclosed head, a sink, a place for a stove, and shelving on the other. Later I might install a two-burner stove and an icebox. Even at the cost of the boat's having a boxy look I wanted enough headroom to be able to stand up in the forward cabin. I also wanted plenty of light: several ports on each side, and two at the bow.

The main cabin would be as roomy as could be managed for a twenty-four-foot boat. If two persons were sleeping aboard, one would use a folding cot there; when I was by myself I could choose between that and using the forward berth, whichever seemed more comfortable. The engine box in the center of the main cabin would be the major limiting factor, but given the length and depth of the boat there was no other place for it to go. I could fit a detachable table top onto it. There would be seats on both sides of the cabin, as well as a pilot chair forward and another across from it. There would be sliding windows with removable screens. The cabin would be fully enclosed.

On the starboard side of the cabin's aft wall, halfway up, would be a removable glass panel, sized so that a small shore-unit air-conditioner could be slipped snugly into the aperture when needed. On a hot, breezeless summer night, particularly when thunderstorms were coming through, it would mean the difference between comfort and misery. With a properly grounded ship-to-shore 115-volt outlet, a small, portable commercial model would work fine, given the occasional use it would receive. When not in place and running it would be left ashore or, if I were on a trip, stored forward out of the way.

An unusual feature of the boat—unusual for pleasure craft—would be the engine exhaust system. I had decided to go with the standard workboat rig—the exhaust pipe running up and through the cabin roof, rather than beneath the deck and through the transom for underwater discharge. My reasoning, inspired in part by the incident with the *Little Eva* of some years back, was that the fewer holes in the hull, the better. A muffler would be installed atop the cabin to keep the noise level down.

The exhaust pipe from the engine would be of stainless steel, two and a half inches in diameter, wrapped in fiberglass for insulation, and placed inside a five-inch-diameter pipe, so that if anybody placed a hand on it, it would be warm to the touch but not dangerous.

The stern cockpit was to be only five feet deep.
This would mean that no more than three persons would
be able to troll from it, and only two if casting rods
were being used. How often had there ever been more
than two persons at a time seriously fishing from any
boat I had owned? Almost never; typically it had been
me and one other person, and most often only me. What
point was there in building a boat that could
accommodate a half-dozen fishermen, when the space
saved by having the smaller cockpit could be used to
good advantage inside the cabin? If more than three
persons were aboard and wanted to fish, they could do so
from the bow.

There was no doubt that the new boat would
indeed have a somewhat boxlike appearance, the more so
because there would be no more than three feet of deck
between the forward cabin wall and the bow. Again,
however, what would be of more use to me: a larger
cabin, or a more capacious bow area? Other than having
to go up there to anchor or tie up at the dock I had
never spent any time at the bow. Anyone who wished to
sit out in the sun would be able to do so on the forward
cabin top. This wouldn't do for rough weather, of course,
but at such times nobody would want to be out there
anyway.

One of the amenities aboard my old Luhrs
Sea-Skiff, the *Mary Simpson,* which I had never

previously enjoyed on any boat I had owned, was her electric windlass. Instead of having to go out onto the bow and grapple with the anchor by hand, I could raise or lower it by remote control, from inside the cabin. The line led through a deck pipe down into a rope locker at the bow. The windlass was a sizeable affair, with a mooring bit built atop it, and it was expensive—close to a thousand dollars if purchased new. I decided to remove the device from the *Mary Simpson* and install it aboard the new boat. I would do the latter, however, after I had taken possession of the new boat and moved her over to Peltier Creek. I didn't have the heart to tell Clem Willis that he would have to remove the mooring bit he had already installed and drill a big hole through the deck.

There was another feature of the new boat that was of importance. The deck leading around the cabin to the bow was a good twelve inches wide even at its narrowest point, so that it would be easier to get to the bow during rough weather. The difference between a half-foot and a foot-wide deck would be the difference between enjoying a reasonably secure footing and having to edge forward, one foot planted in front of the other, while holding on for dear life to a grabrail. I intended to install grabrails, however, and not little teak affairs, either, but stainless steel tubing mounted a good two inches above the cabin top.

It did occur to me that when the day arrived, as it must, that my once-new boat would be put up for sale, to have it built so totally, even eccentrically, to my own needs would make it considerably more difficult to sell. But I was not going to worry about that in the slightest, for this would be the last and, I hoped, best boat I would ever own.

I declared as much to a longtime friend, who knows my ways very well. He laughed. "Famous Last Words," he said, and reminded me of a *New Yorker* cartoon of some years back, which showed a boat, mounted on a cradle near the water, with the name lettered across the transom: NEVER AGAIN III.

So I am not so foolish as to assert that I shall not ever, regardless of what the future might hold, divest myself of this boat in favor of another. If, for example, I were suddenly to stumble into a considerable sum of money, either by writing a best-selling novel or by winning the Irish Sweepstakes, I might change my mind. The chances of either happening are roughly equal.

In January and early February the weather was too poor to think about boating. It was the last week of February before I headed down to the North Carolina coast again with the idea of going out on the water. The *Mary Simpson* was in first-class shape and ready to go, and I was determined to make good use of her while she was still mine. All the previous summer and well into autumn I had waited for George Alletsee to restore her to usefulness. It had been late fall before she was back in action, and I had been able to take her out only a couple of times before the winter closed in.

Was I being extravagant in having the new boat built? Would I really be able to do much aboard her that I could not already do with this venerable but now thoroughly repowered lapstrake Sea-Skiff? In any event it was good to know that in the *Mary Simpson* I at last had a powerboat that I could fully trust.

I drove into Morehead City, turned off at Gillikin's Boat Basin, parked my car, and got out. There was the *Mary Simpson,* ready for service. I stepped aboard, took down the plastic tarp that kept rain out of the cockpit, rolled it up, and stowed it in the cabin. I lifted the engine hatch. No odor of fumes. Even so I switched on the sniffer; the needle was well within the safe range. I opened the fuel valve to let gas flow into the engine, checked to make sure the gearshift was in neutral, pulled out the choke, and turned the ignition key. The rebuilt Chrysler Crown engine roared into action, as if it had been waiting patiently all winter for the chance to see service again. The old girl was raring to go, all right.

I pushed the choke back in and moved the throttle to its lowest setting. While the engine warmed up, I disconnected the shore current, cast off the stern lines and the springs, and unfastened the bumpers and hauled them aboard. I climbed out onto the deck, raised the radio antenna and tightened it into place, then freed the bow lines and draped them over the pilings. I stepped back down into the cockpit, cut on the bilge pump, opened the side windows and watched until there was no more water coming out. I opened the forward-cabin windows, which I had had replaced over the winter. The *Mary Simpson*'s engine was rumbling away steadily and happily.

Anchors aweigh! I was ready to take to the water again. It was a beautiful day to open the season, with the temperature in the seventies and a breeze blowing down the creek from the west. Bogue Sound would be bouncy, but only to the point of invigoration.

I threw the gear into forward, kept it there just long enough to establish forward motion, then put it back into neutral. Slowly the *Mary Simpson* edged out into the creek. When she was clear of the pilings I spun the wheel all the way to port, placed the gear in forward again, and gave her a brief spurt of power. The stern swung around, and her bow was pointed down the creek. Next I swung the wheel back to counteract the turning

---

motion and to let her go forward. The *Mary Simpson* kept right on turning to port.

I threw her out of gear, spun the wheel all the way to starboard, then went back into gear and gave her another brief spurt of power. Still she kept moving to port. The rudder was not responding.

Hastily I threw her into reverse, to keep her from nosing into the stern of another boat. The *Mary Simpson* backed out into the middle of the creek again. I took her out of gear and surveyed the situation. Soon the wind was slowly pushing her down the creek.

For the next twenty minutes I worked at getting the *Mary Simpson* turned around and back upstream to her slip. Whether in forward or reverse she would turn only to port. There in the narrow arm of the creek there was room to move her only a few yards forward or backward before having to reverse directions. So it was back and forth, a second's surge of power forward, a minute's drifting, then just as briefly into reverse. Eventually I got her stern close enough to one of the pilings at her slip to allow me to reach out with a boat hook and retrieve a line. I hauled her back into her slip, secured the lines, dropped the bumpers back over the sides, cut off the engine, and sat down to catch my breath.

It was like old times.

I removed the panel from the console; the steering gear itself seemed to be in working order, and the rod connecting the wheel to the rudder moved as the wheel turned. I lifted off the deck panel at the stern, got on my hands and knees, leaned my head down into the bilge, and peered underneath the compartment housing the fuel tank along the transom. The connecting rod seemed to be lying loose. I got a flashlight in order to see better, and I discovered that the end of the tiller arm had apparently rusted out and snapped. The broken-off tip was hanging from the quadrant. Lying down on my side I reached under the transom compartment until I could take hold of the quadrant. The rudder turned normally.

The connecting rod would have to be taken out and a length of new tubing attached to the end, held in place with a metal sleeve. The rusted-out tip of the tiller arm, and the pin that held it in the quadrant, would have to be removed, and the new tiller arm affixed to the quadrant. Repairing it would not be a major project. The difficulty would be in gaining access to it, for the rudder quadrant was located three feet back under the transom compartment, in an area no more than four or five inches high. Obviously it was beyond my capabilities. So I closed up the boat, got in my automobile, and drove over to Taylor Boat Works, at the eastern extremity of Peltier Creek.

Even though it was Saturday afternoon, John McCallum was there at work on the winch of a boat trailer, which held an aluminum runabout. He had shaved off his luxurious Viking-like red beard. John said that on Sunday he was planning to trail the boat over to the town of Atlantic, fifty miles to the east, put her overboard there, and go in search of the wooden hull of the old mail boat that before the advent of the Cedar Island–Ocracoke ferry had carried mail out to Ocracoke. He believed he had located it, sunk in a creek near there. He had in mind raising it, towing it back to his boatyard, and restoring it, just as he had done with the *Ruth,* his elegant thirty-eight-foot ex-Core Sounder.

I described my problem with the *Mary Simpson.* He would probably want to have my boat towed over to the yard before he attempted to work on it, he said. That way, if for any reason the rudder shaft were to drop out during the process of repairing the tiller arm, he would be able to haul the *Mary Simpson* onto land before she took on too much water and sank. He offered to go and have a look at the problem now, but I told him that Monday would be time enough.

So much for the triumphal return of my old but thoroughly reliable boat to action after a winter's waiting. An old boat is an old boat is an old boat. I felt better about my decision to have the new boat built.

* * *

The following Sunday I drove back to the coast, and with Bob Simpson along for the ride I took the *Mary Simpson* on the run I had planned for the previous weekend. She performed in first-rate fashion. We headed down to the turning basin at a steady 2,150 RPMs, looped around by the Morehead City waterfront, then went back along the Waterway to Peltier Creek, a run of some ten miles. She was a smooth-riding boat, and her rebuilt Chrysler Crown was as peppy as a brand-new engine. At one juncture, just to see what she would do, I moved her throttle all the way forward; she roared along, slicing through the waters of Bogue Sound like a frisky mare at 2,800 RPMs. After a minute or so, however, I edged her down to cruising speed. There was no point in tempting fate.

The next day Bob and I went over to Harkers Island to see how the new boat was faring. Clem Willis was at work atop the forward cabin, sanding down the surfaces of the plywood preparatory to applying a layer of fiberglass. The progress he had made since my previous visit was remarkable. The sides and tops of both cabins were in place, and the openings were cut for the windows. The frames for the forward windows of the main cabin had been installed; there would be three of them, with those on either side angled back slightly from the center window.

Clem's plan was to have only the center window

actually capable of being opened. The idea, however, did not appeal to me, because it would mean that, when operating the boat on hot days in July and August, I would have to stand in the center of the cabin, rather than be seated behind the steering wheel, in order to be in the line of the breeze. So I wanted to be able to open all three windows.

Clem had also finished installing the head and the mandatory holding tank in the trunk cabin. Getting the flexible holding tank properly anchored so that it could expand to full capacity if need be had proved to be a difficult job, he reported. The whole business of the federal government requiring the installation of holding tanks aboard small craft, without an accompanying regulation making it mandatory for all marinas and municipalities to maintain pump-out facilities, was and is absurd, of course. If the latter requirement existed on the books, it was emphatically not enforced by the Coast Guard or anyone else. So far as I had been able to discover, there was exactly one pump-out station for the entire Beaufort area. If there were any in Morehead City, I did not know of it. Certainly there wasn't one near Peltier Creek, despite its hundreds of boats and half-dozen marinas.

Since for obvious reasons most marinas and towns forbade the discharge of waste overboard, boat owners

made use of the facilities ashore when docked. If they did
use their own holding tanks, they simply pumped out the
tanks the next time they were out in the nearest harbor
or river, which was what the federal anti-pollution
legislation was intended to prevent. Theoretically a boat
owner in the Morehead-Beaufort area could take his craft
three miles offshore and discharge the contents of the
holding tank into the Atlantic Ocean—which from
Peltier Creek involves an eight-mile run to the mouth of
the harbor. Few bothered to make the trip. As for the
numerous commercial watermen in the area, they simply
disregarded the holding-tank law and pumped waste
directly overboard. Pleasure boat owners, being less blasé
about such things, dutifully laid out the three hundred to
five hundred dollars required to install holding
equipment, after which most of them either never used it
or else did so in the fashion I have described—which is
to say, illegally and in a way that defeated the purpose of
the whole thing.

When the anti-pollution legislation was first
proposed, opponents pointed out that the total amount of
waste discharged from small craft was infinitesimal
compared to the daily output from towns and industrial
installations fronting on the water, but to no avail. So
Congress enacted a law that, in our part of the country,
at least, was neither enforced nor, with the limited Coast

Guard personnel available, enforceable, and the manufacturers of marine sanitation equipment enjoyed a bonanza.

"What are you going to call her?" Clem Willis asked.

"Algonquin," I said, making up my mind in that instant. I had been thinking about it off and on for some time.

"What's going to be her calling port? Chapel Hill?"

I shook my head. "Morehead City, I guess." I had seen numerous boats with the calling port listed as the place of the owner's residence, no matter that such places were far inland and the boat in question would never get within hundreds of miles of there. It had always seemed silly to me. If my new boat was to be based in Peltier Creek at Morehead City, then the latter was the proper designation.

Clem was puzzled over my choice of name, and I explained its appropriateness. Algonquin was, of course, the name of the book publishing house I had started eight years earlier. But that was not the full explanation for the name. As noted in an earlier chapter, when I was a child growing up in Charleston, South Carolina, the Clyde–Mallory Line's fleet of coastal passenger liners had all borne Indian names: *Cherokee, Iroquois, Shawnee,*

Mohawk, Seminole, and *Algonquin.* On one occasion, in 1929, when I was six years old, we were spending the summer months on Sullivan's Island, across the harbor from Charleston, and my father had gone up to New York City on business. Instead of returning by train, he came back aboard the *Algonquin.*

The ship channel into Charleston harbor led through the jetties at the harbor mouth to a point only a few hundred yards off Sullivan's Island. On the day of my father's return, my mother woke us early, and we walked down to the beach to watch his ship arrive. It was just before dawn, and the morning sky was still gray when the *Algonquin* steamed in past Fort Sumter, seemingly headed directly for the beach, only to execute a sweeping turn and move past us. Although she was a small coastal liner, of less than five thousand tons' displacement, she seemed enormous.

Just as she reached a point abreast of where we were standing, a light began blinking amidship, clearly visible in the still-murky day, as if signaling especially to us. My father had tipped a steward to make available a high-powered blinker light on deck. The ship proceeded on its course and out of sight beyond Fort Moultrie, but thereafter, in the way that children adopt favorite baseball teams, players, aircraft, and warships, my favorite passenger liner was the *Algonquin.*

When a group of us were casting around for a name for our newly established publishing house, we had first thought to call it Bright Leaf Books, after a variety of tobacco grown in Virginia and the Carolinas. But several of our authors and sales representatives objected to the name, arguing that it was both too regional and not regional enough. Those who understood the reference would think we were publishing our books exclusively for and about the southeastern United States, while those who did not might well think it was a reference to marijuana.

So we looked around for another name that was not already being used by a book publisher. Someone said that an Indian name might be nice, and I thought at once of Algonquin. As the name not of a tribe but of an Indian language group, Algonquin, or Algonkian, would be quite appropriate, in that the tribes that inhabited the North Carolina and Virginia coast when the English arrived in the sixteenth and seventeenth centuries had spoken Algonkian.

The name would have the additional virtue of possessing bookish associations, because of the once-celebrated coterie of literary humorists who used to gather at the Algonquin Hotel in New York City, whose members included James Thurber, Ring Lardner, Alexander Woollcott, Dorothy Parker, Heywood Broun, and Robert Benchley. (When I traveled to New York I often stayed at the Algonquin, not because of its literary aura but because its owner had formerly been a resident of Charleston and a semi-pro baseball player of note.)

But the main reason for choosing the name Algonquin Books for the publishing house had been the Clyde–Mallory Line ship, a photograph of which had long hung above my desk. It was only right, therefore, that the new boat be named for a publishing house that had in turn been named after a ship. The contrast between the coastal liner of sixty years ago and my little twenty-four-foot wooden craft would be ludicrous enough. I would also be forever explaining to boatyards, marina offices, and the like how to spell it. But the *Algonquin* she was going to be.

John McCallum had made the repairs on the *Mary Simpson,* and my abruptly undercut confidence in her reliability was restored. When my novelist friend Clyde Edgerton and his wife Susan Ketchin, a onetime student of mine, told me several weeks later that they and another couple were planning to spend a weekend in Beaufort, I invited them to come by Gillikin's Boat Basin and I would take them for a ride out on the Waterway. It was mid-March and time that I began readying the *Mary Simpson* to be put up for sale. My plan was to advertise the boat in early April, in the hope that by the time I brought the *Algonquin* over from Harkers Island in mid-May, my boat slip on Peltier Creek would be available for her.

The Saturday I had expected to take the Edgertons out was rainy, so I did not go down to the coast until Sunday morning. I had just begun removing mildew stains from the underside of the cockpit roof when the Edgertons and their friends showed up. We cast off the lines and took in the boat bumpers, and headed down Peltier Creek toward Bogue Sound and the Waterway. As we passed *Sylvia II,* tied up at Bob Simpson's dock behind his home, I gave a couple of toots on the air horn, and Bob came outside and waved as we went by. We moved along the entrance channel to the Waterway buoy, then turned eastward in the direction of the Morehead City waterfront. It was a bright, clear day, with a light wind and the temperature in the sixties.

We were cruising along the Waterway in fine style and had passed underneath the bridge spanning Bogue Sound between Atlantic Beach and the mainland, when I began to hear, or fancy that I was hearing, a kind of irregularity in the sound of the engine. I tried to ignore it, but I soon had to concede that this was no imagined phenomenon. I shoved up the throttle, and the RPM needle not only did not move up but even faltered for a moment.

This was exactly the way the engine had behaved the previous June, on that fateful day when salt water had gotten into the block. Was it possible that the new engine, rebuilt at a cost of more than $2,500, was doing precisely the same thing?

I swung the *Mary Simpson*'s bow around and turned back toward Peltier Creek, three miles away. After a couple of minutes the engine died out completely. So there we were, stranded in the Intracoastal Waterway without power, several miles from the dock.

I lowered the anchor to keep us from running aground, and opened the engine hatch. The rebuilt engine looked perfectly sound. There was no water in the bilge that I could see, and the cylinder heads showed no sign of dampness. The gasoline filter that George Alletsee had installed seemed clean. There was no way that we could be out of gas, for there were at least thirty gallons in the tank. The batteries were fully charged. Yet for whatever reason, the *Mary Simpson* was again *hors de combat*.

The Edgertons and their friends had to leave for Chapel Hill by five o'clock, and it was well after three. I called the Coast Guard on the radio, gave them Bob Simpson's telephone number, and requested that they ask Bob to come and rescue us.

After a minute the corpsman on duty reported that the *Sylvia II* would be on her way soon. After we had waited for five minutes or so I decided to try to start the engine again. Not only did it turn over strongly but it caught almost at once. So we hoisted anchor and headed for Peltier Creek.

As we passed beneath the bridge I caught sight of *Sylvia II* emerging from the mouth of the creek, so I called Bob on the radio and told him to go on back. *Sylvia II* rounded the entrance marker to the creek channel, however, and headed toward us. *Her* engine, the original Chrysler Crown, always ran nicely—Bob being sufficiently knowledgeable to keep her properly maintained.

It was well that Bob did not turn back, because after five more minutes or so the *Mary Simpson*'s engine gave a repeat performance, losing power and then stopping altogether. So down went the anchor again.

Sylvia II was by now only a few hundred yards distant, so she came up alongside, with Bob at the wheel and Mary at the stern, together with their dog Kudzu, who was jumping back and forth between the fantail and the stern deck, obviously enjoying the proceedings. Bob was a man with long experience at cajoling ancient Chrysler Crown engines into behaving properly, and I wanted him to come aboard and inspect ours, but he would have none of it, insisting that we throw a line to them and be towed in. So with a towline stretched between *Sylvia II*'s stern post and *Mary Simpson*'s bow cleat, we set off up the Waterway, and were soon turning into the Peltier Creek entrance channel.

By now I had again succeeded in inducing the engine to run, and I called to Bob by radio and told him to cast off the towline. Not until we get inside the creek, he replied; if the engine were to cut out again while we were still negotiating the narrow entrance channel, we would be aground before the line could be refastened.

Slowly, ignominiously, the *Mary Simpson* reentered the creek that she had left so proudly a little earlier that afternoon. This time there was no tooting of horns. I thought we could get to the dock under our own power, running slowly, so we freed the towline and set off for Gillikin's Boat Basin at a snail's pace, with *Sylvia II* following us until we were safely into the proper arm of the creek. We made it back to the dock without further incident. By five o'clock the *Mary Simpson* was properly moored and the Edgertons and their friends were on their way home.

I was considerably rattled by the adventure, and more than a little worried at the possibility that the rebuilt engine block might be ruined, just like its predecessor. If another $2,500 reboring and repair job was needed, I would just sell the old boat "as is where is" for whatever I could get for it. Bob Simpson doubted that the problem was as serious as that. If salt water had gotten into the engine block, he said, in all likelihood I wouldn't have been able to restart it and keep it going even for as long as I had. His surmise, which proved to be correct, was that the fuel line was clogged and the engine simply hadn't been getting enough gas. As long as I operated at very low speed, enough gas could make its way to the engine to keep it going, but when power was increased beyond a certain point the flow became insufficient and the engine cut out. He had insisted on towing the *Mary Simpson* rather than trying to diagnose and repair her because he didn't want to be working on a gasoline engine in a crowded cockpit while the boat was pitching back and forth. If we had been caught out somewhere far from home it would have been another matter, but with the entrance to Peltier Creek less than two miles away, there seemed to be no point in doing things the hard way.

George Alletsee, who had installed the *Mary Simpson*'s engine, was working now for Ken Markel. Had I checked to see whether gasoline was getting through both fuel filters? he asked. *Both?* The only one I knew of was the one he had installed, just behind the transmission. George lifted up the deck board behind the engine and showed me another filter, tucked out of sight behind a frame. This one was housed inside a brass cylinder, and looked very dirty. He unscrewed the cylinder and, examining the filter, pronounced it badly clogged. It would have to be thoroughly washed out with gasoline and blown clean with air.

He took the filter to his truck and set off in search of a service station with an air compressor. When he returned he reinstalled the filter, removed the hose from the other filter, and tried blowing into the hose through the one he had cleaned. It was no go; the fuel line was still clogged. What we would have to do would be to disconnect the line from the gas tank—which meant first taking off the panels around the cockpit and stern compartment. To do that we would have to remove some two dozen screws. We finally got the panels off and George detached the copper fuel line from the gas tank. Again he tried blowing through it, without success. It was not until I drove over to Bob Simpson's place, borrowed a bicycle pump and a suction pump, and we attached these to the line and began pumping away that whatever was blocking the flow of fuel worked loose. Bob Simpson had been correct; we couldn't have repaired the boat out there on Bogue Sound.

George's guess was that the line probably had not been cleaned since being installed on the *Mary Simpson* as original equipment several decades earlier. In any event, the gasoline now appeared to be flowing freely. We hooked up the line, started the engine, and it ran nicely. George departed, and I spent the next hour replacing the panels.

Once again the *Mary Simpson* was in proper operating condition. Very well. There was no reason to assume that anything else would go wrong. Indeed, both George Alletsee and Bob Simpson had expressly said they thought it highly unlikely that I would have any more trouble. But, given the convergence of my record and the *Mary Simpson*'s, I was not going to tempt fate. She would be put up for sale at once. And I would not take her out again until a buyer had been found and it was necessary to demonstrate that she was in working order.

The following Sunday I drove back down to Morehead City from Chapel Hill. I spent that afternoon and the following morning cleaning up the old boat, taking off all the accumulated mildew from underneath the roof and inside the cabin, putting another coat of paint on the roof over the stern, vacuuming out the forward and main cabins and the cockpit, and removing all equipment that would not be sold with the boat. I bought a FOR SALE sign, wrote my home telephone number on it, and taped it to the cabin window where it could be seen from the dock. Then I departed. Until Clem Willis delivered the *Algonquin,* I would simply consider myself boatless. It would not exactly be a new experience.

10

THE BOAT THAT DIDN'T GET BUILT

The launching of the *Algonquin* was set for mid-May. Clem Willis had aimed for late April, but several deaths in his family had slowed down his working time. He was seventy-five years old himself by now, and I had no wish to hurry him along.

I was planning to give a party to celebrate the commissioning of the *Algonquin*. The paperback edition of Bob Simpson's *When the Water Smokes* was also due out in May; of all the outdoors books we had published it was my favorite, and I wanted to do something to call attention to the new edition. In talking with the Simpsons one day, we came up with the idea of combining the reissue of Bob's book with the delivery of my boat. We would stage a book-and-boat extravaganza and invite the Algonquin Books staff and various authors to come. The guests would board the *Algonquin* and Bob's *Sylvia II* at Peltier Creek, journey along the

Waterway to the Morehead City waterfront, tie up at the
Sanitary Restaurant, and everyone would go to DeeGee's,
a bookshop nearby, to autograph books. Bob's book was
centered on the raising of *Sylvia II* from where it had
sunk next to the Sanitary Restaurant during the notorious
Groundhog Day Storm of 1976. He tells of buying the
boat for three hundred dollars, rebuilding and
refurbishing it, and exploring the rivers, bays, sounds,
creeks, and barrier islands along the Carolina coast. So the
location of the book-and-boat party would be particularly
appropriate.

The proprietor of DeeGee's, Ed Voorhees, a
longtime friend of Bob's, was delighted at the prospect.
Between us we decided that Saturday, May 26, would be
the best day to stage the event. Bob added an additional
dimension by proposing that we invite John McCallum,
at Taylor Boat Works, to bring along the *Ruth,* the
thirty-eight-foot Core Sounder he had rebuilt and
restored. The *Ruth* had originally been launched in 1930,
and *Sylvia II* in 1940. Together with the *Algonquin,* a
brand-new product of Harkers Island boatbuilding, the
three boats would constitute a nautical processional
spanning some sixty years of traditional North Carolina
wooden boatcraft.

I sent invitations to various authors. Clyde
Edgerton, Jill McCorkle, and Kaye Gibbons agreed to

take part. Another Algonquin author, Larry Brown, of Mississippi, was scheduled to be visiting the Edgertons that weekend, and when told of the plans he was eager to join us. So was a non-Algonquin author, Elizabeth Spencer, a native of Mississippi and a longtime friend of mine who now lived in Chapel Hill. All in all, it would be a literary event such as had not before taken place in Morehead City, North Carolina: five widely known writers arriving by water to join Bob Simpson in autographing books.

Clem Willis felt sure that the *Algonquin* could be delivered by that date. Bob and I drove over to see the progress of the boat, and she seemed all but ready to take to the water. Numerous details remained to be taken care of, but just about everything important was in place. Sides, deck, and cabin were now completed and painted bright white, in characteristic workboat style. If anything, she looked a bit too much like a workboat; I wanted the workboat ambiance for her, but she *wasn't* a workboat, and I felt something was needed that would distinguish her from what must surely be several thousand all-white commercial craft based along the North Carolina oceanfront.

While in Richmond, Virginia, for a speaking engagement, I located a scrap-metal yard specializing in pipe, and for eleven dollars procured enough stainless steel tubing to provide handrails along the topsides of both the forward and main cabins. An hour's work with some metal polish and they gleamed handsomely. Locating surplus fittings to attach them to the cabin tops was considerably more difficult, and I ended up ordering them new, so that the cost came to something over a hundred dollars in all—which was still decidedly less than I would have had to pay had I ordered ready-made grabrails. My younger son, who was handy at carpentry, promised to make nameboards for the cabin sides. With rails, nameboards, and windowed cabins the *Algonquin* would be distinctive enough in appearance. In addition, I ordered a string of brightly colored signal pennants to decorate her for the party.

So everything now appeared to be set for May 26. Barring an act of God or some other calamity, in a little over four weeks the long wait would be ended and the *Algonquin* would be in service.

Memories, however, die hard. I began realizing that I was becoming very nervous about the new boat's actually being finished and delivered to me. I seemed to be hearing a voice, back in the more remote annexes of my consciousness, warning me.

Something is going to go wrong, as it always does. You are riding for a fall. Remember what happened last time.

Last time? What do you mean, last time? This is the first new boat I've ever had built.

Ah, but what about the boat that didn't *get built?*

I did indeed remember. I remembered the most trying summer of my adult life, the summer of

The Boat That Didn't Get Built

It was in 1966. I was forty-two years old, a member of the faculty of Hollins College, Virginia. My family and I had been accustomed to spending our summers on the York River, in Gloucester County, Virginia, fifteen miles upstream from the Chesapeake Bay. Our house—my father-in-law's, to be exact—was located on a cove just off the river. Using my father-in-law's sixteen-foot fiberglass motorboat I had fished all up and down the river. I caught spotted trout, croaker, spot, and blues. Even rockfish—the local name for striped bass—were still in decent supply if one knew where to fish for them. On several occasions I drove over to Kilmarnock, an hour away across the Rappahannock River, and went cobia fishing in the Chesapeake, in successive summers landing fifty-eight- and sixty-four-pounders from a charter boat belonging to a cousin of one of my ex-students.

The more large boats I saw, the more I thought about how nice it would be to own one. A cabin cruiser with inboard power would allow me to venture much father away than was possible with the outboard runabout. I could go out into the Chesapeake, where the cobia were caught and where I could troll for the big blues. More than that, with my wife and two young boys I could go on trips, up the Bay to the Rappahannock and Potomac rivers; we could visit Washington, Annapolis, Baltimore. I could go across the Bay to Tangier Island, down the Bay to Hampton Roads, and up the James River to Jamestown and even Richmond, or I could go down the Intracoastal Waterway.

One day I happened to be over near Seaford, Virginia, and I stopped in to talk with a boatbuilder from whom I had once bought a twelve-foot wooden skiff. His name was Belvin, and I asked him how much it would cost to have a small cruiser built, say twenty-four feet in length, with an inboard-outboard engine. About three thousand dollars, he said. He could install a dinette in it that opened into a double berth, and V-berths forward. There would be room for a small sink, icebox, stove, and a marine head. A 120 horsepower inboard-outboard engine would cost another $1,200. Including anchor, mooring lines, compass, depth-finder, and marine radio, the total cost would be something under five thousand dollars.

The figure was considerably more than I had available, but I thought about the boat all that autumn. Then, shortly after the first of the year, I received a letter inviting me out to the University of California at Santa Barbara in June for a six-week stint as visiting professor.

The stipend offered was generous, and of course it would be in addition to my regular salary. The cost of driving out to the West Coast and back, and the rent for a house for my family to stay in, would all be tax-deductible. Together with a small bequest I was about to receive from the estate of an uncle who had recently died, what I could expect to clear would come to just about enough to pay for the boat.

So I telephoned the boatbuilder and told him to go ahead. The boat would be ready, he promised, by mid-summer, so that when we returned from the West Coast in early August I could expect to spend the remainder of the summer afloat.

We set out for California in our three-year-old Pontiac Tempest sedan. We also owned a Volkswagen, but the Pontiac would be more roomy and comfortable. On the second day of the trip the Pontiac began to misbehave; for brief intervals it would hesitate and lose power. Needless to say, the very thought that the automobile might go bad was enough to dispel any pleasure I might otherwise have taken in the journey.

In Memphis, Tennessee, a mechanic at a Pontiac dealer reported that the clutch needed some adjustment, which he proceeded to do. The day following, from Memphis to Dallas, there was no more sign of trouble.

But halfway through the next day's drive, from Dallas to
Carlsbad, New Mexico, the engine began faltering and
slipping badly. It was Sunday, and there was nothing to
do but keep going.

We arrived in Carlsbad in late afternoon. Early
Monday morning I took the car to the only Pontiac
dealer in town. The service manager examined it, and said
that the transmission would have to be completely rebuilt.
If I would bring the car in on Wednesday morning he
would be able to work on it. I explained that I was 2,500
miles from home, I had a wife and two small boys along,
and I was due on the West Coast that weekend. Couldn't
he possibly make an exception and work on my car
today? No, he told me, Wednesday was the earliest
possible time that he could get to it. He added, however,
that although the gears were slipping from time to time,
it was not likely that they would do anything more
grievous than that for a few thousand more miles. If I
did not drive above fifty-five miles an hour and made
sure to check the oil and transmission fluid every five
hundred miles or so, we ought to be able to get to Santa
Barbara without undue difficulty.

I had no choice but to proceed. With the Pontiac
acting up, I would have preferred to keep heading due
west, but I had promised my aunts that I would stop by
a bank in El Paso, a day's drive to the south, to check on

the status of my uncle's estate. So I picked up several cans of oil and transmission fluid in the event of an emergency, and off we headed for El Paso. I was careful to keep our speed below fifty, and I checked the oil and transmission fluid level regularly.

All seemed well—until about fifty miles from El Paso, in desert terrain, we started down a long hill, whereupon the gears began slipping, the engine lost power, and the temperature needle promptly and swiftly rose to the overheating point. There was nothing to do but put the car in neutral and coast down the hill, at the base of which I could see a small stone structure.

The building proved to be an unmanned shelter with a water fountain. The temperature outside was well above a hundred degrees, and there was nothing in sight for miles but sand, rock, occasional patches of cactus, and, far in the distance, mountains.

Either I could try to flag down a passing motorist—the highway was all but deserted, with cars appearing only very occasionally—or else wait there until the engine cooled down, and try to keep going. It was mid-afternoon. I had visions of our spending the night out there in the desert, with water but no food. It was achingly hot now, but it would be very cold at night on the desert.

My wife took the boys out walking in the desert

while I waited with the car, until finally the heat gauge
dropped down to a reasonable level. I checked the oil and
fluid; they seemed to be adequate. So we started off again.
Driving at no more than twenty-five miles an hour,
air-conditioner and fan turned off, windows wide open,
we crept along Highway 180 toward El Paso, while I
kept an eye on the temperature-gauge needle, while
silently cursing all Pontiacs and Pontiac dealers wherever
and whenever. Occasionally a car or a truck flashed past.
By now it was dusk, but the heat showed no sign of
diminishing.

Eventually we puttered into El Paso and located a motel.
My wife took the boys to the pool for a swim, and I lay
on the bed, still vibrating from the long and wearisome
drive. Should I try once again to get the transmission
repaired? In terms of terrain the worst part of the journey
still lay ahead, in particular the trek across the California
desert, where the temperature was reputed to hover
around 110° and the tourist guides all urged caution.
Suppose the transmission went out there? Nothing that I
had seen in respect to Pontiac repair shops thus far was
calculated to instill much confidence in either their
reliability or their compassion.

    The next morning I called home and arranged
with my bank to cover a check. I read the automobile

advertisements in the newspaper carefully, to determine local car prices as best I could. A Plymouth dealership in downtown El Paso was having a sale on new cars. I drove the Pontiac there and told the sales manager exactly what had happened and why I wanted to trade my car for a new Plymouth eight-cylinder station wagon with a radio and air-conditioning. I did not want to dicker or compare prices at other dealerships, I told him. I knew approximately how much I could expect to pay. If his price was reasonable I would sign the papers, and give him a check forthwith. He could call my bank in Roanoke to verify it. I wanted the car ready to go by noon.

From his standpoint it was all too easy. He wanted to show me the various features of the 1966 Plymouths, and to have me drive one. That was not necessary, I told him; I knew how Plymouths drove. I wanted to buy a car and be on my way.

He showed me a tan station wagon and quoted a price that was several hundred dollars below what I had estimated. While the car was being prepared, I drove over to the bank in the Pontiac and talked with an official about my uncle's estate, returned an hour later, and exchanged cars. By one o'clock we were on our way to Albuquerque, New Mexico.

The Plymouth station wagon was not only

considerably roomier than the Pontiac Tempest sedan, but the air-conditioning worked with markedly greater efficiency. Even so, when we climbed the steep grade of the Piute Mountains west of Needles, California, with the temperature outside at 110° and the desert on either side of the highway, the temperature gauge rose closer to the warning line. The Pontiac would never have made it across.

We arrived in Santa Barbara, located the house that I had rented via mail, installed ourselves in it, and I went over to the University, ready to begin my teaching stint. I wrote to the bank and arranged for a ninety-day loan to cover the cost of the new car. I could not afford both the new car and the boat, but I would sell the car when we returned and buy an older and less expensive car to go along with our Volkswagen Squareback.

The entire episode left me exhausted and edgy. My state of mind was not helped by the house we had rented. It was located out in Lower Suburbia in a sleazy-looking neighborhood, with cheap, uncomfortable furniture and imperfectly functioning kitchen appliances. There was a crack in the toilet bowl, and another in the bathtub. One corner of our bed was propped up with books. The television set did not work. The air-conditioning was inefficient. The decor was depressing; there were plastic flowers in the vases. There were no

---

shopping centers or stores, no parks within walking distance. We had looked forward to being close to the Pacific Ocean, but the nearest beach was five miles away.

Except for one person, a former student of mine who was serving as acting chairman of the English Department and was kept extremely busy with administrative duties, I knew no one on the faculty. There were, in fact, very few faculty members around. Except for my course and a couple of others, all the classes being offered were beginning level and were taught by graduate students. The permanent faculty either stayed at home or were away on trips. My own course had several hundred students in it. I lectured from a dais with a microphone, and a graduate assistant met with discussion groups and handled the grading. It was not my idea of the way to teach.

Each weekday I arrived at the university about ten o'clock, sat around for an hour in the office assigned to me, lectured for fifty minutes, ate lunch in a cafeteria, then returned to my office for "office hours." No students ever came in to talk. At the end of my six-week lecture stint I did not know a single student by name. For all the good I was doing as a teacher I could just as well have sent the University of California at Santa Barbara a series of lectures on video tape.

If there was any community life among the

English faculty, any shared recreational or social activities, we did not discover it. Except for my former student and his wife, nobody paid us the slightest heed. We were never asked out to dinner in the evening, or invited to receptions or the like. Since we had only one car, my wife was forced to wait around the house with the children each day until I got back from the university. She then drove them to the beach, while I stayed at home, napped, and read. We rented a television set so that the boys could watch cartoons before dinner and I could see an occasional baseball game in the evening. One weekend we took the boys to Disneyland; otherwise we mostly went for drives in what for the most part was hot, barren, semidesert country.

The biggest disappointment of all was the ocean. I had brought along my fishing tackle with the idea of renting a boat of some kind and fishing offshore. Surely, too, there would be faculty colleagues who owned boats and fished. But I had misunderstood the nature of the California coast near Santa Barbara. It was not broken up with harbors and inlets, but presented a long expanse of cliffs with an occasional small, crowded beach area below. There was but one boat harbor, with a concrete breakwater and an assortment of yachts and commercial craft moored inside. To walk along the harbor docks, see all those boats, and be utterly land-bound, while 3,500 miles away my own boat was in the final stages of construction, was a frustrating business.

As for my being able to rent a boat, there was only one such agency—a chartering outfit which handled only large yachts. Other than that the only boats available were aluminum skiffs, not tied up at a wharf but located atop a high fishing pier that reached out over the ocean. You paid something like twenty-five dollars for two hours' use of a boat, which was lowered down onto the water with a crane. I tried it once. There was no shoreline with rocks, jetties, or inlets for casting into; all I could do was troll, and given the size of the boat, only close in to shore at that. I picked up a few yellowtails, then turned the boat in.

I did run into one faculty member who fished and owned a boat. The place to fish, he said, was alongside the offshore oil rigs, and he described the numerous large fish he was accustomed to catching at such places. He invited me to meet him at the yacht harbor the following afternoon.

When I got there I found that he had a battered fifteen-foot runabout with an old Sears Roebuck outboard motor, and that he had brought two graduate students along as well. My better judgment told me not to go, but I had done without decent fishing all summer and could not resist. We headed out to an oil rig a half mile offshore. I cast plugs and spinners underneath it and picked up a couple of small fish, but the boat had so little freeboard that I was too uncomfortable to enjoy it. Fortunately the sea was calm; any kind of wave action and we would almost certainly have capsized.

After an hour or so, during which we had caught nothing except for my several small fish, we started back. A quarter mile from the shore the outboard gave out. There was only a single paddle aboard. I ended up doing the paddling—the other two guests were obviously without any experience in boats whatever—while the owner kept trying to start his engine. Occasionally it would sputter for a minute or two, then cut off again. With the help of the current we worked our way inshore, but well to the south of the harbor. Finally we reached a swimming platform a hundred yards or so off the beach of a resort hotel. Trying to take the boat ashore through the surf was out of the question, so one of the group who happened to be wearing bathing trunks swam in to shore to summon help.

By now it was getting on toward evening, and the air was becoming distinctly chilly. After a long hour's wait a Coast Guard launch hove into view around a point, her running lights quite visible in the gathering dark. She came up to the platform, the coastguardsmen tied the runabout alongside, and we headed back to the harbor. When we arrived the runabout was subjected to an inspection, during which it was discovered that, except for the life jacket I had brought along, the safety equipment aboard consisted of two jackets, one of them children's size. There were no flares, no horn or whistle. The running lights did not work. The boat owner was fined twenty dollars. He had no money with him, so I paid the fine. Thus ended my only offshore fishing venture in the Pacific Ocean.

During all this time I was getting bulletins from my father back in Richmond. My mother was very ill with Parkinson's Disease, and her condition was steadily deteriorating. My father was in no way a stoic, and his letters consisted mainly of lengthy lamentations. Each time I spied a letter from him in the mail my insides constricted.

What kept me going was the knowledge that back on the Chesapeake Bay the new boat was waiting. I counted the days until the end of the term. At least the long drive back across the continent would be made in a new car this time. We would head home by the straightest possible route.

Ultimately the time came when we could load up the car and depart. The Plymouth station wagon performed flawlessly. We crossed the desert, drove through Las Vegas and northeastward up a long valley

into Utah, then eastward through the Rockies and across
the long Kansas plain to Kansas City. We crossed the
Mississippi River north of St. Louis, and spent the final
night of the journey in Versailles, Indiana. In the
morning we set out, crossed Kentucky to the West
Virginia Turnpike, then down to Interstate 81. Shortly
after one in the morning we pulled into our driveway on
the Hollins College campus. We had made the trip in
five nights and six days. Our summer-long ordeal was
over at last.

The next morning I called the boatbuilder,
Belvin, and was informed that the boat had not been
built.

It seemed that he had suffered a pinched nerve in his
back, and had been unable to work. The partially
completed hull had been sold to someone, and he was
returning my deposit by mail. We went down to the
York River anyway, and I did some fishing in my
father-in-law's old runabout. On one occasion I drove to
Richmond to see my parents, and was shocked at the
deterioration in my mother's condition. No longer could
she cook or fend for herself. For most of the day all she
did was sit in the living room and stare at the television
screen. In addition to the Parkinson's she was experiencing
hardening of the arteries. I had brought along my older

son, thinking that it might cheer up my mother. She seemed scarcely to know who he was. My father's conversation consisted of a lengthy recounting of my mother's condition.

By the time we returned home and the school year began, I was in a deep depression. Shortly after the school term opened, I walked into a classroom and began to lecture, only to find that I was *hearing myself speak.* I tried to continue, but could not. I dismissed the class and went back to my office, shaking like a leaf. I called a psychiatrist friend and made an appointment to see him. He listened to my description of what had happened during the summer and fall. "A boat," he said. "What a strange thing. A boat—"

There were no more problems with lecturing, and gradually I fell into my normal routine, although it was a month before I was able to resume my writing. I decided later on that it had been a kind of "male menopause." I was in my early forties, and had come to realize that I was not going to conquer the world. My mother's deterioration had not only released the pent-up emotions of half a lifetime's burden of filial guilt but had triggered a confrontation with my own mortality.

Was it caused by the boat not being built? By my mother's condition? Or was it, in some way that I was unable as yet to fathom, that the two were somehow connected—that whatever meaning the idea of the boat had held for me was related to my feelings toward my mother? Sometime in the future, I hoped, I would be able to figure it out more clearly.

The summer following, when we were down at the river again, I ran into the boatbuilder at a marina. "How's your back?" I asked.

He seemed puzzled. "Oh," he said after thinking about it for a moment, "it's fine now."

I realized then what I should have suspected all along. The pinched nerve in his back—if indeed there had been one at all—had been merely an excuse. He had sold my boat to someone else. All the previous summer I had been placing my hopes on a boat that had become someone else's property.

Now, a quarter of a century later, the small voice was speaking to me out of the recesses of my memory, reminding me about what had happened back then. *Don't count on this boat being finished as promised, either,* it was saying. And more than that, *Don't let your mother die of anguish over the way you spend your money.*

Which was absurd. My mother had been dead for nine years, and my father for twenty. My own children were grown now and happily married, and there were two grandchildren. I had owned numerous boats since then, had published several dozen books, had retired after one career and had taken up an entirely new one. My income was reasonably secure.

Moreover, strictly on a practical level the parallel made no sense. Not only was I not a continent's distance away from where the new boat was being built, but I had been checking on its construction regularly, photographing every stage of it. The boat was almost ready for launching. There was no way that it could be sold out from under me.

The small voice that was whispering to me, I realized, was only the lingering and groundless reflexive response of a past that I had both outlived and outgrown. The only meaning the voice could possibly hold for me now was *as* memory. If I chose to let it speak to me still, it would be in order to help in the writing of this book.

11

THE BOAT THAT DID
GET BUILT

Despite my long wait for the launching of the new boat, when it took place I was not present to watch. The *Algonquin* was lowered into the water at Harkers Island on May 21, 1990, when as luck would have it I was in New York City at the sales conference for Algonquin's fall books. With the Book-and-Boat Party set for May 26, what was important was that the sea trial take place as soon as possible, so that any problems that turned up could be rectified in time to take the *Algonquin* over to Morehead City for the big event. I had been cautioned that with a wooden boat that had not been built on a production line to a standard design, modifications were almost certain to be needed. Nobody could say ahead of time just how the particular diesel engine I had chosen would affect the boat's trim when afloat, or how that effect would make itself felt at various speeds.

I returned from New York on May 22, and drove down to Harkers Island the next afternoon. The *Algonquin* was tied up alongside a pier at Barbour's Marina, looking dignified and self-possessed, and seemingly already very much at home in the element for which she had been designed. Clem Willis was not around, so I drove over to Larry Myers's diesel shop to find out how the sea trial had gone. The boat was operative, Larry said, but for reasons unknown to him the engine had been mounted very high and at a considerable angle; during the sea trial, when it was run faster than about 2,200 RPMs, it leaked a little oil and the stern tended to squat. To operate efficiently, the engine would have to be lowered to a more nearly level position. Since the aperture for the propeller shaft had been bored through the keel in accordance with the current position of the engine, the transmission Larry had sold me would have to be exchanged for one of another design, in order to maintain the higher shaft angle with the engine lower down in the hull. This need not be done immediately; the *Algonquin* could certainly be taken over to Morehead City to participate in the festivities of the twenty-sixth. As long as the motor was kept to a comfortable displacement speed and not pushed hard, it would give no trouble.

Clem Willis was still nowhere to be found, so I

worked aboard the boat for a while, assembling the
pilot's chair I had ordered from Boat/US, storing various
items such as life jackets, binoculars, fuel cans,
foul-weather gear, spare line, and toolboxes; setting out
fenders; and otherwise making myself feel Proprietary and
Important.

There is a qualitative difference between observing a boat
on land as she is being built, and going aboard her in the
water—even when, as in this instance, I had been
watching her progress from almost the moment that her
keel was put into place. I had seen her materialize from
the rough sketch I had drawn the previous summer when
I had first gone looking for a builder, observed her lying
bottomside up as her planking was installed, her cross
members emplaced, and her wooden sides constructed.
Then I watched her deck and cabin come into being,
until on my last visit almost everything was in place and
Clem Willis and his grandson were fitting the wheels and
axles underneath the hull preparatory to launching.
       Yet now that she was in the water and moored to
a wharf, she seemed more formidable and imposing—and
at the same time a bit diminished. More imposing,
because she was a *boat,* a thing designed for use in a
particular element and now afloat in it. Diminished,
because her built-in dimensions and accommodations were

finite and set, as they had not been when she was still a creature of possibility, incomplete and therefore amenable to being further shaped.

The forward cabin was as roomy and high-ceilinged as I had specified. There would be no stooping, no need to contort one's body in order to lie down in the single berth. And the berth was a full three feet wide and six and a half feet long, so that I would be able to stretch out in comfort without any sense of being encased in a straitjacket. Although there was no cookstove or icebox, there were places on and below the counter to install both. The enclosed head was accessible and reasonably roomy, too.

The main cabin was more cramped than I had anticipated. I had not realized how much space the engine would take up. Clem had not only mounted the engine very high but had built a large motor box around it, so that the structure dominated the cabin, reducing the available standing or sitting room to about three feet in front and on either side. When someone was seated at the wheel, anybody else desiring to go into the forward cabin, or to leave it, would have to squeeze past.

The main cabin clearly was no place for several people to lounge around in, the more so because the windows were four feet above the cabin floor; anyone seated in a normal-sized folding chair would not be able

---

to see out. If, however, the engine needed to be lowered farther down into the hull, as Larry Myers said, then the height of the engine box could be reduced, and perhaps the length and width as well. Even a few more inches of space would make a great deal of difference to anyone moving about the cabin. Nor would it be a difficult matter to install high folding seats for the pilot and one passenger, using the made-to-order pilot seat I had bought for a third person. With the engine box lowered, passengers could simply sit around it, their feet placed atop it for comfort, with no more inconvenience than when sitting at a bar.

As for the stern cockpit, only two or at most three people could be seated outside in any comfort, and no more than two persons could fish at a time. I had specified precisely those dimensions; I wanted this boat to be built for *my* convenience, and the small cockpit would permit greater cabin space. Even so, it seemed very small now.

What it came down to was that my twenty-four-foot, tailor-made boat had a cabin arrangement appropriate to a twenty-eight- or thirty-footer. That was what I had asked Clem Willis to build for me, and he had done it.

It was on Clem's recommendation that I had purchased the engine from Larry Myers, and I had assumed that

---

there would be ample consultation between the two of them during the installation. Apparently, however, Larry had not laid eyes on the engine from the time that it and the transmission had been delivered to Clem's boat shed back in the late fall, until the completed boat was in the water and ready for her trial run.

I had the sense that there was a certain distance maintained between Clem and some of the other old-time boatbuilders on the island, on the one hand, and Larry, on the other. Larry had lived among them and worked with them for seventeen years, but he was a native New Yorker; he had moved to the Carolina coast because he felt the metropolis was not a good place to raise children. As was true of most of the New Yorkers I knew, he expressed himself fluently and articulately. By contrast, Clem Willis—like most of the other Harkers Islanders I had met—was chary of speech, tended to keep his opinions to himself, and was not quick to volunteer information. His taciturnity was only augmented by his deafness. It was only after I had been coming down to observe the progress of my boat for some months that he seemed to relax in my presence and to enjoy my visits. By then he had apparently decided that I could be counted upon to live up to my part of the bargain, that I was not going to second-guess his every action, and that I was not merely attempting to flatter him when I expressed my genuine admiration for his painstaking craftsmanship.

For my part, I liked both Larry and Clem. I had known and worked with New Yorkers for more than forty years, and had long since learned not to be put off by the way that many of them come on so strongly. And as for the Harkers Islanders, I had grown up in a small southern coastal city, and I had known and frequented the company of people like them from my earliest days. I had found early on that in associating only with other academics, a certain access to everyday reality seemed to be missing. So instinctively I had made a point of also seeking out the company of the Clem Willises of the world, frequently to the bafflement of some of my academic colleagues, especially those from the Northeast. I had noticed, too, that other southerners who were academics tended to do the same thing. It had something to do, I thought, with the fact that we had all grown up in relatively small middle-class communities in which there wasn't a strict separation into specialized economic, social, and professional groups. The result was that those of us who had gone on to become "intellectuals," as it were, seemed to wear our academic robes a bit uneasily.

In any event, both Clem Willis and Larry Myers were now in agreement that the diesel engine was mounted too high and at too steep an angle, and were prepared to rectify it. Both agreed, too, that if the engine were kept to a moderate speed until the operation was

---

accomplished, the boat could be used in safety and without trouble. As for her reported tendency to dig in at the stern when run fast, Clem recommended that trim tabs be installed, while Larry favored placing wooden wedges beneath the stern. The likelihood was that the specifications I had set for the boat—not only the lengthy cabins and small cockpit but a ceiling high enough in the forward cabin to permit me to stand erect, upon a hull whose length was to be no more than twenty-four feet—had resulted in an unusually heavy boat for its size. In terms of stability and seaworthiness this was no drawback. But if I was to derive full advantage from the eighty-two horsepower engine, the problem would have to be rectified. I had no burning desire for a planing hull and high over-the-water speeds. What I *did* want was the full displacement speed possible for a twenty-four-foot workboat hull, so, if the stern of the boat was digging in once it reached a certain RPM output, then it would have to be elevated, whether with trim tabs as Clem proposed or with wedges as advocated by Larry.

After listening to what both men had to say on the subject, I decided on the trim tabs, mainly because installing the wooden wedges beneath the stern would entail removing the boat from the water again. I was in no mood to wait for my boat any longer. If the trim tabs proved inadequate, I would consider having the wedges

added when the time came to have her bottom scraped
and repainted next spring.

It was necessary now to get the *Algonquin* from Harkers
Island to Peltier Creek in west Morehead City, with the
engine still at the original angle and without trim tabs,
for the Great Book-and-Boat Party on Saturday. By car
it was a drive of thirty minutes or so. By water it was a
fourteen-mile trip, which at a moderate speed would
require from two and a half to three hours, much of the
journey along a narrow channel running between wide
flats of shoal water, with the markers set fairly far apart.
I had covered the first six miles or so—the less well
marked portion—only once before, some eight years ago,
in an outboard motorboat. Since I had no wish whatever
to install the *Algonquin* upon a mudbank on her first
voyage, someone would have to be found to make the
trip with me, someone who was well acquainted with the
waters off Harkers Island.

I had to admit to myself, too, that I was *afraid* of
the engine. What if it were to go out en route? I would
have no idea what to do about it. So many of my recent
experiences with marine engines—the Atomic 4 on the
Virginius, the *Mary Simpson*'s Chrysler Crown—had
involved just that happening. The *Algonquin*'s engine had
been completely rebuilt and her transmission was

---

brand-new, so there was no reason to anticipate trouble. Even so, to make that inaugural run I wanted someone with me who not only was familiar with the waters but would also have ideas about what to do if the engine began acting up.

Clem Willis, though thoroughly acquainted with the route between Harkers Island and Cape Lookout, had not taken a boat over to Morehead City in forty years. Larry Myers promptly offered to make the trip, but said that I would have to wait until five o'clock, when he had finished his work for the day. So I spent the afternoon driving around Harkers Island sightseeing and working on the boat. Shortly after five Larry showed up. We started the engine and took in the lines. There was a great deal of vibration, but Larry assured me that it would decrease when we got under way, which indeed proved to be true. The vibration was due to the manner in which the engine was mounted, he said; when it was properly lowered and made level, much of the shaking would be eliminated, although any four-cylinder diesel engine would vibrate to some degree.

With Larry at the helm we made our way up the Harkers Island channel. We threaded the narrow pathway through the Middle Marshes and then headed westward to the dredged cut leading to Lenoxville Point, at the eastern end of Taylor Creek. From here on it would be safe

---

navigating, with a channel that was both broad and amply deep, and I took over the wheel. We moved down the wide creek between Carrot Island and the mainland, along the Beaufort waterfront with its hundreds of sailboats—many of them obviously bluewater veterans—then around Radio Island into the mouth of the Morehead City harbor. I was in familiar water now. Here for the first time we encountered considerable wave action from the current sweeping in from the inlet, and I was impressed with the solidity and firmness of the *Algonquin* as she breasted the waves with a minimum of pitching and rolling. Whatever the adjustments remaining to be made to the angle of the engine and transmission, old Clem Willis obviously knew what he was about when he designed a hull.

At the Morehead turning basin we joined the Intracoastal Waterway and headed westward along Bogue Sound for the final four-mile stretch. By now the sun was on the horizon, and when we turned into the Peltier Creek entrance channel I glanced down at my watch; it was just before eight o'clock. Earlier in the afternoon I had telephoned Bob Simpson to say that we would not be leaving Harkers Island until after five, and now as we drew close to the narrow mouth of the creek, the Simpsons were standing at the edge of the shore, Mary waving a welcome and Bob aiming his camera to capture

on film the *Algonquin*'s arrival at what would henceforth
be her home port. Given my previous record and
remembering what had happened when I had last taken
the *Mary Simpson* out for a run, I felt reasonably sure
that Bob had spent the last several hours waiting for a
call asking him to come out with *Sylvia II* and tow us
in.

The Great Book-and-Boat Party was scheduled for
Saturday. The three wooden boats—the *Algonquin,* Bob
Simpson's *Sylvia II,* and John McCallum's *Ruth*—were to
leave from Taylor Boat Works at two o'clock, arrive at
the Morehead City waterfront about three, and tie up at
the Sanitary Restaurant. Then everyone would go across
the street to DeeGee's Books and Gifts. Bob would
autograph copies of the new paperback edition of *When
the Water Smokes.* Clyde Edgerton, Jill McCorkle, Kaye
Gibbons, Elizabeth Spencer, Larry Brown—who was
visiting the Edgertons in Durham—and myself would
also autograph our recent books. All except for Elizabeth
were Algonquin Books authors, and in that sense the
occasion would have a very special meaning for me.

Eight years earlier, when Algonquin brought out
its first list of books, neither Clyde Edgerton, Kaye
Gibbons, Jill McCorkle, nor Larry Brown had published a
book of any kind. Now they were among the more

---

talked-about young fiction writers in the nation. Their new books—the first three would have new works of fiction on the forthcoming Algonquin fall 1990 list, and Kaye was completing a novel that would come out the following spring—would be eagerly awaited by reviewers and readers from coast to coast, and would doubtless appear in Great Britain and be translated into various foreign languages.

That all four of them would have eventually become published authors if my publishing house had never existed, there can be little doubt. But the fact remained that Algonquin Books had recognized their incipient talent, had helped them materially in bringing it to fruition, and had sent them off on their literary careers. We were doing what no other publisher outside the metropolitan Northeast had been able to do in the twentieth century: show that talented young southerners could write books and get them published without having to conform to what the New York and Boston establishment thought was appropriate to fiction set in the South.

I had set up Algonquin Books after more than three decades of teaching, almost all of it in southern colleges and universities. Throughout that time, the subject in which I specialized was southern literature and history. I had also been teaching fiction writing, and found that most of my students by far were from the

South. When Algonquin Books came into existence it was with the specific intention of helping to launch the literary careers of worthy young southern authors—although of course neither our fiction nor our nonfiction list was by any means restricted to that.

What I am getting at is that the presence of those four young southern novelists—Clyde Edgerton, Kaye Gibbons, Jill McCorkle, and Larry Brown—on the porch at DeeGee's Books and Gifts on the Morehead City waterfront, with people waiting in line to buy their books and get them autographed, was important to me because it embodied so much of what I had set out to do with my life. I had taught and written about southern literature, I had encouraged numerous young southerners to write more of that literature, and now I had been able to launch—the word is used deliberately—a group of them on their careers by editing and publishing their books.

In the opening chapter of this book I told of building a leaking, tippy little skiff in order to go out upon the tidal marsh to the edge of the Ashley River, and I described it as a liberating act, an assertion of freedom. As indeed it was—and also an assertion of ambition. I remarked, too, that every other boat I have since owned and operated could be said to constitute an attempt to reproduce that early experience.

These things being so, it was scarcely surprising

that an occasion for the display of the accomplishments of
a group of young authors whose books were published by
the company I had founded, would also be one for
celebrating the completion of a boat designed by and
built specifically for me. Or that on the day when my
boat was to take part in the big event, I would be
nervous, uneasy, and apprehensive that something would
go wrong.

The autograph party at DeeGee's had been widely
advertised, and newspaper stories had made much of the
procession of North Carolina–built wooden boats that
would carry the participants from Peltier Creek to the
Morehead City waterfront. To give the occasion a
properly festive air, we strung lines of signal flags from
stem to stern on all three boats. The marine weather
forecast had called for light winds and the possibility of a
late-afternoon thunderstorm, which would mean that
while we might be able to get to the waterfront without
incident, the return trip, which was to begin at about five
o'clock, might very well run into trouble. By
mid-morning on Saturday, however, the weather was not
behaving as predicted. Instead there was a high blue sky
with cirrus ice-clouds, the wind was blowing briskly out
of the southwest, and it was apparent that a cold front
had already come through the coastal area, so that the

arrival of a thunderstorm anytime soon was extremely unlikely.

My younger son, Bill, arrived shortly after ten o'clock on Saturday. He brought an extra supply of life jackets and a pair of handsome nameboards with the letters "Algonquin" cut neatly out of a slab of walnut-stained plywood and backed by a slab of light yellow, so that the name shone through clearly. Ordinarily my older son, Robert, would have been very much involved, too, but he was away for the weekend to attend his tenth class reunion at Kenyon College in Ohio.

I should have been happy to have both of them along to help me with the *Algonquin,* because this was going to be the first time that I had operated her by myself, without a diesel mechanic going along. I had not thus far attempted to maneuver the boat alongside a dock, and I had no real idea of how she would behave when in reverse. I did not yet know how rapidly or how slowly she would drift in front of the wind. And despite the fact that the engine had performed flawlessly two days earlier, I had visions of it cutting out while we were out on the Waterway en route to the waterfront, and one of the other two boats having to tow me in, with all my friends looking on. The last time Clyde and Susan Edgerton had been out on a boat with me, aboard the *Mary Simpson,* that was precisely what had happened. Theoretically the

---

Algonquin's diesel was far less likely to fail than the Chrysler Crown gasoline engine on the old boat. But when I was at the controls anything was possible.

John McCallum had committed himself to a Boy Scout outing that day, so Bob Simpson's younger brother Bill and Bill's wife, Susan, were scheduled to operate *Ruth*. As we ate lunch at the Simpsons', it became evident that although both Simpson brothers were far more experienced than I with boats, they too were feeling some anxiety. Bill would be handling a thirty-eight-foot boat that belonged to someone else and that he had operated only once before, and he would have along a boatload of adults and children. I would be operating my boat for the first time. As for Bob Simpson, while he was thoroughly familiar with the ways of *Sylvia II*, he was also more or less responsible for the overall operation. This would include not merely the boats but the well-being of more than thirty passengers, including at least a dozen youngsters most of whom were less than six years old. For I had blithely invited the authors and the Algonquin Books staff to bring their families along.

The time for my son Bill and me to bring the *Algonquin* over from its slip at Gillikin's Boat Basin to Taylor's dock could no longer be postponed. We drove to the dock, started the *Algonquin*'s engine, and took in the lines and the fenders. I placed the gear into forward and we

---

began edging out of the slip. It was the simplest of maneuvers, yet my heart was in my throat and I was sweating profusely as we started out.

We headed down the arm of the creek, then into the branch that led to Taylor's. The wind was blowing briskly from the stern, and I decided to go on past Taylor's dock, turn, and maneuver into the dock while facing the wind. There was ample room for swinging the *Algonquin,* but I misjudged her turning radius and had to go into reverse before I got her headed back downstream. Then I failed to recognize Taylor's installation in time to come alongside, and went on past it. There was nothing to do but turn the *Algonquin* around again, this time in a narrower area of the creek. Ordinarily there would have been no trick to the maneuver, but I had no feel yet for just how much power was needed to swing the stern without beginning to move forward, or for how long at a time. I ended up working back and forth across the creek several times, while people aboard the numerous other boats moored along the sides gazed in puzzlement at what was going on. Finally I got the *Algonquin*'s stern near enough to the dock for Bill to grab hold of a piling with the boathook, and we were able to haul her alongside and tie her into position with her bow pointed toward the creek. My debut as skipper of my new boat had not exactly been an auspicious one.

The guests began to arrive, and Bob Simpson

brought *Sylvia II* around and tied her alongside. John McCallum's *Ruth* was already there. By now everyone who was to go along was on hand, and it was time for the flotilla to set out for the Morehead City waterfront. *Sylvia II* would lead the way. Next it would be *Algonquin*'s turn. *Ruth* would come last.

The wind was blowing steadily up the creek from the west, and the one thing I didn't want to happen when the *Algonquin* cleared the pier was for the bow to be blown in the wrong direction, forcing us to execute yet another turnaround with everybody watching. I told Bill to stand on the bow and loop a line around a piling, holding onto both ends, so that at the proper moment he could simply let go of one of them and push off. Then I got someone else to free the stern line and shove the stern away from the dock. The wind swung it out farther, and when it was several yards away from the wharf I told Bill to push off. When he did I threw the engine into forward. We curved out into the creek with the bow pointed downstream, and moved off in pursuit of *Sylvia II.* Again, an extremely simple maneuver, but given my state of mind, the direction of the wind, my lack of familiarity with the *Algonquin,* and the presence of an audience, I was much relieved when it was done, and with decidedly more efficiency than my earlier effort.

As if that departure had been an augury, the

Great Book-and-Boat Celebration proceeded to come off without a hitch. Signal pennants and American flags waving in the breeze, the three wooden boats cleared Peltier Creek and the entrance channel, cruised up the Waterway, turned into the Morehead City waterfront channel, and headed for the Sanitary Restaurant dock paralleling the creek. A crowd of several hundred people was on hand to greet us. *Sylvia II* swung around and, bow to the breeze and currents, eased up to the head of the wharf. *Algonquin* followed, carefully duplicating the maneuver but angling for the foot of the wharf. As we drew alongside the dock the wind pushed us neatly in, our lines were passed to waiting hands and secured, and we climbed up onto the wharf. *Ruth* pulled in between *Sylvia II* and *Algonquin*.

The bookstore was crowded with customers. Bob Simpson took up his place at a table inside, with copies of the paperback edition of *When the Water Smokes* ready for autographing. On the front porch a counter had been fitted onto the bannister, and signs indicated where each author was to stand. Kaye Gibbons, Elizabeth Spencer, Jill McCorkle, Clyde Edgerton, and Larry Brown dutifully took up their stations and began signing their books as people brought copies up to them.

I did not. It was not a matter of modesty on my part—though as an author I had much to be modest about. It was rather that I wanted to be able to stand back and look at the whole spectacle—the crowds of people, the young novelists who because Algonquin Books existed were now well-known writers, the Algonquin staff and their families, all together there on the waterfront. After a while I walked back to where the boats were tied up, and let my son Bill, who was standing guard, go over to the autographing. I sat in the cockpit of the *Algonquin,* watching the stream of small craft as their owners came by to look at the three pennant-bedecked wooden boats, chatting with occasional onlookers up on the wharf, taking snapshots of the scene, absorbing the occasion—the sun and the breeze and the high sky and busy holiday waterfront. It wasn't so much that I was relaxed—I wasn't—as that my initial apprehension had given way to a kind of subdued anticipation. Later, when Bill returned, I took my camera and went back over to DeeGee's, where I photographed the goings-on.

For almost three hours the autograph party continued. Inside the store Bob Simpson, who as the local author of a book about the coastal area was the star of the show, inscribed book after book. A newspaper reporter interviewed the various authors. She asked me whether I thought the occasion was a success. "It certainly is," I told her. Why? she wanted to know. "Oh, we're selling lots of books," I said, for want of a better reply. As indeed we were—but what I did not tell her was that selling books was not the reason so much as the excuse for the party.

The run back to Peltier Creek was somewhat rougher than the outbound trip had been, both because we were moving against the wind and waves and because we were constantly being passed by boats large and small going in both directions, their wakes hitting us on either side and often simultaneously. Still, it was not really uncomfortable, and the *Algonquin* showed herself to be sea-kindly and stable as she moved along, several hundred yards behind *Sylvia II.* When we turned into the entrance channel to Peltier Creek and headed for the dock it was close to seven o'clock.

After tying up the *Algonquin* securely at Gillikin's Boat Basin, Bill and I headed over to the reception and picnic dinner at the home of the bookstore proprietors. Almost everybody else was already there. The children were playing croquet out in the side yard, the adults were standing and sitting around, drinking, eating, and talking. I found a large reclining wooden chair out on the porch, and sprawled in it. I began to realize that I was very tired. I had been going at full steam all day long, and the two preceding days as well. But it wasn't just fatigue. For most of that time I had been tensed up, anxious, apprehensive—and the anxiety and apprehension had built up as the time for the boat processional had drawn nearer. Once it became obvious that the *Algonquin*'s diesel engine was not going to conk out, and I was not going to put her on a sandbar, and everything was working out as I hoped, the trepidation had been replaced by excitement. It was not until the boat had been returned to her slip and her engine turned off that I had ceased trying to anticipate all possible developments.

Now it sank in on me that it was *over*. The Great Book-and-Boat Celebration had taken place. Like the young writers who had autographed their books at DeeGee's, the new boat had been launched. She had been brought over to Peltier Creek, and I had operated her successfully.

Next week Larry Myers would come and take her back to Harkers Island, where the engine would be lowered, a new transmission would be hooked up, and Clem Willis would install a set of trim tabs. While this was taking place I would be away on the West Coast on business. When I got back three weeks later I would run the *Algonquin* back to Peltier Creek, and begin building and installing screens, building a frame for the aft window so that it could be opened, moving the hatch-adjuster so that it no longer blocked egress from the cabin via the hatch, constructing a removable awning

---

for the stern cockpit, building fold-down cabin seats,
installing cabin fans and an automatic battery charger, and
doing the numerous other jobs large and small that
needed to be completed before my boat was fully
equipped and ready for use.

It was clear that the trip down the Waterway to
Charleston that I had originally planned to take in late
June would have to be put off. Not only did I want to
complete all the various projects, but I would need more
time to get to know my boat better. And although I
intended to make the trip eventually, it now seemed to
me that in order to complete the full-circle imaginative
journey I had planned when I first decided to have the
new boat built—from looking out at the river more than
fifty years ago to looking in toward the land—the actual
physical trip home might not be appropriate. The
important thing was that the *Algonquin* had come
through her initial test successfully—as, indeed, had I.
The time of waiting, and planning, and anticipating was
over. I could lie back in the chair and relax.

In an odd sort of way, the events of the weeks following
the Great Book-and-Boat Party seemed almost designed
to reenact, as if in order to rectify and so cancel out, the
memories of that dreadful summer of 1966, twenty-four
years earlier. It was not merely that, unlike the boat that

I had arranged to be built that year in Virginia, this boat *was* completed and delivered to me. In early June I also drove across the continent, just as I had done that earlier summer.

In order to get down to the Great Book-and-Boat Party I had been forced to rent a car, for mine was in the shop once again. A long-ago student of mine, the novelist Sylvia Wilkinson, who lived in California and was also a much-in-demand timer for sports-car races, had some connections with the research and development divisions of several Japanese car manufacturers. She was able to arrange for me to buy a 1987 Honda Accord sedan that had been driven only about eight thousand miles during three years. I had become disgusted with my three-year-old Buick station wagon, which, late in 1988, while still under warranty, had developed carburetor trouble. Sixteen trips to the repair shop had failed to fix the problem properly and permanently.

For years I had stuck with American automobiles, ignoring the telltale rows of black dots alongside our cars in *Consumer Reports* that signified "much worse than average" frequency-of-repair records, and the equally significant rows of red dots indicating "much better than average" performance for the imported cars. But the Buick's misbehavior was the culmination of a series of American-built cars—new and used, made not only by

General Motors but also Chrysler and Ford—that seemed
to produce progressively greater problems. The callousness
and idiocy of our long-spoiled domestic automobile
industry, and the hypocrisy of Detroit's efforts to
substitute flashy advertising for quality control, were too
much to take.

It so happened that the American Booksellers
Association convention, at which Algonquin Books had
an exhibit, took place in Las Vegas during the first week
of June. So when the convention was over I flew to Los
Angeles and picked up the new car. Before I left for
home, I spent a night in Pacific Palisades with a friend
from my college years, whom I had not seen since my
stay out there in 1964. We went out for dinner at a
restaurant overlooking a yacht harbor, so that once again
I found myself gazing at the Pacific Ocean and thinking
about a new boat a continent away—a boat, however,
that was built and delivered, not merely promised. The
cross-country drive this time involved no transmission
breakdowns or fruitless stops at unsympathetic Pontiac
dealers. My Japanese-made car cruised along smoothly,
and I listened to classical music on cassettes as I sped
down Interstate 40 across deserts, mountain ranges, and
plains at a steady seventy miles an hour.

And there was something else. My wife used to
joke about my decision to get involved in Algonquin

Books—in my late fifties and following three decades in an academic career—as being motivated by my wish to prove to my now dead parents that I could develop a viable business venture. If so, and I suspect there is some truth to it, then the conjunction of the autograph party featuring writers that I had published successfully, and the completion of the boat that *did* get built, must surely have been some kind of a symbolic corrective for what had happened twenty-four summers before.

For after all, the boat was named after the publishing house, and the publishing house had in turn been named for the ship that, long years ago, had borne my father home to Charleston following a business trip to New York City, and that my mother had taken us down to the beach at Sullivan's Island in the early dawn to watch arrive—the *Algonquin*.

The weekend after I got back from the West Coast I headed for Harkers Island. The new boat—trim tabs installed and her engine now mounted considerably lower in the hull and at markedly less of an angle—was ready to go. This time I would take her over to Peltier Creek by myself.

Operating solo, I headed out into Back Sound and turned up the Harkers Island waterfront, westward bound. There was plenty of water, so I pushed up the

RPMs and tried various angles with the trim tabs. She now ran smoothly and steadily, without any noticeable squatting. At 2,700 RPMs I figured that she was making her full displacement speed, and in no way straining to do so. So I eased the throttle back to 2,350 and we moved along at a comfortable cruising rate.

Sticking close to the channel markers, we threaded our way through the Middle Marshes, cut into the North River, then cruised along the narrow channel to another cut leading to Taylor Creek and the Beaufort waterfront. After a time we were swinging along the waterfront, past the clusters of sailboats and powerboats. Anchored out in the channel were the larger sailing craft, including not a few that were obviously rigged for blue water.

I could well imagine some of the sailboat people watching the *Algonquin* churn by, wondering just what kind of prosaic and plebeian soul would want to own such a craft, with her boxy profile, small cockpit, and dry exhaust. Well, let them wonder. She was mine, built to my specifications by a master boatbuilder, and she was now performing handsomely and even, I thought, a trifle jauntily. She would take me wherever I wanted to go in comfort and safety.

We swung past Radio Island, then turned into the Morehead City channel close to the harbor entrance. There was a brisk breeze blowing in off the open ocean, producing a decided swell. Numerous boats, small and large, were moving past, too, so that the water was well churned up. The *Algonquin* took it in stride, scarcely rocking as she handled whatever came her way. Never, of all the boats that I had owned, had I known one that was so steady. I will not say that her engine purred, because diesel engines don't purr, but it droned along without so much as a missed beat. She handled beautifully, satisfyingly responsive to the wheel as power cruisers roared past. She was going to be some boat, all right, and old Clem Willis was some boatbuilder.

Moving along at what I estimated was a steady eight miles an hour, she was quite fast enough for a retired university professor who was in no great hurry to get anywhere anymore, and who had spent the larger part of a lifetime wanting to do exactly what he was now doing.

12

SO SAID THE
WATER RAT

The *Algonquin* spent the next several months at Taylor
Boat Works rather than at her permanent berth at
Gillikin's Boat Basin up the west branch of Peltier Creek.
John McCallum said that he had plenty of room during
the summer months, and that I was welcome to leave her
there until I had completed all the work I planned to do.
I was quick to accept his offer, not only because the
facilities for working on her were better there but also
because I would have the benefit of his advice as I
proceeded. The *Mary Simpson* remained at Gillikin's,
unsold despite the FOR SALE sign and advertisements in
several newspapers. On each trip I made down to
Morehead City I stopped by to start and run her engine,
which was now performing perfectly. The paint in her
cockpit and along her coaming was in poor shape, so I
hired someone to touch her up. Prospective buyers came

by to look at her, but even though I lowered the asking price several times, there were no takers. Meanwhile she was costing me eighty dollars a month for slip rental. She was too large and heavy to be loaded onto a trailer, even if I had someplace to keep a trailer, and, being wooden-hulled, she was better off afloat so that her planks would not dry out and the seams open. Of all the various old boats that I had owned over the years, I had gotten the least use out of her; there could be no doubt of that. When I had needed her she had been out of commission, and now that she was running well she was superfluous. What I wanted to do now was to sell her and get rid of the monthly slip rental. Instead of naming her *Mary Simpson,* I should have christened her *Jonah.*

The *Algonquin,* however, was performing in first-class fashion. Except for a problem with an improperly attached twelve-volt connection—which drained her batteries one weekend when I had planned a fishing trip and had to be tracked down and remedied—she gave no trouble whatever. I had John McCallum remove the electric windlass from the *Mary Simpson* and install it on her bow, and I also put in a backup bilge pump and float switch.

I drove down to Morehead City every two weeks or so for overnight stays. Sometimes I took the *Algonquin* out for runs, and sometimes I merely stayed at the dock and worked aboard. The latter activity was baffling to my wife, who does not understand the ways of boat ownership. "Did you catch any fish?" she always asked when I returned home.

"No, I didn't go fishing."

"What were you doing, then?"

"Just working on the boat."

She would shake her head sadly. To drive so far in order to *not* go out on the boat was beyond her comprehension.

Kenneth Grahame and the Water Rat, however, would have understood. Of Grahame (1859–1932), author of *The Wind in the Willows,* I know only that he was a Scotsman, that for many years he was secretary to the Bank of England, and that he understood exactly why people own boats. *The Wind in the Willows* is what is known as a Children's Classic. Nobody thought to present me with a copy at Christmastime or for my birthday when I was a child, and I am sorry for it, because the opening pages of that book would surely have caused me to elevate it to the top shelf of my favorites, right next to *The Adventures of Tom Sawyer,* to be read and reread.

Readers familiar with *The Wind in the Willows* will recall that a certain Mole, after a morning of cleaning and refurbishing his underground home, goes out for a stroll in the sunshine, and comes upon the bank of a river. He has never seen such a thing until then. He strikes up an acquaintance with a Water Rat, who invites him to go rowing—or sculling, as the Rat puts it, for he is a British rodent. The Mole is much taken with the Rat's boat: "It was painted blue outside and white within, and was just the size for two animals; and the Mole's whole heart went out to it at once, even though he did not yet fully understand its uses."

They set off, and the Rat extols the joys of boating as follows: "Believe me, my young friend, there is *nothing*—absolutely nothing—half so much worth doing as simply messing about in boats." The remark has acquired a measure of fame, and it has been lettered onto a plaque now sold in boat-supply stores (along with others reading *O God thy sea is so great and my boat is so small* and *The Captain of this ship is authorized to perform marriages for the duration of the cruise* and other such inanities). But it is the Water Rat's next pronouncement that best speaks to Grahame's insight into the ways of boats and boat owners:

"In or out of 'em, it doesn't matter.
Nothing seems really to matter, that's the
charm of it. Whether you get away, or
whether you don't; whether you arrive at

your destination or whether you reach
somewhere else, or whether you never get
anywhere at all, you're always busy, and
you never do anything in particular; and
when you've done it there's always
something else to do, and you can do it if
you like, but you'd much better not."

There spoke my kind of boatman. On my trips
down to Peltier Creek and the *Algonquin* I measured,
sawed, hammered, drilled holes, installed screws and bolts,
strung wires, sanded, and painted. When thus occupied I
do not think about the problems of the publishing house
I operate, or the book or essay that I am currently
supposed to be writing, or the condition of the family
exchequer, or politics, or the situation in the Middle East,
or of anything else that is Important. I am totally
occupied with working on the boat. I contort my ageing
body into all manner of odd positions to get at what I
am doing. By the time I leave for home my back hurts
and my muscles ache, because my customary way of life
is sedentary in the extreme and I am Out of Shape. No
matter; I feel contented and at ease.

I am neither a skilled carpenter nor painter nor
electrician. I make mistakes constantly, and must start
over. In terms of dollars and cents what I accomplish

---

makes little sense. That I would be better off financially if I left all such projects to the boatyard and spent the time writing, at which I am more nearly skilled, goes without saying. The revenue from the magazine and newspaper pieces I could knock out in the same amount of time would cover most or all of the cost, even at the hourly rates that boatyards charge, and beyond question the work would be done far more neatly and capably. But logic, and fiscal responsibility, have no bearing on the case. What is involved is pleasure—the therapy, or tonic, of Messing About in Boats.

I proceed at my own pace. Nor am I averse, when the spirit moves, to laying down the tools, removing the accumulated impedimenta from the berth in the forward cabin, and enjoying an hour or so of napping. And if I become so wrapped up in the current project that I do not get around to taking the boat out that day, what of it? Again, if all this is puzzling, just check it out with the Water Rat. Or any other owner of a wooden boat.

Make no mistake. This is diversion, all the way. I enjoy it *because* it is not what I do for a living. If I were forced to perform physical labor on boats for a livelihood, and my day-by-day routine consisted of sawing, hammering, working with electric drills and sanders, and stripping and painting wooden surfaces, I would quickly grow tired of it, and yearn for the privilege of again earning my living while seated before a keyboard. For people like myself, boating and fishing are purely recreational activities. When not Messing About in Boats, which is most of the time, I am a workaholic: the writing, reading, and editing that I do are my chosen vocation. I work willingly, keep no nine-to-five hours, and make no distinction between weekdays and weekends.

I have never been seriously tempted by the thought of retiring to the coast so that I could maintain my boat on an uninterrupted basis and go fishing every day of the week. I have had friends who have done this, and for the most part they have not seemed to be notably happy. I know myself better than that.

In regard to anything having to do with the care and operation of boats, therefore, I am, and shall always remain, an amateur. But the root of the word is the Latin *amare,* to love, and what I love is Messing About in and with Boats. A new boat is an opportunity. I no sooner move to acquire a boat but I begin planning projects that I can do aboard her. I get out the boating catalogs—Boat/US, Defender Industries, Goldbergs', West Marine, E&B—to see what equipment is needed: additional lines, anchors, antennae, bilge pumps, cushions, navigation instruments, deck chairs, vents, fire extinguishers, fenders, rod holders, ladders, life jackets, lights, shock cords, switches, pillows, and so on. I measure walls, decks, spaces, windows. I plan carpentry. I get to work.

The first priority, once all the lines, safety equipment, and navigation instruments were installed on the *Algonquin,* was to do what was needed so that I could sleep aboard in peace. I had a mattress made for the berth, and bought several pillows and pillowcases. But staying aboard at night would be impossible without adequate ventilation and window screening to keep out the mosquitoes. Clem Willis, accustomed as he was to building workboats, had installed fixed windows at the stern of the main cabin, so that when the door was closed no breeze could blow through the cabin. I removed the pane from the starboard window, built one that could be swung open, and built and installed a removable screen; eventually I could slide in a portable air-conditioning unit.

The side windows of the main cabin were of the sliding type, so the open apertures had to be screened. Building the screens, however, was not a simple affair, because the space to be screened on each window was not rectangular, nor even a true parallelogram, but only approximately regular in shape—that is, there was sufficient irregularity so that none of the four sides was the same. Moreover, the apertures on either side were not

identical in shape or dimension, so that each frame had to
be constructed somewhat differently.

I measured the spaces and set to work building
the screens in my workshop at home; there is not much
work space on a small boat. The boards for the frames
had to have a half-inch lip into which the screening
material could be fitted, and molding affixed atop the
screen. My assumption was that I could purchase precut
lumber for framing, but this is the day of the aluminum
storm window, and lumber companies, in my part of the
country at least, no longer carry boards cut to
accommodate screening. I do not own and have never
used a router, so I had to have the boards shaped to
order.

To cut the angles so that they fitted neatly, I
needed a miter saw. Instead of buying one, I tried to do
the job with a ripsaw, and in the process made a mess of
things. Not only did the angles not fit together but
several times I ruined sections of boards by cutting the
angles in the wrong direction. I finally fit the boards
together, filled in the more unsightly gaps with plastic
wood, cut the screening to fit, tacked it into place, cut
and nailed in the strips of molding—and only then
remembered that the wood needed to be painted. Instead
of dismantling the frames and removing the screens, I
applied masking tape along the edges of the screens to

keep the paint from getting on them. Alas, it did not work; when I removed the tape there were white streaks all along the screening. Oh well.

I took the screens down to the boat. They did not fit. Either my original measurements, or my carpentry, was considerably off. It would be necessary to cut tapered strips of wood and place them along the sides. So I measured for these, took the screens home, cut the strips, and fastened them into place with glue and wood screws. On my next trip to the coast I tried the screens again—and found that I had managed to place the strips onto the wrong sides of the wrong screens.

I decided to start all over. This time I measured the open window spaces very carefully. At home I cut new frames—knowing my skill at such things I had ordered several times the number of boards needed—and fastened them. I also cut new sections of screening material and molding, this time painting the wood before attaching the screens and nailing the molding in place. When I brought these screens down to the boat they fitted, though still with some gaps. But a screen with even small gaps around it is not mosquito-proof. To get them to fit any more snugly was beyond my skills, however, so I conceded defeat, placed foam weather stripping over the remaining gaps, and resolved to figure out a better system later on.

* * *

Anyone who has ever spent a rainy summer night in the
cabin of a small boat knows how uncomfortable it can
get with the hatch cover down and the ports shut tight.
To enable me to leave the hatch partway open during a
storm, I built a hinged plywood square that would extend
beyond the cover far enough to keep the rain from
coming in. The easiest way to keep the mosquitoes out
would be to apply strips of Velcro to the edges of a
piece of mosquito netting and around the hatch molding.
But Velcro tends to pull loose, and moreover the
protruding hatch-adjuster would prevent a tight fit. So I
bought some netting, had sleeves sewn along the edges,
bought several dozen small egg-shaped lead sinkers, strung
and knotted them on lengths of cord, then pulled them
inside the sleeves. The netting could then be draped over
the hatch cover, with the lead sinkers holding it down
along the cabin top.

As for the ports, it is possible to get them with
rain shields; in the event of a really heavy rain blowing
in at an angle, however, the shields are ineffective,
because the protective lip does not extend sufficiently far
out. If it did, it would block the view. At a hardware
store I came upon some adjustable covers of thin plastic
which slanted out and down below the lower rim of the
port. They were intended for use on the metal window

frames of motor homes and house trailers, and there were magnets along the edges to hold them in place. I bought a couple, mounted them upon narrow plywood strips, and fastened them over two of the ports. So far as keeping the rain out was concerned, they worked nicely. What I failed to take into account was their vulnerability. It wasn't long before, engaged in fastening the spring lines after a day on the water, I leaned my weight against a cover and broke the thin plastic into several pieces.

In my workshop at home I happened to have several four-by-eight-foot sheets of heavy plexiglass, each a full three-eighths of an inch thick, left over from before aluminum storm windows were installed in our house. I sawed two six-by-fourteen-inch rectangles from the plexiglass for the tops and small triangular shapes for the sides, glued them together, reinforced the edges with strips of wood, and placed these over the ports. While these too could be broken by a sufficiently powerful blow, as covers they are far tougher than the thin plastic affairs they replaced, and any rain that manages to make its way past them into the open ports will have to be falling upward at the time.

With screened windows, hatch, and ports, and a couple of electric fans at work, it became possible to sleep aboard the *Algonquin*. Now I could concern myself with the amenities. To be able to sit out on the stern on hot

---

sunny days, I would need some kind of an awning. I intended eventually to have a vinyl canopy made to order, with flaps that could be rolled down when the sunlight was coming in at an angle. For the time being, however, I rigged up something with a polyester tarp and some PVC tubing. Two vertical lengths of pipe were fitted into the rod holders at the corners of the cockpit. To the top end of each I bolted another length of tubing horizontally across the cockpit. One edge of the tarp was fastened to the edge of the cabin top, and the tarp was pulled over the horizontal length of tubing and held in place with shock cords running down into the cockpit. I had put together similar rigs on previous boats; they work nicely, and can be assembled and disassembled in a matter of minutes, the tubing easily stored when not in use.

I had ordered and bolted together a pilot's chair for the *Algonquin,* but, as noted earlier, there was only so much floor space around the motor box in the main cabin, and the chair proved to be much too bulky. In addition, it tended to teeter whenever the *Algonquin* negotiated waves of much size. I could have bolted the chair to the deck, of course, but then it would be in the way at dockside. So I set out to design and build a pair of seats, one for each side, which when not in use would fold down against the cabin sides. I looked through half a

dozen boat-project books for a suitable model, but found
next to nothing on the subject. One old tome published
by *Motor Boating*—back when it was still written
"MoToR BoatinG," when small craft and automobiles
alike used six- rather than twelve-volt batteries, and
fiberglass had not reared its sleek and immensely practical
head—had a design for a pilot's chair that involved
building a seat on top of a length of two-inch metal pipe
mounted in a socket on the deck. Presumably one
unscrewed the chair from the pipe, then the pipe from
the socket, and stored them both when not in use. Not
only was the thing ugly and cumbersome, but the
thought of a length of two-inch steel pipe rolling around
on deck at two in the morning after not being stored
away properly, was daunting. The pilot's chairs featured
in the boating catalogs were all large, padded affairs,
which would defeat the purpose of providing more room
in the passageway. I wanted something that could fold
down out of the way when it wasn't being used.

At a boat store I found some seat brackets at a
reasonable price. I cut seats and backrests out of half-inch
plywood, installed them into the brackets with screws and
reinforced them with pieces of one-by-one-inch board,
then mounted the chairs atop the narrow sides of parallel
one-by-three-inch boards. The outside ends of the
one-by-threes were closed off by an additional piece of

---

one-by-three. The two parallel lengths extended well
beyond the edge of the seat and were also closed off with
additional pieces of board both above and below. This in
turn was hinged to a slab of inch-thick Douglas fir,
twelve inches wide and eight inches high, which was
bolted to the side of the cabin. The chair was supported
by a length of two-by-four, one end of which would fit
between the closed-off parallel boards underneath the seat;
the other end would wedge against the angle where the
deck and the cabin side joined. When not in use, the seat
would simply be lifted a little, the support removed, and
the seat would then be lowered down against the cabin
side, with the seatback folded in.

I built the seats at home, then took them down to
the boat, drilled holes in the cabin sides, and bolted the
twelve-by-eight-inch board into place. At this point I
discovered that I had mounted the hinges on top of rather
than underneath the closed ends of the parallel boards, so
that the chair folded upward instead of down, which
would not do at all. So I remounted the hinges
underneath, lifted up the seat, installed the two-by-four
support, and climbed into the seat to try it out.

I am not a lightweight; I usually weigh between
215 and 220 pounds. There was a ripping sound, and the
chair collapsed, with me in it. The slab of Douglas fir
had split horizontally at the bolts, right across the middle.

While I was surveying the wreckage, John McCallum came along. My mistake, he declared, was twofold: I had used a piece of light wood like fir, and I had mounted it with the grain running horizontally instead of vertically, so that it had quickly parted along the line of the bolts. I would have done much better, he said, to have made the slab out of half-inch laminated plywood, which could support far more weight.

So I took the seats back home, cut twelve-by-eight-inch pieces of plywood, and mounted the hinges on those. The following week I again bolted the chair to the cabin side, inserted the supporting piece of two-by-four, climbed into the seat, and it worked nicely. There was, however, a flaw. In order to be able to see out the forward window comfortably, I had mounted the seat so high that my feet could not reach the floor. With the pilot seat I had bought this had been no problem, for the chair had horizontal rungs joining and supporting the legs. Now there was nothing to place my feet upon except thin air.

It was necessary, therefore, to build a footrest and attach it to the front of the control console at the proper height. For good measure I also nailed a couple of short lengths of two-by-four onto the cabin floor up against the side, into which the nether end of the supporting two-by-four could fit and thus be prevented from sliding out during rough weather and depositing me on the floor.

* * *

One of the problems with a twenty-four-foot "pocket cruiser" like the *Algonquin,* for all that the outside deck area had been sacrificed to roominess within, was storage space. Among the items that had to be put away where they would not slide around during a rough passage were life jackets, foul-weather gear, tools, fishing tackle, clothes, bed linens, cushions, blankets and towels, electric fans, a heater, electrical equipment and power cables, paint cans and paintbrushes, a case of engine oil, several bottles of transmission fluid, window screens, the folding plywood cover for the hatch, lines, groceries, tableware, flares, a set of spare battery-operated running lights, cleaning equipment, charts, books, binoculars, a first-aid kit, a six-gallon can of spare water and another of diesel fuel, a spotlight, a collapsible swimming ladder, the PVC tubes and tarpaulin for the canopy, a canvas suitcase, a camera and flashgun, and assorted other objects.

It was necessary not only to find a place to store such things but also to group them together in some kind of coherent and accessible way, so that in an emergency what was needed could be located without delay and confusion. When an additional dockline is needed, or a suit of foul-weather clothes, or a toolbox, or a chart, it is needed at once, then and there. So things have to be stored away in accordance with some system—tools and flares in this locker, clothes and raingear in that, rope here, charts, documents, and navigational equipment there, and so on. That, at least, is the theory. In practice the system usually gets out of hand after a few weeks.

Because of the presence of the engine box in the center of the main cabin, there was little room for cabinets or shelving there. Just about everything would have to be fitted into the forward cabin. The area up under the bow, above the fresh-water tank, served to house the lines of two anchors, which were led down into it through deck pipes. There was an area perhaps four feet wide, a foot long, and four feet deep between the forward end of the single portside berth and the counter along the starboard side, into which the spare fuel and water cans, the screens, and several life jackets could be jammed. Other than that, the only space available was beneath the berth and the counter. Clem Willis had fronted these with plywood and cut several openings for access. Not only was the available room there limited but the openings were too small, and when I needed something I found myself groping blindly under the berth, trying to identify what I was looking for by touch alone. So I enlarged the openings with a saber saw and mounted plywood doors outside; the doors were hinged so they would open downward. I also nailed boards inside to divide the space into separate compartments.

Although the storage area below the counter on

the starboard side was higher than that under the berth, it was also considerably more truncated because of the enclosed head just inside the cabin. Moreover, because the single berth had been built for comfort, it was quite wide, and it took up more space than a normal half-V-berth would have done, with the result that the counter narrowed considerably toward the bow.

Roughly a fourth of the countertop—the portion nearest the wall of the enclosed head—was occupied by a recessed sink, which took up space below and from which a two-inch-wide drainpipe led downward and back to a through-hull fitting. The area under the narrowed forward portion of the counter was not very accessible, because no opening had been cut in the plywood side. That area could be gotten to only by getting down on one's knees and reaching into it from beneath the sink. It would be the logical place to install an icebox, but that could wait until I was ready to set out on an extended trip. For now a portable Igloo cooler in the main cabin would suffice.

Where in the world was all the stuff that couldn't be stored under the berth or counter going to go? The only solution would be to mount several cabinets against the cabin sides and under the roof, in the space above the berth and the counter. After all, the only area where I needed to have full standing room was along the center line of the cabin. At the same time it would not do to block off the light or the breeze from the ports, so cabinets and shelving could be fitted only into certain places.

Building plywood cabinets that were sufficiently sturdy would be difficult enough under any circumstances, but my task was complicated considerably by the fact that I would not be able simply to put together even-sided wooden boxes, with doors in front and shelves within, and attach them to the cabin wall. For the cabin sides were not flat, but curved inward and downward to conform to the narrowing bow of the boat. In addition, there were curving ribs at intervals along them, and arching cross-members overhead to reinforce the deck and cabin roof. Any cabinets I might build, therefore, would have to taper inward at several places and have notches cut into the top and back.

It was a job, really, for an experienced cabinetmaker, not for a heavy-handed book publisher and retired university professor in no way noted for his prowess with tools. But the cost of having a boat-carpenter design and build the cabinets to fit into the odd-shaped places where I wanted them to go would be prohibitively high. If I were to have additional storage space, therefore, I would have to build the cabinets myself.

I decided to make two cabinets, both of them to
fit between and be anchored to ribs on the cabin sides.
One, for groceries and the like, would go above and
behind the sink. It would be small—just enough to fit
into the available space. There would be a shelf inside it,
halfway up, and underneath it I would build racks for
dishes and smaller cooking implements. The other cabinet
would be larger, with a front that hinged so that it
opened downward, and that space would hold linens,
blankets, and clothes.

From my experience with making the screens for
the main cabin I knew better than to try to measure the
curves and angles involved in fitting the cabinets snugly
against the cabin sides, and then attempt to cut plywood
to shape in my workshop at home. Instead, I built the
cabinets in my workshop, extending their plywood sides
several inches beyond the desired size. Then I took them
down to the boat, held them up against the cabin sides,
and by trial and error notched and contoured them with
a saber saw until they fitted with reasonable snugness.
Any gaps resulting would be covered over with strips of
three-eighths-inch plywood cut to fit.

Building the two cabinets involved the usual
errors, such as cutting the plywood for the larger
cabinet-front across rather than with the grain, promptly
causing it to warp; affixing the catches for the cabinet

doors on top of instead of beneath the shelf; and so on. To my considerable surprise, however, when completed and taken down to the boat, both cabinets fit into the spaces where I meant for them to go, and could be edged and patched reasonably tightly, as planned. For good measure I built several more shelves for the forward cabin and head, cut out rod racks from plywood and mounted them overhead in the main cabin, built a box for the binoculars, added a bookrack below the linen cabinet, installed assorted clothes hooks here and there, and replaced the bare-bulbed porcelain 110-volt light sockets that Clem Willis had installed with shaded brass fixtures.

It was obvious that the cabins would need some movement of air to keep mildew down to manageable proportions, so I ordered a solar-powered vent fan, cut a hole in the roof of the forward cabin, and installed it. At the stern end of the main cabin, above the motor box and battery compartment, I cut a rectangular space and installed a louvered vent, which could stay open when the *Algonquin* was not in use. Around the vent I built a rack, into which a small mosquito-net screen could be inserted at night during the summer, and a slab of plexiglass in cold weather when I was aboard.

No one, seeing all these cabinets, screens, shelves, and vents, would ever mistake the builder thereof for a Hepplewhite or Sheraton, or even for a reasonably skilled

---

boat-carpenter. Not only was my woodworking technique on the crude side but the equipment available to me was limited. A generous use of plastic wood and several coats of paint or stain, however, can cover over a multitude of gouges, false starts, uneven surfaces, irregular seams, plugs, stripped-in inlays, and the like.

There was one project that I tried to carry out, failed, and had to get help. It had to do with the engine box, and the eighty-two horsepower Mazda diesel it hid from sight. When Clem Willis lowered the engine, he had reduced the size of the box, but, though the engine no longer vibrated so badly, it was still extremely noisy. I knew that diesel engines ran more loudly than gasoline engines, but I had not realized just how much so. On the only other boat with a diesel engine that I had owned, the *Bill James,* the ancient 3-71 engine and engine box were located outside the main cabin on the open deck. There was no such outside space available on the *Algonquin,* however, and the engine and box had to go in the main cabin.

The resulting din was awesome. When the engine was running it was impossible to hold a conversation. More than that, it was potentially dangerous, for along with my partial deafness it meant that I could not hear what was being said over Channel 16. Were the Coast

Guard to announce, for example, that a tornado was making its way up the coast and all boats in the area should seek shelter at once, or that an Iraqi submarine was currently engaged in shelling the Morehead City harbor, I would never know it.

I drove over to a building-material store in search of soundproofing material, but all I could find were some polystyrene foam slabs. I asked a clerk whether these might do the job, and was assured that numerous local watermen used them for just that purpose. So I purchased several packages, along with some copper roofing-tacks, and spent an afternoon cutting and fitting the slabs into the inside of the motor box. It was a messy business; the polystyrene tended to disintegrate into hundreds of little bubbles, which got into everything and had to be vacuumed up to prevent the bilge pumps from being clogged. When finally I got everything into place and turned on the engine, I could detect no difference whatever in the decibel level.

I ordered some more soundproofing material, of the best quality I could find listed, from a mail-order boat-supply company. When it arrived and I read the instructions I was chagrined. It would not be a matter of merely cutting it to fit and tacking it into place; the stuff had to be glued, fastened, and sealed. The result, at my hands, was likely to be appalling, and unless done properly the stuff would probably be dropping off all the time. So I asked John McCallum to have it installed for me. Thus, despite the pleasures of Messing About in Boats, I left that particular job to the experts. Besides, I had more than enough to do to keep me occupied as it was.

Slowly and steadily, the *Algonquin* was becoming not only a boat built to my specifications but *my* boat. I was also getting the hang of how to operate her properly. I had to learn, for example, how to use the trim tabs. My assumption had been that the purpose for which they were devised was to get the bow farther up in the air, by digging into the water. This was, to put it bluntly, thoroughgoing asininity, inasmuch as the trim tabs had been installed specifically to prevent the stern from squatting—digging in and raising the bow. After a day in which Bob Simpson's brother Bill and I shoved the *Algonquin* against an incoming tide up the Waterway to get out into the ocean and fish offshore, then did the same against an ebbing tide on the way back, at a speed over the bottom of no more than four miles an hour, I was forced to reexamine my premises—that is, to read the trim-tab instruction pamphlet carefully. Only then did it dawn on me that the purpose of the tabs was to get the bow *down*. Lowering the fins caused the water to shove the *stern* up, thereby presenting more wetted surface and permitting greater speed. The tabs should thus be level when going with the tide, to permit better control of the rudder, and extended down when bucking it. I tried it that way on my next run, and the improvement in my boat's performance was gratifying. She broke no speed records—she was built to run slowly and steadily—but now she made her way sturdily against the tide.

I was impressed with how nicely the *Algonquin* handled. Backing her into a slip could be managed with a minimum of trouble; her transmission worked smoothly and decisively, and because of her weight and wide beam she responded to the wheel neither too rapidly nor too sluggishly. I could edge her bow slowly up alongside a dock, then throw her into reverse, give her a quick burst of power, and she would come to a halt only inches away. For all her boxlike design and abundance of exposed surfaces, she was not blown about easily by the wind. By using the rudder and power properly I could turn her within a very small radius. Indeed, though having only a single screw she was every bit as easy to maneuver as my old twin-engined, twin-screw Chris-Craft of years back, the *Little Eva*. And she used far less fuel.

My boat was a Success. She was built well. She could do what I wanted her to do. I had yet to take her on any extended trips, of course, or concentrate on some serious fishing. And, now that cold weather was coming on, the chances were that for some months to come I'd not be using the *Algonquin* for anything more than occasional tours of the harbor area or, on days when it was warm enough, a little fishing. But what was comforting, and mattered so much, was the knowledge that I *could* make excursions large and small, if and when I wanted to.

That conviction, and the pleasure and diversion of being able to leave my duties at home behind me and drive down to Peltier Creek and work aboard her as and when I wished, was what I wanted in a boat. "Whether you get away, or whether you don't; whether you arrive at your destination or whether you reach somewhere else, or whether you never get anywhere at all, you're always busy, and you never do anything in particular; and when you've done it there's always something else to do, and you can do it if you like, but you'd much better not." So said the Water Rat. So too say I.

Now, if I could just find a purchaser for the *Mary Simpson.* . . .

13

WANING OF THE
SEASON

In the two Carolinas and Virginia, where I have spent
almost all my life, the best days come in the fall. Frigid
Canadian air may drift down for brief visits in
November, and occasionally there will be a snowfall in
the foothills and mountains, but, from early October
onward, on most days the temperature is in the sixties
and seventies during the morning and afternoon, and dips
into the forties and fifties at night. The sun is almost
always shining, the winds are light, and the sky is a high
cerulean blue. In the piedmont, leaves spin down from
the trees in reds, yellows, and browns and cover the
ground. Although the panorama is not as spectacular as in
the mountains, it is equally intense. Not until December
have most of the leaves fallen from the trees and turned a
uniform drab along the ground. Our neighbors are
assiduous in heaping them into piles to be carted off so
that their bright green winter lawns will be visible. At

our house we tend to be less energetic about it; we like
the thick carpets of leaves under the oak trees in our
yard, and prefer to let them stay until the winter winds
drive them away. Our lawn suffers accordingly, to be
sure, but we manage somehow to bear up under the
ordeal.

Along the coast the colors are less dramatic; the
marsh grass stays green until late in the season, and there
is more brown and ochre to the foliage, and less red and
gold. Somewhere about the scene there is always some
green. The water reflects the high sky and the
fair-weather cumulus. There is only the trace of an edge
to the breeze, not so cutting as to cause discomfort. The
shimmer and heft of the hot weather is gone, the
atmosphere is clear and clean, and it is possible to see for
miles across the water. The South Carolina poet Henry
Timrod, looking seaward from Charleston in 1862 in
expectation of an attack from Admiral DuPont's Union
flotilla, noted the way that the Indian Summer held on:

> *But still, along yon dim Atlantic line,*
> *The only hostile smoke*
> *Creeps like a harmless mist above the brine,*
> *From some frail, floating oak.*

It is a phenomenon of reed grass that it is at its
deepest green in the early fall of the year, after the trees

have already begun to shed their leaves. Not until close
to winter will the green of the marshland give way to
brown and then to gray. When growth resumes in the
spring the green will begin to creep up from below, and
as the summer comes on the drabness will give way to
green higher and higher along each stalk and blade, until
by late June only the tips will remain dun. By late July
the gray will be gone entirely, and everything will stay
green until close to wintertime.

Peltier Creek, where the *Algonquin* is berthed, is a
quiet place in the late fall. There is no longer the steady
processional of boats streaming past which is common on
summer weekends. Most of the power cruisers and
sailboats docked along the shore seem to go unused. The
forklifts at the several dry-storage marinas only
occasionally are called upon to extract runabouts from the
tiers of boats and lower them down into the water,
where they can go roaring off toward the entrance to the
creek and out into Bogue Sound.

The "creek" isn't really a creek at all so much as
a protected bay, a small lake almost entirely landlocked
except for a narrow entrance from the sound at the south,
which opens into an area several hundred yards across and
perhaps twice that in length. At the head of the creek
several arms branch out east and west, and it is along
these that most of the boats are berthed.

Although Peltier Creek is populated principally

---

by local boats, as a protected anchorage for craft bound
up and down the Intracoastal Waterway it is unexcelled.
There is six feet and more of water throughout, and the
entrance is so sharply angled that from no point inside,
away from the entrance itself, can one actually see out
into the sound. Only in the event of a full-fledged
hurricane would a boat moored in the creek be
endangered. Thus all year long, but especially in the late
spring and early fall, a number of sailboats are to be
found anchored out in the creek or tied up at docks
along its banks. Seagoing sloops and ketches, easily
identified by the self-steering apparatus at the stern, the
mass of impedimenta secured fore and aft, and the
laundry hung out to dry along the deck, mingle with the
resident sportsfishermen, cruisers, and day-sailers. The
transients put in for overnight stays or for longer visits;
there are no fees for anchoring, and the size of the visitor
is limited only by the four-and-a-half-foot mean
low-water depth of the entrance. Even then, a wait
outside until high tide will enable boats of deeper draft
to enter and depart. Once inside, there is abundant room
to swing an anchor, and it is no more than a few
hundred yards by dinghy to one of the marinas along the
northern edge. Peltier is also an excellent place to have
repairs done; not only John McCallum's Taylor Boat
Works but several other installations are available.

Two days after Thanksgiving I drove down to

Morehead, and with the help of my friend Bob Simpson moved *Algonquin* from the dock at Taylor Boat Works, near the tip of the eastern extremity of the creek, to her permanent berth at Gillikin's Boat Basin on the western branch. Bob's role was to ferry me back from Gillikin's in his van to where I had left my car at Taylor's, a distance of no more than a half mile. I hated to leave the slip at Taylor's, where the *Algonquin* had spent the summer, partly because John McCallum was always there to keep an eye on my boat and perform any repair or installation work needed. Also, however, there was always more activity at that end of the creek, where a marina and several boatyards are located, than at Gillikin's, which was at the end of a narrow arm of water. But John had told me that during the winter and early spring months he would be using every bit of his dock space, because there would be one boat after another brought in for hauling and painting. Gillikin's had the advantage, too, of being almost completely sheltered from storms; across the water from the dock was a bluff with numerous trees. In fact, when a blow seemed imminent, that arm of the creek was a favorite hurricane hole.

I tied up *Algonquin* next to the *Mary Simpson,* which remained unsold even though I had been running advertisements in newspapers all summer and fall long. I had started out asking $5,500 and had steadily lowered the asking price until now it was $2,700—$300 less than I had paid for her, not counting the $2,750 it had cost to have her engine replaced and another block rebored, resleeved, and rebuilt. The old Luhrs lapstrake Sea-Skiff was now in perfect running order, the engine had less than four hours running time on it, yet I could find no takers. Since her bottom had not been painted for more than a year, I had had John McCallum haul her out, scrape her, and apply fresh paint. Now all I could do was to keep placing classified advertisements in newspapers, and hope that a buyer would come along.

The next morning my intention was to go fishing. *Algonquin*'s rebuilt diesel roared into action at once, and I cast off the lines, edged out into the creek, and headed for the entrance. It was another beautiful day, sunny and crisp. There was no activity in the creek. Near the entrance Bob Simpson's *Sylvia II* lay at her dock, handsome as ever. Bob and Mary were off on a canoeing expedition. The weather forecast had called for light airs only, but when I negotiated the narrow entrance and proceeded out onto Bogue Sound the wind was blowing from the southwest at a brisk rate against the incoming tide, and there were low whitecaps on the waves.

The Waterway, which on Sunday mornings in the summer and early fall was always heavily traveled, was largely free of other boats. I swung past the entrance marker, turned east, and headed up the sound toward the harbor. Across the tidal flats to the south lay the low outlines of the houses and trees of the barrier island that was Bogue Banks. The likelihood was that the streets were all but deserted now and most of the summer homes boarded up for the forthcoming winter. I was glad I was not there to see; few places seem more forlorn and melancholy than an oceanside resort after the summer season is over and the crowds have gone home. All the life is missing, and only the tasteless tawdriness of beachfront architecture remains, bare, faded, and windswept.

The sound, by contrast, was as inviting as ever in appearance. The absence of motorboats, water-skiers, fishermen, waterscooters, and other craft, far from causing the scene to seem deserted, offered the pleasant feeling that one had the water to oneself. The movement of the waves, and the flash and play of the sunlight on the water, are all the activity needed. On a cold, gray, windy day it would doubtless be less attractive, but as it was, to be there at the wheel of one's boat, moving along steadily and holding her on course while the wind from off the stern strove to shove her about, was a satisfying experience.

A half-dozen boats were anchored under the tall spans of the bridge across Bogue Sound that links

---

Atlantic Beach and Fort Macon with the mainland, and just east of the bridge were several dozen more. This was obviously where the fish were stationed that day. The question was, what kind of fish? I tried to keep my binoculars focussed and trained on the activity, while also holding the *Algonquin* pointed along the channel. If the people in the boats were casting and retrieving, that meant sea trout, or possibly blues; if they were bottom-fishing, the quarry was almost certainly Norfolk spot. I am far from turning up my nose at the latter; a plump nine-or-ten-inch-long spot, fried so that the moisture of the flesh is retained yet free of soupiness, is as sweet a panfish as ever God gave mankind dominion over. But the bait that attracts Norfolk spot best is bloodworms, and I had brought none along—had brought, indeed, no organic bait of any kind. Sea trout, whether speckled or yellow-fin, are amenable to green plastic bucktails attached to a leadhead jig, while blues, if present at all, will strike at almost anything placed in their way, but especially at a Hopkins jig with a bit of red or white feather on it.

It was soon clear that it was spot that the fisherfolk were after that morning; the fish were being hauled in two at a time. Were trout also present? I did see some people who seemed to be casting and retrieving lures rather than waiting for bites. When I got right down to it, however, I didn't really wish to anchor there by the bridge and fish, a mere three miles from Peltier Creek. For one thing, it might be a trifle breezy; those fishing seemed to be wearing windbreakers over sweaters. But the true reason was that I wanted to cruise on my boat while I could still enjoy a day out on the water in reasonable comfort. As far as I was concerned, she was still an end in herself, not a means to catch fish or to get somewhere. Perhaps after I had owned and sailed the *Algonquin* for a year or so the experience of simply being aboard her, guiding her, moving her along the water would become more nearly routine, and I would place more importance upon what I could do and where I might go with her. For now, however, the pleasure of operating the *Algonquin* was quite adequate by itself. So instead of anchoring and fishing there at the bridge where the fish were, I would continue on out to the harbor, in the hope that the blues were running and the gulls working above them. What the hell, it was *my* boat, wasn't it?

I steered eastward along the Waterway, passed by the Morehead waterfront channel, and moved alongside the State Ports Authority docks. Bucket cranes were removing what appeared to be some kind of ore from the holds of a small, blue-hulled cargo ship with Cyrillic lettering across her stern. I reached the turning basin and

---

headed for the harbor entrance a mile away. So far as I could see there was only one other boat on the scene; even the customary contingent of fishermen anchored along the shoreline and bottom-fishing was missing. Along the eastern edge, on Radio Island, some persons were fishing from the shore.

Out toward the harbor mouth there was some gull activity, but not the frantic circling and diving that would signify the presence of active schools of feeding blues. The gulls seemed to be hovering and skimming over a wider area, which might be an indication that blues had been feeding but were now running deep and looking for more schools of small fish. On the other hand, it might merely mean nothing more than that a few small fish were in the vicinity. Certainly the gulls didn't appear to be enjoying any particular success at their chosen profession.

As I drew near Fort Macon and the Coast Guard installation, the boat that had been located out there off the beach turned toward the inner harbor and moved past the *Algonquin*. She was a sportsfisherman, with outriggers, and if those aboard had been fishing, they had apparently thought better of it. I looked along the inner edge of Shackleford Banks, to see what was going on at the deep hole a mile or so eastward. Not a single boat was in evidence. There were *always* boats anchored there; if blues were anywhere in the harbor, they could be counted on to congregate in the deeper water near the buoy there.

Oh well. I thought about going outside into the ocean, but with no barrier island to screen the brisk southwest wind, the water there looked to be decidedly choppy. If there had been any gull activity I might have tried it even so, despite the absence of any other boats, but I could not see so much as a single bird. There was no point in getting the *Algonquin* so completely doused with salt spray that I would have to give her not merely a hosing down but an extensive washing and mopping when we returned to her berth on Peltier Creek.

I decided to move over to the area just inside the harbor mouth where the gulls were hovering and to cast while drifting. Maybe the dozen or so hovering and dipping gulls did know something, and there were blues running deep. I cut the throttle, placed the gear in neutral, extracted a spinning rod and reel from the overhead rack, and took a seat out in the stern to rig up. What I should have done was to have prepared everything while still at the dock. Threading monofilament through the guide rings of a six-foot casting rod, extracting lures from a tackle box, tying improved blood knots, attaching lures, and so forth while a twenty-four-foot boat is pitching and tossing about in the swiftly moving current of a harbor mouth, is not handily managed. By the time everything was in order and I was ready to begin casting, the *Algonquin* was drifting decisively toward shoal water on the eastern side of the channel buoy, so I had to put down the rig and return to the controls. I moved her back across the channel, close in to the Fort Macon shore, then returned to the stern. By then most of the gulls that had been moving about had departed for parts unknown, and the few that remained settled down to float on the surface of the water. It occurred to me that perhaps they were watching to see whether *I* knew something that *they* didn't. Poor, deluded creatures they were, if so.

I devoted half an hour or so to the diffident casting of Hopkins jigs, green bucktails, and plugs, both large and small, working them at various water depths, retrieving them at assorted speeds. During that period I managed to haul in one—*one*—leaf of kelp grass. Well, damn it, I had discharged my duty as a fisherman; now I was going to run my boat some more. The plugs were replaced in the tackle box, the rod and reel in the overhead rack, and the *Algonquin* placed in gear again and her bow pointed harborward. Instead of returning toward Morehead City, however, I swung toward the starboard side of the channel, toward Beaufort. I rounded the buoy off Radio Island, and headed along the eastern shoreline of that diamond-shaped island, which divides the harbor into Morehead City and Beaufort channels.

The Beaufort waterfront along Front Street was

as usual crowded with small craft, largely sailboats, and there were several dozen or more of them anchored out in Taylor Creek. Although considerably fewer visitors were in view along the docks than on summertime weekends, the place still possessed all the appurtenances of a tourist mecca—small shops with quaint signboards, flags and pennants on mast-style flagpoles, gabled and shingled roofs, wooden buildings painted lemon-yellow or ultramarine blue with white trim, and several large sailing schooners at the public docks with ostentatious bric-a-brac and ropework and harbor-tour signs.

The remarkable thing was that the quaint atmosphere had been established here largely within the past fifteen years or so. Until then, the waterfront had offered no more than the usual deteriorating frontage of a commercial fishing town come upon hard times, with the expected rotting pilings, swayback planking, dilapidated fishing shacks, and moldy-green-planked warehouses that accompany such a decline. Only after every bit of the once-active waterborne commerce and much of the commercial fishing had vanished in the wake of improved highway transport and long-distance refrigeration techniques did it begin to occur to the state tourist industry and the local authorities in North Carolina towns such as Beaufort, Elizabeth City on the Pasquotank River, Edenton on Albemarle Sound, and, on the Pamlico

River, the communities of Bath and "Little Washington" (so called to distinguish it from the Larger, Johnny-come-lately installation on the Potomac River) that inland-dwelling landlubbers would travel for considerable distances to visit harbors and look at watercraft.

With block after block of colonial and early federal dwellings lining its tree-shaded streets, Beaufort was particularly well endowed for the housing and feeding of tourists. Moreover, its location, at the point where the Intracoastal Waterway turns sharply southwestward along the coast after its lengthy inland traverse down from the Chesapeake Bay, made it an ideal jumping-off point for tropic-bound sailboats, whose skippers could thus avoid having to battle the powerful current of the Gulf Stream in order to keep away from the protruding and dangerous shoals of Cape Hatteras. Not only the spectacle of dozens of such bluewater craft, but the ubiquitous presence ashore of numerous unshaven and uncombed bluewater mariners, attired in colorful Henri Lloyd and Patagonia foul-weather garb and carefully haberdashed and coutured, provided a nautical atmosphere that was the more commercially valuable for being free of charge. All that was needed was some waterfront remodeling and refurbishment—the tearing down of structures too far gone in desuetude to be made safe and usable, the building of waterside parks and

---

parking lots, and the installation of public dockage. Thereafter private enterprise could and did take over in high style.

I took *Algonquin* up the creek a mile or so, beyond the moored sailboats and the business district and along Front Street with its once-dilapidated but now handsomely groomed residences. In the early 1970s a writer friend of mine, Max Steele, whose eye for real estate is at least as good as his eye for fictional scene-setting, bought one of these residences for eleven thousand dollars, dock and all, and it was sold a year ago for twenty times that. What would happen if a full-fledged hurricane, style of Hugo, decided to come ashore in the area would be fearsome to contemplate; between Front Street and the open ocean the sole impediment to the full force of wind, water, and tidal surge would be a low-lying sandbank and marsh just beyond Taylor Creek, and the somewhat wider but entirely treeless dunes of Shackleford Banks two miles to the south. But until and unless that dismal event occurs, it is prime property.

Think of being able to tie up one's sailboat or cruiser directly in front of one's house, with the mouth of the harbor and the open ocean only a few miles distant! Well-heeled northeastern citizens possessing yachts, I am told, snap up Front Street homes as they

come on the market, sight unseen; all they ask is a
photograph. And why did I not buy a house on Front
Street as my friend did? Because I did not have eleven
thousand dollars, because I had neither nerve nor
intelligence enough to think to borrow it, and because
where money is concerned God did not see fit to endow
me with the perspicuity that He gave to the mud
minnow.

I came back along the waterfront, enjoying the
air and sunlight. I considered returning to Morehead City
and the Waterway via Town Creek, behind Beaufort,
having a look en route at the fancy new marina there and
perhaps dropping off a commemorative buoy near the
spot where Bob Simpson and I had put the *Virginius*
aground the previous winter. But since I had not yet
gotten around to measuring the height of the *Algonquin*
from waterline to tip of mast, I could not be certain that
she would pass beneath the Highway 70 bascule bridge,
which according to the harbor chart provided for eleven
feet of clearance at mean low-water. It did not seem right
to cause the bridgetender to open the span just for me,
and thus back up motor traffic for a half mile in either
direction, when I could just as easily go back the way I
had come. So I steered *Algonquin* back around Radio
Island again and into the harbor, then northward toward
the Waterway.

It was after one o'clock, and there was still ample time for a tour of the Morehead City waterfront before I headed back to Peltier Creek. The difference, both in style and function, between the two neighboring waterfronts, separated as they are by the Newport River and Radio Island, is remarkable. Although someone had now built a high-rise condominium between the downtown harbor and the Ports Authority terminals along the Newport River and fronting the turning basin, so that there was now a respectable collection of sailboats there, too, nothing is very glamorous about Morehead City. Not only is it of less antiquity than Beaufort, but it is basically utilitarian and plebeian in nature. Between the various waterfront restaurants and seafood companies were dozens of charter boats, docked stern-in. Many were of Harkers Island construction, with the characteristic flared bows. These were not picturesque sailboats but fishing machines with powerful engines and wide cockpits, designed to speed their customers fifty miles out to the Gulf Stream, troll for pelagically inclined fish all morning and early afternoon, then speed them back again by mid-afternoon. There were also a number of shrimp trawlers, several harbor pilot boats, and other working craft in view. As for the restaurants, no picturesque little havens here, but shore-dinner houses catering to large crowds. Nor were there any little public parks along the waterfront. The scenic view plays almost no part in

Morehead City's economy, and the buildings along the water were not restored, for they had not been allowed to become dilapidated.

In the summer the Morehead waterfront is always crowded. As the charter boats and head boats arrive home from the Gulf Stream and Continental Shelf in late afternoon, the results are very much on display, as those who landed dolphin, bonita, and snapper pose for photographs alongside their catches. Parking lots are crammed with automobiles. The oddly named Sanitary Restaurant, which dates back to the mid-1940s, is the oldest and most popular of the available eateries; it features an abundance of freshly caught seafood, caters to a family clientele, and serves no alcoholic beverages of any kind. The food is plentiful, prepared tastefully but with nothing of the gourmet about it, is very reasonably priced, and the guests are seated and fed with rapidity. On summer weekends in particular the line of waiting customers stretches well along the sidewalk; indeed, nearby restaurants owe no small part of their prosperity to the overflow of would-be diners from the Sanitary who chose not to stand in line for an hour or so before being assigned a table. DeeGee's Books and Gifts, across the street, offers an abundance of souvenirs and an assortment of books, including any title having remotely to do with the area.

There is no pretentiousness about Morehead City;

---

it is functional all the way. The place has neither scenic district nor historical aura; it is only and self-sufficiently a small working seaport, with railroad tracks running along the middle of the main street. The assumptions of my middle-class origins responded comfortably as I steered my boxy little cabin launch with her workboat hull up the channel, her name and home port lettered prominently on the wide stern:

ALGONQUIN

Morehead City

Meanwhile the wind had picked up, and now as my boat proceeded steadily toward Peltier Creek the spray from the waves was being lifted up and hurled against the cabin windows, so that the windshield wiper saw steady duty. Near the buoy marking the western junction of the waterfront channel and the Intracoastal Waterway I passed a sloop proceeding under power, her skipper and his lady attempting to hold the folds of what was obviously a Waterway chart sufficiently still in the breeze to read from it. The sloop was a bluewater craft, twenty-nine or thirty feet in length, with steering vane, storm stay, baggywrinkles, ratlines, jerry cans lashed to the lifelines, spare anchors lashed to the pulpit, halyards

___

leading from the mast to the cockpit, a Charlie Noble atop the cabin, and so on. I looked back, saw them head into the waterfront channel, then execute a sharp turn and return to the Waterway, where they fell into line westward several hundred yards behind me. They were no doubt looking for the entrance to Peltier Creek, or perhaps Spooner Creek further down the channel, and had overshot their objective. I reached for the VHF microphone: "Calling the sailboat at Marker Number 4," I said. "Are you looking for something?" No answer. I tried again; still no reply. Either their radio wasn't on or else they didn't care to admit they were lost. In any event they were in no danger; it was early afternoon, with several hours of daylight remaining.

Moments later the sailboat made another 180° turn and headed eastward. Perhaps they were searching for Morehead or Beaufort after all. I continued on my way, then looked back after a few minutes, only to see them in the process of reversing directions yet another time. I decided to give the radio another try. "Calling the blue-and-white sailboat near the Morehead City channel entrance!"

After a moment the reply came. "This is the blue-and-white sailboat," a female voice responded.

"Are you looking for something?"

"Yes, we're looking for Pell-le-tieh Creek." To judge from the accent of the speaker, she was English.

"It's a couple of miles beyond the bridge," I told them. "I'm headed there myself. Just follow me."

"Thanks. Are you aboard the white powerboat?"

"That's right."

I cut the power back to 1,900 RPMs so as not to leave them too far behind—*Algonquin* was no speedster, but obviously the sailboat was slower still—and proceeded along my way, glancing back occasionally to see whether the sailboat was still following along behind me. Most of the boats I had seen fishing for Norfolk spot near the bridge were gone now. It was only a little after two o'clock, but the sun was already decisively on a downward orbit in the sky to the southwest.

When I turned into the Peltier Creek entrance channel I called back to the sailboat. "Calling the blue-and-white sailboat. How much water do you draw?"

"Just under four feet," came the answer.

I advised them to stay on the starboard side of the channel on the way in, and I reduced speed still more to allow them to follow *Algonquin* into the creek mouth, keeping close to the right-hand shore until I was opposite the point across from Bob Simpson's place, then turning sharply to port to skirt the sandbar there. The sailboat copied the maneuver, and followed me into the creek.

"Is there a particular location where it's best to anchor?" the female voice asked.

Most of the sailboats I had seen anchored in Peltier Creek, I told her, had positioned themselves out toward the northern end. If they intended to go ashore in a dinghy, I added, most of the docks were along the creek's eastern arm.

"Thanks, but we plan to remain aboard." The voice proceeded to thank me for my help, and as I moved on toward the western fork of the creek I looked back and watched the sailboat circle, and the man aboard go out onto the bow and prepare to drop anchor.

I backed *Algonquin* into her slip, cut off the engine, fixed all her lines, and lowered the bumpers into place. Home is the hunter, home from the hill, and the sailor home from the sea. Sans fish. I hooked up the shore power, set the battery switch at the off position, emptied the water and ice cubes from the ice chest, placed the folding chairs and ring buoy inside the cabin, closed and tightened all ports and windows, dumped the contents of several trash buckets into a plastic garbage bag, and carried the bag ashore along with my camera and other items to be taken back to Chapel Hill. I connected the water hose to a spigot on the dock and gave *Algonquin* a thorough washdown with fresh water. Then I got into my car and drove off. It was 3:05 p.m. With any luck I would be home in time for dinner.

The feeling of having gone somewhere on a boat,

spent some hours on the water, and returned without
incident is one of quiet satisfaction. In my own instance,
perhaps, it is all the more decisive. Helping the couple in
the blue-and-white sailboat to find Peltier Creek, then
guiding them in to a safe anchorage, added to the
satisfaction. My last experience with communication via
VHF radio en route back to the creek had been the
previous year, aboard the *Mary Simpson,* when I had
taken Clyde and Susan Edgerton boating, only to have
the engine die and be forced to summon Bob Simpson to
tow us in. The *Algonquin,* by contrast, had behaved
perfectly, as indeed she had done every time I had ever
operated her. For once in your life, my wife had said, get
a boat that works, a new boat that won't break down
every time you use it. There was and is, of course, no
such watercraft in existence, new or old; it is the nature
of marine engines to break down, and beyond doubt the
time would come when *Algonquin*'s rebuilt eighty-two
horsepower Mazda diesel would get its licks in, too.

Yet there was no question that the twenty-
four-foot boat that Clem Willis had built for me,
equipped with the engine that Larry Myers had sold me
to power her, was by far the most reliable I had ever
owned. Who knows but that the day might yet come
when, upon first going aboard my boat after a layoff of
several weeks, I would no longer feel my insides tighten

---

in apprehension as I prepared to turn the ignition key? It might, after all, be possible that I would not forever be locked into the reflexive stance of a batter who, having once been hit in the head by a pitched baseball, ever afterward remains wary of being beaned as he steps into the batter's box. Stranger things have happened.

As I drove westward along Highway 70, I thought about the couple in the blue-and-white sailboat. Even given the fact that wind and waves were making it difficult to read the marker numbers on the Waterway chart, how could they *not* have been able to locate Peltier Creek without trouble? The chart must have shown them that the creek was three miles west of the bridge—the only bridge across Bogue Sound for twenty-five miles. Yet they had been looking for the entrance a mile east of the bridge. Could it be that there were people out there operating boats who were even less competent at the job than I?

I thought of the woman's calm, casual voice, with its clipped British pronunciation—"Pell-le-tieh," she had called the creek, and the chart did give it as "Peletier" rather than "Peltier." If indeed she was English, and not a Sarah Lawrence graduate with elocution lessons and acting ambitions, had she and her husband, or boyfriend perhaps, sailed that blue-and-white sloop across the Atlantic Ocean? It was difficult to imagine anyone being able to

manage the navigation involved, yet then be unable to
locate a well-marked creek entrance several miles west of
the only bridge in the area. Or had they acquired the
boat over here, perhaps, and planned to take her home
the following summer, via the Leeward Islands and the
Azores? If so, God help them, for they might well end
up somewhere along the coast of Africa, or else becalmed
in the Sargasso Sea.

　　　　If they could do such things, why couldn't I? Not
cross the Atlantic Ocean, to be sure—I was no sailor, and
sixty-seven years of mostly sedentary life had not left me
in a physical condition conducive to bluewater or even
offshore sailing. But whatever my deficiencies in muscular
fitness, I could obviously read a nautical chart with
considerably more facility than the couple in the sailboat.
Why could I not take the *Algonquin* down the Waterway
to southern Florida, then across to the Bahamas and down
into the islands? I was looking forward to extricating
myself from my publishing commitments within the year
ahead. Why not then head south? My wife would be
decidedly dubious about my doing so, to be sure, but she
would not stand in my way. I could do the thing in
stages—go down to Florida, then, after a month or so at
home, continue on to the Bahamas and, after another
break, on to San Juan. And so on. With Loran-C and a
good radio, the navigation would be no problem, and I

would take no chances with the weather. I would be in no hurry; I could afford to wait for the calm days. Before I tried any such thing, of course, I would have to put an end to my blissful ignorance of the inner and outer workings of diesel engines. I would have to learn how to assemble and disassemble every part of the engine, and to make any and all repairs to it.

If all this sounds familiar, it is because I have written about it in an earlier chapter. It was not exactly a new idea, nor the last time it would ever occur to me; I knew that. What I lacked was what even the oceangoing British couple, if that was what they were, possessed, for all their apparent inability to read a Waterway chart— nerve. The capacity for taking chances, and not waiting until everything was in order and all contingencies covered.

It had been that way all my life.

After college I had wanted to earn my living as a writer, but I had never had sufficient boldness to consider quitting my newspaper job, working only enough to pay for minimum lodging and food, and *write*. I had wanted to go to Europe the summer after my first year of graduate work. Instead I had taken a job on the copydesk of a newspaper. I had very little money, it's true, but others had gone there with no more. I could have managed it somehow, if I had dared to try it. And after I

was married, I could still have gone; my wife would
have been willing, if I had really wanted to do it. She
would have been willing, too, if I had wanted to leave
my teaching position and write. Not once had she ever
cautioned financial prudence, insisted upon security,
discouraged me from taking risks. Yet I had never
seriously considered anything of the sort.

I had played it safe, had insisted upon having an
assured income, a tenured appointment, and had been
unwilling to turn loose and take my chances. In the long
run it had worked out reasonably well, to be sure. I had
done the writing I wanted to do, or much of it; we had
traveled, spent time abroad; we no longer had to think
twice now before every expenditure we made. It was too
late to fret about such matters. Marked paths had been
taken, charted courses set and followed. But what was it
that had caused me then, and still caused me now, at the
age of sixty-seven, to pull back from the unknown, avoid
the risk, not take the chance?

14

ON RISK-TAKING

Risk-taking. When I was ten years old, I was made to take swimming lessons at the YMCA in Charleston. The third lesson involved letting go of the railing around the edge of the pool and pushing off into the water. I could not do it. When I let go and found myself in the water with nothing to hold my head above the surface but my own exertions, I scrambled for the poolside, grabbed onto the railing, and clung to it for dear life. Nothing could persuade me to abandon the security of the poolside and trust to the water. The instant there was no support for my body, I lost control of my actions. The swimming lessons were a complete failure, and the frustration and humiliation were such that I came to dread the mornings on which they were scheduled. Ultimately my parents were compelled to accept the fact of my failure, and ceased to require me to attend the lessons.

Not quite a decade later, when at the age of
nineteen I was inducted into the Army, as part of basic
infantry training I was required to learn how to float.
Again I could not make myself push off from the side of
the pool and try to support myself. The lieutenant in
charge of the platoon did his best to encourage and cajole
me into letting go of the side of the pool, and at one
point even tried to push me under the water, whereupon
I promptly took a swing at him. Fortunately he was wise
enough to realize that at that point I was not in control
of my actions, or else I might have been in serious
trouble.

The winter following, during specialized Army
area-and-language training at Yale University, the famous
Olympic swimming coach, Robert Kiphuth, worked with
me alone for hours, doing his level best to teach me to
swim. I went into the pool, and he held out a long pole
with a float attached to the end, which I grasped while
he walked along the edge of the pool, pulling me
through the water. I wanted very much to let go of the
float and start swimming, but for the life of me I could
not. I was able to force myself to release my grip and
drop off into the water, but no sooner did my head go
under than I lost control and leaped for the edge of the
pool. Eventually even the great Robert Kiphuth knew
when he was licked, and he gave up. Only years later, at

---

a lake in Virginia, did I manage to thrash across a
half-dozen yards of water, my arms flailing, out to a
platform, and then, after I had recovered my breath, back
again. I never tried it again.

At first glance it might seem odd that, with this
background, I should be so fascinated with boats, so eager
to own them and go out in them. Yet there is no
incongruity involved. On the contrary, going out on
boats is a way of going onto the water without the need
of having, figuratively, to release my hold on the railing.
It is the way I can come closest to the element which
represented for me, as a child, uncertainty and lack of
support. I venture out upon the water, I operate my boat,
I can even think of myself as a boatman, a sailor; yet I
am in reasonable control of the situation, as I was not
when as a child and youth I tried so hard to let go of the
railing and suspend myself in the water, without being
able to do so.

Sigmund Freud, in *Beyond the Pleasure Principle,* wrote of
having observed an eighteen-month-old boy—his
grandson—repeatedly playing a game with a wooden reel
attached to a string. The boy would throw the toy out of
his crib and out of sight, then haul it back in,
accompanying the latter activity with expressions of
pleasure. The child in question was notably well behaved,

and never cried even when his mother, with whom he was very close, left him alone for hours at a time. What Freud came to perceive was that, with the objects he had on hand, the child was dramatizing the disappearance and return of his mother. But why, he wondered, would the child deliberately wish to reenact what was surely a highly unpleasant experience?

The answer was that in repeating the experience over and over, the child was seeking to convert the trauma of his mother's disappearance into a repetitive game, in order to assert, to a degree at least, his own control over it. Freud was also struck with the actions of soldiers who had been severely wounded during World War I, and who returned to the event compulsively, as if by ritualizing and repeating a traumatic experience they could somehow control their responses to it. In the same way, it seems to me, my own longtime fascination with boats and boating is related, in part at least, to the experience of being unable to learn to swim as a child. It is a way of taking a risk—but a controlled risk, conducted on my own terms. (Call me Captain Chicken, as they say.)

It would be a considerable oversimplification, however, to think of the swimming incident as a *cause*. For the larger question, of course, has to do with the reason, or reasons, for my unwillingness and inability to

---

trust myself to the instability of the swimming pool, to let go the railing, take the chance.

Joseph Conrad, in *Lord Jim,* put these words into the mouth of his character Stein:

> "A man that is born falls into a dream
> like a man who falls into the sea. If he
> tries to climb out into the air as
> inexperienced people endeavour to do, he
> drowns—*nicht wahr?* . . . No! I tell you!
> The way is to the destructive element
> submit yourself, and with the exertions of
> your hands and feet in the water make the
> deep, deep sea keep you up."

The fear is of lack of control, of being unable to exert authority over one's experience. But the result is that in declining to take the risk one denies oneself the experience itself. It is something on the order of a verse, of the sexist variety, that I once heard:

> *Here lie the bones of Susan Jones.*
> *For her, life held no terrors.*
> *She died unwived at sixty-five:*
> *No hits, no runs, no errors.*

L O U I S   D .   R U B I N ,   J R .

What has kept me, throughout my life, from taking the risk of losing control in the water? I have been told that, when I was very small, I once fell into the waters of the Colonial Lake in Charleston and had to be pulled out, and that I witnessed a drowning at the beach, as well, and a human chain being formed in an effort at rescue. I do not recall either event, though I do have a dim memory of a gray day, a beach, the surf, and people shouting—unless I only imagined it. Moreover, the earliest dream I can remember having is a recurrent one, which I have not had for many years, in which I was falling over the side of a ship into the water, and sinking down, down to the bottom—only to find myself asleep in my bed. Again, however, it is not the water itself but the insecurity that caused it to play the role it did which is important.

My wife has pointed out to me that my fear of taking risks seems to manifest itself in only two ways: with boats and the water, and with money. Intellectually, and in matters involving my professional life, I have taken great risks at various times, and thought nothing of doing so. Apparently the fear of risk-taking that is associated with boats and boating, as these figure in my life, involves a certain *kind* of risk-taking. And to try to understand what that fear is and is not, I shall have to go into still more personal history.

* * *

My father, one of a family of seven children, was raised in dire poverty. His own father, who died long before I was born, had no talent for business, but for want of any other vocational skills was forced to earn a living by operating a succession of small retail clothing and general stores in the Low-country of South Carolina around the turn of the twentieth century. The stores did not prosper, and when in the early 1900s he was taken ill with a heart condition and for several years was unable to do any work whatever, it became necessary for my father and two of his brothers to be sent off to a Hebrew orphanage in Atlanta, Georgia, for several years, until matters improved and the family was reunited. But like all three of his brothers before him, my father was forced to drop out of school after the seventh grade and go to work as a stockboy.

Starting from scratch, he taught himself to be an electrician, began his own repair service, then opened an electrical-appliance store and construction business, and by the time I was born, in 1923, he had become a prominent and quite successful businessman, known for his innovativeness and his civic involvement. My mother, whom he married in 1921, had grown up in less straitened circumstances in Richmond, Virginia, where her father was a jeweler and watch repairman, but if not actually in actual want, the family was by no means well off. For her father, too, was not gifted at moneymaking, and she was well acquainted with the nature of limited circumstances.

During the middle and late 1920s my father's business prospered, and his reputation grew. When the Depression hit in the 1930s, like all businesses his own suffered, but undoubtedly he would have been able to survive and, once the worst was over, flourish. Late in 1930, however, he came down with a severe head cold, which, incorrectly diagnosed as mastoiditis, was operated upon. Thereafter his condition grew worse, and it developed into a severe brain abscess. He had to be taken to a specialist in Richmond, and we lived there for the next two years; he was operated on several times and on two occasions was given up for dead.

Somehow he pulled through, although for a time his left side was paralyzed, and in late 1932 we were able to return to Charleston. But his electrical business, which he had left in the hands of an assistant whom he trusted completely and who proved to be dishonest, failed. He was forced to declare bankruptcy, and the ex-assistant and another employee purchased what was left of the assets.

Fortunately, he had taken out ample insurance on his health, no doubt because of his own childhood experience, and with the proceeds of the insurance and a disability pension for his Marine Corps service in World

War I, he had an adequate income. But his health, both physical and mental, was shattered. Several years elapsed before the paralysis in his left side was completely gone, and for years thereafter he remained subject to what the medical terminology of that day described as "nervous spells," which incapacitated him for days at a time. An outgoing, extroverted person who had always been buoyant and optimistic, he was thrown on his own inner resources and left to brood on his condition.

He wanted to go back into business for himself, but he could not, for he would have been forced to give up his disability insurance and pension. With a wife and three small children to support, it was a risk he could not take. That he felt his helplessness keenly, and experienced a degree of humiliation at the need to live on his insurance and his pension, cannot be doubted. Having set out to succeed as a businessman, he had failed, and he must have seen the failure not only as a bodily affliction but as a moral deficiency—a failure, in other words, of nerve as well as nerves.

There were times when, unable to sleep, he would leave the house late at night; my mother would awaken to find him missing, and would dress and go in search of him. She would find him standing at the seawall on Murray Boulevard, some blocks from our home, staring at the water. It was for this reason that in 1935, in order

---

to give him something to do, we built a new house up in the then-undeveloped northwest of the city, looking out on the Ashley River.

By the mid-1930s my father had made a fairly advanced recovery, so that he could work for long hours out in his vegetable and flower garden. Though he was only in his early forties, however, his "nerves" were in such poor condition that he could not possibly stand the strain of going back into business for himself. Quite possibly the real stumbling block was less his health than the financial gamble involved in giving up an assured income to reenter the competitive business world. He had lost his self-confidence.

As the oldest child, it was vital, of course, that I understand both the importance of financial security and the perils of failing to protect oneself in a treacherous and uncertain world. The result was that throughout my childhood and youth I was reminded of the advantages of earning money and saving it. I was not to take risks that might jeopardize my financial security; I was to be conservative, prudent, frugal, and to avoid being victimized. I was to be exceedingly suspicious of any and all schemes proposed by others, since I might be deceived and cheated as my father had been (though this last thought was never voiced). Which brings us back to the matter of risk-taking and the blue-and-white sailboat.

* * *

I had no idea, of course, whether the oceangoing couple
in the blue-and-white sailboat intended to sail for the
Leeward Islands and the far-off shores of Europe. I was
hypothesizing only from the bluewater gear they had
aboard their boat. But it is true that the bluewater sailors,
the mountain climbers, the auto racers, and the great
generals, charismatic politicos, scientific discoverers, and
also the marauders and gangsters of this world have been,
whether by inheritance or rearing or earliest disposition,
risk-takers, whose instinctive responses to their experience
have been to pursue opportunities rather than covet
security. The same is true of businessmen and financiers.
"Faint heart ne'er won fair lady," etc.

Yet risk-taking can be foolhardiness, too. If the
couple in the sailboat were indeed ocean-bound, and their
navigational ability was as dubious as the episode I had
witnessed seemed to indicate, clearly they had no business
taking such a risk, or encouraging each other to do so.
Risk-taking that imperils the welfare of others can be a
very selfish and egotistical affair.

Was my father's decision not to go back into
business heroic? To have done so would have jeopardized
not only his health but his wife's and children's financial
security. From that standpoint, one could say that genuine
courage on his part involved being able to resist the

desire to prove, to himself and to others, that he was not finished, that he could go back into business and succeed.

In our home were mementos of what he had been—trophies, awards, citations, and above all two thick scrapbooks of newspaper and magazine clippings and letters exhibiting the awards, distinctions, and triumphs of his business career, the commendations he had received, the esteem in which he was held among the business and civic community. I read them over and over. *This* was what my father had done and been, before his illness. If the fathers of my friends figured importantly in local affairs now, he had at least been similarly important once; I had that consolation. But what I would really have liked was for him to have gone back into the arena and regained his former stature.

I would have to say that neither my father's example, nor the constant admonitions of my mother not to run financial risks, succeeded in making me prudent and foresighted in matters involving money. Instead, the impact of those years—my father's abrupt illness, being uprooted from our home and moving to Richmond, the greatly altered condition of my father when he returned from the hospital, the loss of his business, the dislocations (from ages six to twelve I changed schools seven times), the constant references to his illness and the medicines he

---

was taking, the whole confusing and disturbing experience—would appear to have had a very different effect.

What resulted was a kind of flight into my own world of the imagination, which was shaped to avoid ugliness, helplessness, and hopelessness, and in which reality was kept at arm's length. The circumstances of my existence were made to conform to what I desired them to be, and whatever could not be fitted into that was dismissed as of no importance. Imaginatively I inhabited a world in which all things were possible; any barrier, any hindrance or unpleasantness, was temporary and transitory. Irrationality, error, and confusion did not exist; all was controllable and rational.

To insulate myself against disappointment, I developed an abhorrence of money-making and financial considerations. I did not want even to think about money. To concern myself with ways to make it would be crass and mercenary. To recall the quotation from Conrad's *Lord Jim,* finances became the "destructive element" (had they not wrecked my father's life?). Instead of being willing to immerse myself in that element and to learn to use money-making to achieve what I wished to achieve, my response was precisely what it had been when I was forced to turn loose the railing of the pool and go into the water—which is to say, panic,

---

irrationality. Forced to immerse myself in instability, my uncontrollable reaction was to try to climb out into the air.

There is a well-known saying: *A boat is a hole in the water surrounded by wood into which money is poured.* Nowadays the boat is more likely to be fiberglass, but the principle remains valid. I cannot speak for other owners of boats, but I know that the amount of money I have poured into the boats I have owned has been out of all proportion to the amount of time I spend using them. My friend John McCallum, to whose Taylor Boat Works I have contributed no small amount of money for services amply rendered, is quite correct when he says that the only way for a recreation-boat owner to think about his boat is as an irrational and illogical pleasure; because the cost of keeping one cannot possibly be justified on any rational scale.

I have already suggested some of the elements that I think are involved in my own choice of that particular kind of pleasure. (Which is not to say, of course, that there are not intrinsic virtues in boats and their use that no other kinds of pleasure can provide, for certainly there are. And I do not for a moment wish to convey the notion that my love of boats is no more than a matter of a psychological compensation for deficiencies in my upbringing. Freud once remarked, or is said to have remarked, that there are times when a cigar is merely a cigar; the same is obviously true of boats. What I am trying to get at is, why the insistence upon this particular form of pleasure?)

The *Algonquin,* as noted, was my first new boat (I except several trailerable outboard boats for fishing), the first constructed especially for me. The *Bill James,* the *Little Eva,* the *Groundhog,* the *Diane,* the *Virginius,* and most recently the *Mary Simpson*—these were all used boats, and all of venerable standing. All but the *Groundhog* and the *Diane* turned out to require extensive and costly repairs, and, significantly, the latter two boats were the only ones with outboard power, which had not been part of the purchase but had been installed by me.

Had I at any time been willing to purchase new or recently built boats, in the long run I would have been much better off. With all those boats, the amount of money eventually paid out in repairs, if invested in the purchase price of the boat, would have enabled me to acquire boats that were much newer and far less likely to break down. In most instances, with boats as with other things, one gets what one pays for; and I paid far less than I should have paid, with the result that there was constant trouble.

To acquire those boats I had in each instance to

borrow money—and I was simply afraid to borrow enough money to buy better boats. Unless absolutely necessary I have never resorted to installment buying. To contract such debt would have caused me to worry about it, and I did not want to have it on my mind. For the same reason, when I have had money to invest I have declined to place it in stocks; I did not want to follow the market or to worry about gains and losses.

Apart from financial considerations, why *do* I like old boats, preferably ex-workboats? I have already traced my preference for them back to my youth, when I spent so much time down at Adger's Wharf on the Charleston waterfront, and watched the aggregation of venerable trawlers, cargo craft, launches, and fishing boats collected there. What those boats exemplified for me, I think, in a way that the pleasure craft at the Yacht Basin could not, was a lack of pretense. They offered a status divorced (for me) from considerations of wealth, lineage, or reputation; they belonged, they were part of the harbor scene, they contributed to the picturesque attraction of the old city, yet there was no striving, no question of maintaining a stance, no ambition or stressful competitiveness associated with them.

In a competition, whether between sailboats or baseball teams or politicos or rival businesses or the

military forces of nations, there must be a winner and a
loser. Victory produces emotion—pride, vaunting,
exultation, insolence, even. The same is true of
defeat—disappointment, humiliation, resentment, hatred,
the desire for revenge. Either response transcends
rationality, jeopardizes reason and balance. If there must
be competition, let it be kept as orderly and as friendly as
possible. Otherwise there will be disorder, chaos.

Something of that kind of reaction must be
involved in my response. If I do not discipline my
competitive instincts and keep my ambition under wraps,
I expose myself to explosive anger, jealousy, and
retaliation. The thing to do, therefore, is to seek outlets
for such emotions that will not challenge or threaten
others.

What has this to do with boating and
boat-owning? Think of it this way.

*No one, observing the "Algonquin" as she moves
along the Waterway, would be envious of her, or resent her
presence. No one would think to challenge her to a test of
speed, or attempt to compare the luxuriousness of her
accommodations to those of a yacht. Nor would she be expected
to prove her seaworthiness in conditions of storm and stress.*

Yet she can go anywhere I dare to take her.

15

CRAFT AND CREDULITY

Between craft and credulity, the voice of reason is stilled.
—Edmund Burke, *A Letter to the Sheriffs of Bristol*

I went down to the coast once more, in early January, after winter had descended fully upon North Carolina. The air was chilly, and although the sun was out, the bent light-rays it cast seemed too enfeebled to apply more than a lemon-pale glow to the line of white boats tied up along the creek. It was Saturday, and not a soul was in sight anywhere. The tide was low, and upon the water was a wafer-thin sheet of ice.

The *Algonquin* waited alone at the upstream end of the dock, the slip at her starboard side vacant now, for the *Mary Simpson* had finally been sold. A waterman from the area to the east of Beaufort had bought her via telephone. Built as a pleasure craft, she would henceforth work for a living. I was happy to be divested of her, and of the monthly dockage bill that went along with her.

One boat, and one dockage bill, would henceforth be quite enough for me.

I stepped onto the stern, opened the door, and went inside. The cabin was empty and cold. The red and white lights of the battery charger indicated that the battery was properly primed. Although it is not really necessary with a diesel engine, from force of habit I lifted up the top of the engine box to check for fumes, then I moved the battery switch from "off" to "both," and turned the key. The engine growled briskly, then after a moment caught, and rumbled into action. The moment of truth, when going aboard a boat that has been sitting unused for a while, is starting the engine. It is always a relief to hear it turn over, catch, and go into full motion.

Letting the engine idle, I stepped down into the forward cabin. Everything was precisely as I had left it, but frigid to the touch. The solar vent fan was whirling away, creating some movement of air within the cabin. The unpainted strips of plywood around the cabinets and the compartment doors under the berth reminded me that there was work remaining to be done. I had no intention of taking care of it, however, until March or April, when the spirit would begin to move me more vigorously.

Should I take her out for a run? I would let the engine warm up for a while, until not only the engine itself but the exhaust pipe leading through the cabin roof,

wrapped in fiberglass, began heating up to normal
operating temperature. Somewhere in the forward cabin,
beneath the sink probably, was a small electric heater,
which I could hook up while at dockside; but I left it
alone. I wanted to see whether the warmth from the
engine and exhaust pipe would be sufficient to make the
cabin interior endurable.

When the average person acquires a boat, it is
usually during warm weather, and it never occurs to him
to think about how well the boat is equipped for cold
weather operation. There is an amusing episode in the
early chapters of *Life on the Mississippi* in which the cub
pilot, having set out with his mentor, Horace Bixby,
aboard a steamboat to begin learning the trade, is
surprised to be routed out of his berth in the dead of
night and told to join Bixby in the pilothouse. Until then
it had not crossed his mind that steamboats must be
piloted at night as well as during the day, and that,
unlike the passengers, the people hired to pilot the boat
must work night shifts.

In the same way, one difference between
commercial watermen and weekend recreational boat
owners such as myself is that the professionals must
operate boats during fair weather and foul, in winter as
well as summer. (There are other differences as well, but I
shall not go into them here.) If the cabin of the

Algonquin turned out to be insufficiently comfortable I could decide to stay at dockside and use shore power to operate a heater. A tugboat captain, or a commercial fisherman dependent upon the taking of fish or oysters for his livelihood, must bundle up in long johns and heavy outer garments and make the best of it.

The Morehead City–Beaufort area of North Carolina is only forty or fifty miles from the warm current of the Gulf Stream, and the temperature benefits accordingly. But Arctic air spreading down from the North behind a cold front can thoroughly dispel any residual balminess. Indeed, given the right set of conditions, a belt of low pressure trapped between cold fronts and squeezed northward up from Florida can deposit a thick blanket of snow over the Carolina coastal areas.

I have lived in the Virginia mountains, where winds from the Midwest stab into the area like a razor-sharp blade. One winter we lived in an old and poorly insulated farmhouse atop a hill on the edge of the town of Fincastle, Virginia, and the water froze overnight in the glasses left on the dinner table, even though there was a furnace grate in the hallway just beyond the door to the dining room. Yet the wet cold of the seacoast has a penetrating quality all its own. It seems to ooze into everything, permeating windbreakers, coats, jackets, sweaters, and settling into undergarments. It diffuses itself over the skin, frigid and clammy, and seeps into one's bones.

"But chiefly I remember/how Dick would hate the cold," Housman's poem goes. I don't know who Dick was, but I share his sentiments. I've no use whatever for winter. When I was growing up in Charleston, the January chill would spread over the city from the waterfront like a pall, covering and coating everything. Waiting for an uptown bus down at King and Wentworth streets, I could feel its soggy presence, cumbrous and damp, infusing the air. Since then I've done time in Connecticut, far upstate New York, and Pennsylvania, lived in mountains, piedmont, and coastal places, but I cannot recall ever feeling more uncomfortable than in Charleston on a drizzly January afternoon.

We never saw snow back then. Ice was rare enough. On certain mornings in the winter there would be a film of ice over our neighbor's fishpond, only a fraction of an inch thick, as if a layer of transparent skin had hardened. Picked up, it would shatter into wet fragments and vanish. The snow halted fifty miles to the north, however; all we got was cold rain. In assembly at James Simons School we sang, "Over the fields and through the woods/To Grandmother's house we go/The horse knows the way/To carry the sleigh/Through the white and drifting snow," but it was all Yankee propaganda. I remember one wintry evening when snowflakes were swirling in the wind, only to melt when they reached the ground. I was nineteen before I first actually experienced a true snowfall, and then it was up in frigid Virginia. (In recent years there have been several snowfalls in Charleston, but there were none in my time.)

Since those days I have seen more snow than I ever wanted to see, and once the novelty of it wore off—which is to say, about half a century ago—I lost all enthusiasm for it. A Louisiana friend of mine once voluntarily spent two weeks in a large plywood-cabined motor van on the shores of Hudson Bay, photographing polar bears. He got some marvelous pictures, but if close-up views of picturesque white predators in the wild are desired, I believe I would opt for photographing albino sharks in the Caribbean—from a safe location, of course.

By now the cabin of the *Algonquin,* although not exactly cozy, had warmed up sufficiently to take the cutting edge off the chill. So I stepped outside into the frigid wind, unhooked the power cable and freed the lines, then threw the gear into forward and eased away from the dock. There was just enough ice to provide a crackling effect as

the bow shattered it. In the open part of the creek near
the entrance to Bogue Sound the water was clear of it. I
made my way through the entrance and along the access
channel, and into the Waterway.

I thought about the couple in the blue-and-white
sailboat again; by now they were doubtless somewhere in
Florida, and, if Caribbean-bound, preparing for the
jump-off to Bimini or Freetown. If, that is, they hadn't
misread a chart en route and ended up on a barrier island
at high tide.

The water of Bogue Sound was choppy, the
breeze on the brisk side. Presently the far-off January sun
disappeared behind a cloud bank, so that the surface of
the sound, instead of sparkling with light, was opaqued to
a pasty gray-green. *Algonquin*'s sturdy hull cut through
the water handily, and her diesel engine drove her
forward in a steady throb, but there was not much charm
in the bleakness of water and shore. If Indian Summer
there had been on my last outing, by now the Native
Americans in charge of the weather had retreated inside
their lodges somewhere, wrapped bison robes about
themselves, and were crouched around a fire keeping
warm. I remembered some lines from another poem by
Henry Timrod, in which the nineteenth-century
Charleston poet was using the imagery of the Low-
country to describe the feeling of gloom that the War
Between the States portended:

Now it has been a vessel losing way,
Rounding a stormy headland; now a gray
Dull waste of clouds above a wintry main

It was because Timrod was from Charleston, and used the scenes and objects of the Low-country for his imagery, that his work appealed to me. He was the closest thing to a really good poet that my native city has ever produced.

There were no other boats out on the Waterway. No doubt all the sailboats and yachts that were bound for Florida and the Caribbean had already made the trip, while those that were foregoing the journey either were in boatyards for winter storage, or, if in the water, were equipped with electric devices alongside to prevent the water from freezing fast around them. The tugs and barges were working, as always, but none were in sight today.

The sky overhead was battleship gray now. The houses along the shoreline seemed to be huddled against the land for warmth. The owl, for all his feathers, was a-cold. More poetry. Brrr! There was no point to this. Enough! I turned *Algonquin* in a sharp arc, cut across the wake, and steered for Peltier Creek. "Shall I be carried thro' the skies 'mid flow'ry beds of ease/While others fight to win the prize and sail through frigid seas?" By all means, if it can be arranged.

Inside the entrance I headed for the dock with rather more speed than I ordinarily employ; any wake I kicked up, which would in any case not be much, would annoy no other inhabitants of boats today, for so far as I could tell nobody else was out on Peltier Creek. I backed into the slip, stepped outside, and grabbed a line. Clambering about the hull resetting the mooring lines, I could almost feel the foul fiend's icy breath. I hooked up the shore power again, located the little heater, and turned it on full blast, training it in the direction of the berth in the forward cabin.

The heater soon had the air quite comfortable, the more so once I realized that the solar vent was busily funneling cold air inside, and closed it off. On a powerboat, fortunately, there was no framework of mast and rigging affixed to the hull and collecting cold air. A few years ago a young friend of mine, who was working as an editor in New York, decided to make ends meet the better by living aboard a ketch tied up at a dock on the Hudson River. The boat had shore power, a Shipmate stove, and so on, and appeared to be comfortable enough. But when the really cold weather set in, the hollow metal masts, which came down into the cabin, acted as refrigerating shafts, collecting the cold air and conducting it into the interior, whence it fanned out in all directions. The more fiercely the winter wind blew, the colder the

---

masts became and the more efficiently the refrigerating process worked; it was as if an enormous icicle were mounted in one's bedroom. After several nights of trying to co-exist with it, my friend, though living on short rations at the time, had to pay the tariff to have the masts stepped for the winter.

The increasing warmth of the *Algonquin*'s cabin, following the chill I got while outside tending to the lines, was conducive to drowsiness. A brief nap? Well, why not? It's a free country, isn't it? The thick vinyl cover of the mattress was cold to the touch, so I removed a blanket from the cabinet, unfolded it over the berth, propped a couple of pillows against the bulkhead, and assumed the horizontal. After a few minutes I turned over on my side, and shut my eyes. Awareness of the oddness of the surroundings began yielding to vague shapes in my mind, which soon folded into a steady procession of images and observations. When I realized that I had been asleep I looked at my watch. I had napped for almost an hour. The cabin was now, if anything, too warm; it was necessary to turn down the thermostat on the heater. I looked outside through the port; all was winter gray. I lay down again and enjoyed being warm and comfortable. It was if the boat were a cocoon, or a return to the womb.

It struck me as odd that I had driven 150 miles in order to take a nap, and would shortly get in the car and drive another 150 miles back. I could have done just as well at home; the couch in my study was if anything more comfortable. Nor was this the first time that I had traveled several hours by car to my boat, then either remained at the dock or, as had just happened, made only a brief run. I could not blame an uncalled-for change in the weather, either, for the forecast had predicted cloudy skies and temperatures in the thirties.

The truth was that when I decided to go down to the coast and my boat, it was without any real expectation of being able to take her out for an extensive run. Why, then, had I bothered to do it? For the same reason that inspires the purveyors of boating and fishing equipment to mail out hundreds of thousands of expensive catalogs in late January and February. What the authorities at Defender Industries, Boat/US, West Marine, Goldbergs', E&B, Orvis, M&S, and all the rest discovered years ago was that it is in the dead of winter, when boat owners and fishermen are restricted to barracks and cannot pursue their obsessions outdoors, that the absolute and unavoidable need to replace equipment and buy new gadgets and devices asserts itself.

When there is snow on the ground, ice on the creek, when the need to don gloves makes it difficult to

tie bowlines and improve clinchknots, when the spray is
icy and the breeze is dagger-edged—it is then that cabin
fever becomes virulent. The bluewater sailor rereads
Joshua Slocum, dreams of horizons, remembers that he
needs a better pair of binoculars and that he could use a
better self-tailing winch. The powerboat skipper orders a
new sonar unit, the better to search out those shoals when
he goes exploring new territory next summer. The
fisherman dreams of taking eighteen-pound stripers now
that they have come back into the Chesapeake Bay after a
long absence, prepares for them by ordering a new casting
rod and a reel with greater line capacity.

As a substitute for actuality, the imagination takes
over. Just as in prehistoric times our blood kin painted a
musk-ox on the wall of the cave or sacrificed a captured
maiden or two to bribe the solar disk, so now, with the
help of a fountain pen and an order blank, the sportsman
declares, *Let the springtime come again!* What
anthropologists and literary critics call a Symbolic Gesture
has been made.

To speak of such ritualistic activities as a
substitute for actuality, however, is misleading, for the
fact is that at no time of the year—winter, spring,
summer, or fall—is the imagination not a vital part of
boating. The hardware salesman who goes in weekend
pursuit of bluefish has been thinking fondly about doing

so throughout the week. The investment broker whose
twenty-six-foot Ericson rests unused in the slip at the
marina has an eight-by-twelve-inch color photograph of
her, red-and-yellow spinnaker trimmed, on his office wall
across from his desk; he has been gazing at it between
and even during appointments, and yearning for vacation
time to come around. There is far more to boating than
the actual doing of it.

       In short, I drove 150 miles down to the coast at a
time when the odds were all against my being able to
enjoy a day's outing on the *Algonquin,* because it was a
symbolic gesture—a way of assuring myself that she was
undeniably *there,* and would be there when the good
weather returned. It is as simple, and also as complex, as
that.

I do not for a moment claim that what is true for me
necessarily holds for all others who enjoy messing about
in boats. From what I have observed, however, I do
contend that the cultivation of boats by other than
professional watermen can be and often is just such a
symbolic activity. The watercraft in question, in addition
to being a boat and thus intrinsically pleasurable to own
and use, serves psychological needs that bear no logical or
necessary relationship to the boat itself. More than that,
the intensity of such relationships is apt to be obsessional,

going beyond ordinary attraction and verging on outright possession by spirits. Anyone who has ever watched a sailboat owner willingly spend an entire weekend sanding, cleaning, and rubbing Deks Olje into brightwork will surely concede that.

Some twenty years ago, in or about 1970, I started a novel, my second. Like my published novel of a decade earlier, this one also took place in Charleston, South Carolina, in the 1930s, and boats and the waterfront were central to its meaning. Neither the plot nor the situation, however, were in any way drawn from my own experience. I worked on it for three years, put it through several drafts, tried it on several publishers, and was ultimately forced to concede its impossible shortcomings as fiction.

At one point during the writing, I constructed a model of the ex-workboat that my character was living aboard at Adger's Wharf. I based its dimensions on what I knew of the shallow-draft launches that had once been the principal means for transporting cargo and passengers over the rivers and creeks between Charleston and the various sea islands along the Carolina coast, and which had fallen into disuse in the 1920s following the development of paved roads and bridges that linked the islands directly to the mainland.

Someone told me that, although half a century
had elapsed since most of the craft had been removed
from service, one of those launches was still in existence,
moored behind a store in Georgetown, South Carolina,
sixty miles up the coast from Charleston. I stopped by to
see her. She was about thirty feet in length, with a large
cabin and benches built around the stern cockpit. She was
painted a grayish white, though not anytime recently.
The model that I built was on a scale that would have
made the boat somewhat larger, because the novel
required that the living quarters be more commodious.

I painted it bright red, with a black hull—I
wanted the boat in the novel to look more garish. I
mounted a rowboat on top, with a davit for lowering it
into the water, and with straightened-out hairpins I made
a frame over the stern cockpit, with a rolled-up piece of
tan cloth to serve for a canopy. I also gave the boat a
pilothouse with running lights, a horn, and a searchlight,
a water tank atop the cargo cabin, steps leading down
into the cockpit and a ladder leading up to the cabin top,
a forward-hatch cover, sampson posts fore and aft, a
metal propeller and rudder, a vent pipe, and a mast.

Model-building is not among my skills, and it
was a crudely constructed affair, but what the urge to
build that model should have told me, but did not, was
that it was the boat, and what it signified for me, that

interested me, not the particular story I was attempting to tell. When I think back on the abortive attempt to write the novel, I realize that what was wrong with it was that, despite the choice of setting, it was an effort to avoid almost everything that was important to me about my own experience as a child and youth in Charleston.

What is the relationship between that model boat and my new boat, the *Algonquin,* which, though a full-sized twenty-four-foot boat, is constructed of wood on a workboat hull, has the high cabin and boxy appearance of a cargo launch, an exhaust pipe leading through the cabin roof, old-fashioned light boards characteristic of workboats, and in other ways has been made to look utilitarian rather than recreational?

Is it not that both are in crucial respects icons of the imagination—symbolic gestures intended to anchor that imagination in tangible, everyday actuality?

EPILOGUE, 1991

I did not take the *Algonquin* down the Intracoastal
Waterway after all. It was not merely that I was busy,
and that to go and to return would have required at least
several weeks. It was that there was no longer any reason
to do so. I did not make the trip home in the *Algonquin*
because I had already made it in my imagination, by
writing this book.

Certainly I could have taken the *Algonquin* down
the Waterway, through abandoned rice fields and behind
the barrier islands—Bull, Dewee's, the Isle of Palms,
Sullivan's—into Charleston Harbor, made my way up the
Ashley River and gone looking for the location of the
creek that once led through the marsh to the little dock
at the shore behind Sans Souci. The creek mouth itself
would be there no more, of course, because the river
bottom had been dredged several years before we moved

away in 1942, when I was eighteen years old, and islands
of sand created all along the river's edge had sealed off
the entrance. Yet I could have found the approximate
position where the creek had once flowed into the river.
Had I found it, however, what I would have seen was
not what I was looking for, for what I sought could
never have been found on a journey aboard a boat to a
place where I had lived when I was young.

No doubt I could have looked through binoculars
at the shore from the river, peered through the oak trees
along the bluff, and caught sight of the porch of what
had once been our house; it is still there. What I could
not have seen was my mother as she stood on that porch
and watched anxiously for her son, who could not swim,
as he went out upon the surface of the river in a clumsy,
leaking little boat. I could not have seen her, because I
would have been looking in the wrong place. I would
have been looking outward, at things—the marsh, the
trees, a bluff, a roof, a porch—instead of inward, at
meanings. All that I now required was available within
me as memory. It was through memory that the pathway
existed; I would mistakenly have been seeking it in a
physical, geographical place, had I been so foolish as to
make the trip for the purpose I had originally intended.

Paradoxically, the very mortality that bears each
of us along to a finite conclusion also gives us, through
its unfolding, the means to repossess what we believe we

---

have lost. It is in memory, given its true shape through the imagination, that we can truly possess our lives, if we will only strive to regain them. And by this I imply no Proustian notion that art is the sole reality, unless by "art" is meant the working of the imagination upon intelligence, an activity that is by no means limited to those who style themselves "artists." The latter, if sufficiently talented, can leave behind them magnificent records of what they possessed, but it is in the ongoing process of repossession itself, not the record that may or may not be left for others to read or hear or see, that we make sense of our experience and come to see it for what it really is: the shape of Time.

Such a process can take many forms. Common to all of them, however, is the use of our imagination to interpret what our memory offers for interpretation. We *are* our memory. Truly to possess what we are, we must uncover it, which means looking at the images thrown up for us to see, searching for the emotions that these embody, and tracing out the relationships that fuse them into the single entity that we comprise—an entity that time has arranged for us.

It was by having the boat built that I was able to undertake the process. That was my way of doing it. Others may choose—or more accurately, be impelled by—different ways, since there are as many ways of doing it as there are people to undertake the task. Nor is it even necessary that the process be thought of *as* a process; what it involves is what matters.

I do, however, intend to make the trip to Charleston—the actual trip, down the Intracoastal Waterway with the boat, to the harbor and city and river—someday soon. I will make it not to recover meanings and emotions that no such trip in itself can recover, but for its own sake, in the boat that Clem Willis built for me, made of wood on a workboat hull, named for a certain steamship that my mother took me to see when it brought my father home, long ago in the early morning.

P.S. It turned out that the *Mary Simpson* wasn't sold after all. The waterman who supposedly bought her proved to be both a knave and a fool. A knave, because he neither paid me for her nor returned her. A fool, because he moored her on a tidal flat, and when the tide went out she was left high and dry, bow pointed outward and downward, inclined to one side by weight. When the tide came in, it flowed into the hull through the scuppers and kept on rising, but the *Mary Simpson* did not. She ended up being sold "as is, where is." Raised and repaired, she is now at work. The person who now owns her is reported to be delighted with her. I am delighted that she is now his boat, not mine.